lonely planet

Best Road Trips

ITALY

GREGOR CLARK, BRETT ATKINSON, ALEXIS AVERBUCK, CRISTIAN BONETTO, DUNCAN GARWOOD, PETER DRAGICEVICH, PAULA HARDY, VIRGINIA MAXWELL, STEPHANIE ONG, KEVIN RAUB, BRENDAN SAINSBURY, REGIS ST LOUIS, NICOLA WILLIAMS

CONTENTS

FRANCE
GERMANY
AUSTRIA
HUNGARY
SWITZERLAND
SLOVENIA
CROATIA
BOSNIA & HERZEGOVINA
SAN MARINO
FRANCE
Corsica
SARDINIA
SICILY
ITALIAN ALPS p91
NORTHERN ITALY p35
CENTRAL ITALY p121
SOUTHERN ITALY p167
THE ISLANDS p215
Bressanone (Brixen)
Bolzano
Cortina d'Ampezzo
Tarvisio
Locarno
Sondrio
Trento
Vittorio Veneto
Udine
Lecco
Aosta
Verbania
Como
Bergamo
Treviso
Trieste
Biella
Milan
Brescia
Verona
Vicenza
Venice
Vercelli
Cremona
Mantua
Padua
Turin
Alessandria
Piacenza
Parma
Ferrara
Asti
Modena
Bologna
Cuneo
Ravenna
Savona
Genoa
Imperia
La Spezia
Massa
Pistoia
Rimini
Ventimiglia
Lucca
Pesaro
Pisa
Florence
Ancona
Livorno
Arezzo
Siena
Macerata
Perugia
Montepulciano
Ascoli Piceno
Grosseto
Orvieto
Terni
Pescara
Viterbo
Rieti
L'Aquila
Chieti
Civitavecchia
Rome
Vieste
Frosinone
Campobasso
Isernia
Foggia
Benevento
Bari
Santa Teresa di Gallura
Olbia
Sassari
Avellino
Naples
Matera
Brindisi
Alghero
Salerno
Potenza
Vico Equense
Taranto
Lecce
Nuoro
Orosei
Gallipoli
Oristano
Sapri
Iglesias
Cosenza
Cagliari
Crotone
Catanzaro
Vibo Valentia
Messina
Palermo
Trapani
Cefalù
Reggio Calabria
Taormina
Marsala
Enna
Catania
Agrigento
Syracuse
Gela
Ragusa
0 200 km
0 100 miles

WELCOME TO ITALY

There's no better place for an epic road trip than Italy. With your own car – an Alfa Romeo, say, or an open-top Fiat – you can experience the very best the *bel paese* (beautiful country) has to offer: romantic cities and iconic monuments, regional cuisines and a landscape that encompasses snowcapped peaks, remote wildernesses and swoon-inducing coastlines.

The 40 trips outlined in this book run the length and breadth of the country, leading from alpine passes to smoking Sicilian volcanoes, from hilltop towns in Tuscany to fishing villages on the Amalfi Coast. They stop off in high-profile cities and under-the-radar sights. And while some routes are more challenging than others, they all promise new discoveries and unforgettable adventures.

So whether you want to tour gourmet towns and historic vineyards, idyllic shorelines or pristine national parks, we have a trip tailor-made for you.

The Dolomites (p106)

ARTUR DEBAT/GETTY IMAGES

MY PERFECT ROAD TRIP

GREGOR CLARK

TRIP 36: WONDERS OF ANCIENT SICILY, p218

Sicily's exuberant history comes alive on this incomparable round-the-island journey. The Byzantine mosaics and Arabic *muqarnas* ceilings of Palermo's Cappella Palatina, the temples of Segesta, Selinunte and Agrigento, the mountaintop eyrie of Erice, and the spectacular Greek theatres of Syracuse – each alone would be worthy of building an entire trip around. Combining them all showcases Sicily's remarkable wealth of cultural influences, encompassing 25 centuries of history on one of the Mediterranean's most captivating islands.

ALTRENDO IMAGES/SHUTTERSTOCK

Segesta, Sicily (p219)

BEST LONG DRIVES

1. **Cinematic Cinque Terre** Follow the clifftops along the Riviera.
2. **Grande Strada delle Dolomiti** The Dolomites are the background for this grand trip.
3. **Piero della Francesca Trail** Follow the footsteps of Piero della Francesca.
4. **Calabrian Wilderness** Take in the beauty and ancient towns of Calabria.
5. **Wonders of Ancient Sicily** Traverse the coastline of the island.

Erice, Sicily (p219)

TRAMPER79/SHUTTERSTOCK

ARCHITECTURE, ART AND RUINS

Home to some of the world's greatest artistic and architectural masterpieces, Italy is a visual extravaganza. Everywhere you go, you're reminded of the country's tumultuous past, from ancient Roman ruins and martial monuments to majestic basilicas and breathtaking frescoes. Works by Renaissance heroes and baroque maestros grace churches, palaces and museums, while fountains and marble sculptures adorn medieval piazzas and cobbled streets.

① GRAND TOUR

A whistle-stop tour of Italy's headline cities and their priceless treasures. p22

② NORTHERN CITIES

Treasured Giotto frescoes, medieval cityscapes and Venetian canals await on this northern drive. p58

③ PIERO DELLA FRANCESCA TRAIL

From Urbino to Florence, discover the frescoes of the Renaissance master. p146

CHURCH ART

You'll find plenty of heavyweight art in Italy's richly decorated churches, most of which are free to enter.

④ ROAMING AROUND ROME

Explore thrilling ruins and a perfectly preserved ancient city in Rome's hinterland. p124

⑤ WONDERS OF ANCIENT SICILY

Pore over Greek temples, baroque basilicas and Byzantine jewels in sun-baked Sicily. p218

Left: Marriage at Cana by Giotto, Cappella degli Scrovegni, Padua (p33); Right: The Colosseum, Rome (p27)

LEFT TO RIGHT: SPATULETAIL/SHUTTERSTOCK, RENBRINS/SHUTTERSTOCK

MONDAY CLOSINGS

Many museums and attractions are closed on Mondays, including Florence's Uffizi and Accademia galleries.

BOOK AHEAD

Book tickets online for popular attractions. Many places now require pre-booking and it will save queuing at the site.

MEAL TIMES

Italians typically sit down to *pranzo* (lunch) between 1pm and 2.30pm and *cena* (dinner) between 8pm and 9.30pm.

WINERY VISITS

Book ahead as walk-ins are not always accepted. Tasting fees may be waived if you buy some wine.

FOOD & WINE

Superb produce, culinary traditions and world-beating wines combine to make Italy a food-lover's dream destination. Every region has its own treasured specialities, while graceful piazzas and scenic seashores provide a ready supply of romantic settings. So whether you're savouring pizza in a Neapolitan pizzeria, pasta in a Bolognese trattoria or Chianti at a Tuscan vineyard, you're in for a tasty trip.

① GOURMET PIEDMONT

Feast on cheese, chocolate, truffles and red wine in Italy's Slow Food heartland.
p44

② VALPOLICELLA WINE COUNTRY

A tasting tour of historic wineries in the vine-clad hills west of Verona.
p82

③ TUSCAN WINE TOUR

Savour great reds as you traverse Tuscany's Chianti wine country.
p150

④ FOODIE EMILIA-ROMAGNA

Taste iconic dishes and culinary specialities in foodie cities Parma, Bologna and Modena.
p162

⑤ SOUTHERN LARDER

Revel in decadent pastries, creamy mozzarella and lemon liqueurs on the Amalfi Coast.
p176

Left: Vineyards, Tuscany (p150);
Above: Cheese, meat and wine platter, Orta San Giulio (p67)

BEACHES & COASTAL SCENERY

With four seas and a 7600km coastline, Italy boasts coastal marvels at every turn. From the plunging cliffs of the Amalfi Coast to the pastel villages of the Cinque Terre, from Sicily's volcanic seascapes to Sardinia's dreamy beaches, you're sure to find somewhere to suit your style. Add crystal-clear waters and a wide range of watersports and you've got the perfect recipe for a sunny seaside holiday.

1 CINEMATIC CINQUE TERRE

A picture-perfect coastal stretch sets the backdrop for this week-long tour.
p52

2 AMALFI COAST

Bask in the beauty of Italy's celebrated coastline, a classic Mediterranean pin-up.
p180

3 SALENTO SURPRISES

Join Italian holidaymakers and sun-loving beach-goers in Puglia's summer playground.
p198

4 SARDINIA'S SOUTH COAST

Sardinia's less-trodden southern seaboard reveals glorious scenery and idyllic beaches.
p230

5 THE EMERALD COAST

Watch out for celebs on the dazzling beaches of Sardinia's northern coast.
p234

Left: Sardinia (p238); Right: Amalfi Coast (p180)

LEFT TO RIGHT: LARRAEND/SHUTTERSTOCK, ALEXIS DOYLE/LONELY PLANET

FREE BEACH

You'll have to pay to access private beach clubs. To go free, search out the *spiaggia libera* (free beach).

ISLAND FERRIES

A fleet of ferries serve Italy's many islands. Services and ticket prices increase in summer.

The Dolomites (p106)

MATT MUNRO/LONELY PLANET

WINTER ROAD CLOSURES

High-altitude mountain passes such as the Passo dello Stelvio are often closed in winter, typically October to May.

OUR PICKS

MOUNTAIN LANDSCAPES

For a taste of the high life, buckle up and head to the mountains. Stunning roads weave through the Italian Alps, Dolomites and central Apennines, snaking over hair-raising passes and through silent valleys framed by snowy summits. The driving can be challenging, but you're rewarded with thrilling scenery and superlative sport: skiing and snowboarding in winter; hiking, climbing and cycling in the warmer seasons.

① VALLE D'AOSTA

Explore pristine national parkland en route to Mont Blanc, western Europe's highest mountain.
p102

SNOW CHAINS

Make sure to have snow chains and/or winter tyres when driving in the mountains between mid-October and mid-April.

② ROOF OF ITALY

Drive the fabled Passo dello Stelvio as you explore northern Italy's high-altitude borderlands.
p98

③ GRANDE STRADA DELLE DOLOMITI

This soaring drive winds through the epic landscapes of the Dolomites.
p106

④ ABRUZZO'S WILD LANDSCAPES

Keep your eyes peeled for wolves and bears in Abruzzo's remote national parks.
p128

⑤ ACROSS THE LUCANIAN APENNINES

Go off-piste in the tough mountain country of southern Basilicata.
p202

ALEXIS DOYLE/LONELY PLANET

Ravello (p184)

OUR PICKS

VILLAS & GARDENS

Ever since ancient times, Italy's rulers have spared no expense in employing the top artists and architects of the day to design their residences. The result is a remarkable collection of imperial palaces, royal retreats, aristocratic mansions and lakeside villas. Many are now home to museums and important art collections as well as extensive gardens that can often be visited independently.

① WORLD HERITAGE WONDERS

Visit imperial palaces and art-filled palazzi (mansions) in Rome, Siena, Florence and Venice.

p28

FLOWERING SEASON

Italy's gardens are at their most seductive in April, May and early June.

THE ORIGINAL PALACE

The word 'palace' derives from Palatium, the Latin name for the Palatine Hill, site of the imperial palace in Rome.

② SAVOY PALACE CIRCUIT

Tour the Savoy family's royal palaces in Turin and the Piedmontese countryside.

p38

③ THE GRACEFUL ITALIAN LAKES

The villas and gardens of Italy's northern lakes promise romance and elegant floral displays.

p66

④ A VENETIAN SOJOURN

Andrea Palladio's Renaissance villas impress on this drive through Veneto's wine country.

p76

⑤ AMALFI COAST

Swoon at the views from Ravello's hilltop gardens, above the Amalfi Coast.

p180

WHEN TO GO

Hit the road in spring and autumn for magnificent colours, blissful temperatures and brilliant food.

DRIVING HERE

Duncan Garwood
Lonely Planet writer

A favourite memory is of my first drive through Abruzzo. It was winter and everything was blanketed in snow. The leg from Sulmona to Pescasseroli was particularly special: it was a beautiful blue-sky day, biting cold but sunny and crystal clear, and with virtually no one else on the roads I had the stunning mountain scenery all to myself. Another great trip was a spring drive along Sardinia's south coast. The colours were incredible: the vivid yellows and reds of the wildflowers, and the glorious blues of the sea and sky.

Spring and autumn are the best periods for road-tripping, sightseeing and seasonal food. The weather's pleasant and, away from the main cities, the driving is pretty easy-going.

Summer is good for festivals and beach-going, but watch out for heavy traffic on the coast and on the main north–south arteries, particularly on August weekends.

Winter brings the risk of snow and ice in mountainous areas. Routes into major ski resorts are well maintained, but high-altitude passes are often closed for the season.

Heavy rain, which can strike anytime, can make driving challenging, particularly on smaller rural roads where potholes are a perennial hazard.

ACCOMMODATION

There's no precisely defined high and low season in most Italian cities. As a general rule, accommodation is cheapest between November and March. On the coast, prices skyrocket in August, so try to come in June, early July or September. Book early for the best deals.

SNOWFALL

You can usually expect snow in the Alps and Apennines from November or December through March, possibly even later. It also snows at lower altitudes, although when and how much is far less predictable.

WEATHER WATCH: ROME

JANUARY
Avg daytime max: **12°C**. Days of rainfall: **7**

FEBRUARY
Avg daytime max: **13°C**. Days of rainfall: 7

MARCH
Avg daytime max: **16°C**. Days of rainfall: **7**

APRIL
Avg daytime max: **19°C**. Days of rainfall: **7**

MAY
Avg daytime max: **23°C**. Days of rainfall: **6**

JUNE
Avg daytime max: **27°C**. Days of rainfall: **4**

DIETMAR RAUSCHER/SHUTTERSTOCK

Il Palio di Siena (p159)

HOT WINDS

In southern or central Italy, it's not uncommon to wake up on a spring or summer morning and find your car dusted in sand. This is due to the *scirocco*, a hot wind that blows in from north Africa bringing sand from the Sahara Desert.

DROUGHT

Images of Venice's canals running dry in February 2023 shone a stark light on the water situation in northern Italy. A severe drought in summer 2022 was followed by a dry winter in 2023, leading to alarmingly low levels in many lakes and rivers.

BLOCKBUSTER EVENTS

Carnevale
In the run-up to Lent, Carnevale sees an outbreak of partying, dressing up and extravagant parades. Masked balls are staged in Venice and giant papier-mâché floats are paraded around Viareggio. **February**

Pasqua
Easter is celebrated across the country with solemn processions and explosive firework displays. In Rome, the Pope leads a candlelit procession on Good Friday and gives his traditional blessing on Easter Sunday. **March or April**

Il Palio di Siena
Costumed horse riders thrill the crowds as they race bareback around Siena's showcase piazza. Emotions run high amid all the medieval pomp and pageantry. **July and August**

Estate Romana
Rome's historic streets and ancient monuments set a unique backdrop for a summer season of events, concerts and performances. **June to September**

JULY
Avg daytime max: **31°C**. Days of rainfall: **3**

AUGUST
Avg daytime max: **31°C**. Days of rainfall: **3**

SEPTEMBER
Avg daytime max: **27°C**. Days of rainfall: **7**

OCTOBER
Avg daytime max: **22°C**. Days of rainfall: **8**

NOVEMBER
Avg daytime max: **17°C**. Days of rainfall: **9**

DECEMBER
Avg daytime max: **13°C**. Days of rainfall: **8**

GET PREPARED FOR ITALY

Useful things to load in your bag, your ears and your brain

WATCH

- **La grande bellezza** *(Paolo Sorrentino; 2013)* Lavish depiction of Rome as a complex, beautiful city with a morally bankrupt heart.

- **Inspector Montalbano** *(1999–2021)* Hugely popular TV series starring a food-loving detective and stunning baroque locations in southeastern Sicily.

- **Call Me By Your Name** *(Luca Guadagnino; 2017)* Timothée Chalamet adorns several north Italian locations in this languid love story.

- **A Room with a View** *(James Ivory; 1985)* Florence provides the alluring backdrop to this tale of passion in 19th-century Tuscany.

- **Pane e Tulipani** *(Silvio Soldini; 2000)* A sweet, slow-burning romance set in the seductive streets of Venice.

CLOTHING

Staples For driving and daytime sightseeing, comfort is key, so keep it casual and loose. For going out in the evening, smart casual is the way to go: trousers and shirts or polos for men; skirts, trousers or dresses for women. In summer, shorts, T-shirts and sandals are fine for sightseeing and relaxed beachside lounging. Bring a light waterproof jacket for spring and autumn, and cold-weather gear for winter.

Comfy shoes Practical shoes are a must as cobblestones and uneven surfaces can play havoc with ankles – Pompeii in heels is not a good idea. As a general rule, pack a pair of shoes or trainers for daytime use and a smarter pair for the evening.

Accessories Sunglasses are essential for long hours behind the wheel, particularly along the coast or high in the mountains. A hat can be a summer lifesaver too, especially at the big archaeological sites where it can get ferociously hot and there's often little shade.

Dress codes Many religious sites enforce dress codes, so if you want to get into St Peter's Basilica in Rome or Venice's Basilica di San Marco, play it safe and cover your shoulders, torso and thighs.

CLOCKWISE FROM TOP LEFT: DENDRACREATIVE/SHUTTERSTOCK, THE_MOLOSTOCK/SHUTTERSTOCK, ANTON STARIKOV/SHUTTERSTOCK, KARTINKIN77/SHUTTERSTOCK, ALEXIS DOYLE/LONELY PLANET

Amalfi Coast (p180)

WORDS

ciao hi/bye (informal)
buongiorno/buonasera good morning/good evening
arrivederci goodbye
per favore please
grazie thank you
prego you're welcome
scusa/scusi excuse me (informal/formal)
Non capisco I don't understand
Parla inglese? Do you speak English?
una macchina a car
noleggiare to hire
manuale/automatico manual/automatic
Quanto costa? How much is it?
assicurazione insurance
incidente accident
Come si arriva a ...? How do you get to ....?
destra right
sinistra left
dritto straight ahead
semaforo traffic light
Dove posso parcheggiare? Where can I park?
benzina petrol
gasolio diesel
benzinaio petrol station
Il pieno, per favore Fill it up, please

LISTEN

Rush!
(Måneskin; 2023) The third album by Italy's all-conquering glam rockers topped charts across Europe.

Viva la Taranta
(Orchestra Popolare La Notte della Taranta; 2015) A live album introducing the mesmeric sounds of Pugliese folk music.

La voce del padrone
(Franco Battiato; 1981) The best-selling album that catapulted Italy's much-loved singer-songwriter to pop superstardom.

READ

My Brilliant Friend
(Elena Ferrante; 2012) An international bestseller chronicling the friendship between two girls in postwar Naples.

La Bella Figura: A Field Guide to the Italian Mind
(Beppe Severgnini; 2007) Journalist Severgnini wittily explains the Italian mindset.

SPQR: A History of Ancient Rome
(Mary Beard; 2015) Celebrity classicist brings ancient Rome to life in this authoritative history.

Vroom with a View
(Peter Moore; 2011) Australian travel writer Moore pootles through Italy on a 1960s Vespa.

ROAD TRIPS

Passo Gardena, The Dolomites (p112)

OKSANA.PERKINS/SHUTTERSTOCK

CONTENTS

01

EPIC TRIP: GRAND TOUR

★ BEST FOR:

HISTORY

Rome, the repository of over 2000 years of European history.

The Colosseum (p27)

DURATION: 12–14 DAYS

DISTANCE: 1390KM/864 MILES

GREAT FOR: HISTORY, FOOD AND DRINK

BEST TIME TO GO: SPRING (MARCH TO MAY) IS PERFECT FOR URBAN SIGHTSEEING.

BY DUNCAN GARWOOD

From the Savoy palaces of Turin and Leonardo's *The Last Supper* to the disreputable drinking dens of Genoa and pleasure palaces of Rome, the Grand Tour is part scholar's pilgrimage and part rite of passage. Offering a chance to view some of the world's greatest masterpieces and hear Vivaldi played on 18th-century cellos, it's a rollicking trip filled with the sights, sounds and tastes that have shaped European society for centuries.

LINK YOUR TRIP

24 Tuscan Wine Tour
Linger in the bucolic hills around Florence and enjoy fine gourmet dining and world-renowned wine-tasting.

29 Amalfi Coast
Play truant from high-minded museums and head south from Naples for the Blue Ribbon drive on the Amalfi Coast.

01 Turin

In his travel guide, *Voyage Through Italy* (1670), travel writer and tutor Richard Lassels advocated a grand cultural tour of Europe, and in particular Italy, for young English aristocrats, during which the study of classical antiquity and the High Renaissance would ready them for future influential roles shaping the political, economic and social realities of the day.

First they travelled through France before crossing the Alps at Mt Cenis and heading to Turin (Torino), where letters of introduction admitted them to the city's agreeable Parisian-style social whirl. Today Turin's tree-lined boulevards retain their elegant, French feel. and many gilded cafes, such as **Caffè Al Bicerin** *(bicerin.it)*, still serve its signature coffee and chocolate drink – as it has since the 1760s.

Like the Medicis in Florence (Firenze) and the Borghese in Rome (Roma), Turin's Savoy princes had a penchant for extravagant

architecture and interior decor. It seems they might have pined for their hunting lodges in Chambéry, France, from where they originated though, as they invited André Le Nôtre, Versailles landscaper, to design the gardens of **Palazzo Reale** *(museireali.beniculturali.it)* in 1697.

THE DRIVE: The two-hour (170km) drive to Genoa is all on the *autostrada*, the final stretch twisting through the mountains. Leave Turin following signs for the A55 (towards Alessandria), which quickly merges with the A21 passing through the pretty Piedmontese countryside. Just before Alessandria turn south onto the A26 for Genoa/Livorno.

DETOUR

Milan

Start: 01 Turin

No Grand Tour would be complete without a detour up the A4 to Milan (Milano) to eyeball Leonardo da Vinci's iconic mural *The Last Supper (Il Cenacolo)* in Leonardo's Last Supper Museum *(cenacolovinciano.org/en)*. Advance booking is essential.

From his *Portrait of a Young Man* (c 1486) to portraits of Duke Ludovico Sforza's beautiful mistresses, *The Lady with Ermine* (c 1489) and *La Belle Ferronière* (c 1490), Leonardo transformed the rigid conventions of portraiture to depict highly individual images imbued with naturalism. Then he evolved concepts of idealised proportions and the depiction of internal emotional states through physical dynamism (St Jerome), all of which cohere in the masterly *Il Cenacolo*.

While you're here, take time to walk around other parts of the city, too.

02 Genoa

Some travellers, shy of crossing the Alps, might arrive by boat in Genoa (Genova). Despite its superb location, mild microclimate and lush flora, the city had a dubious reputation. Its historic centre was a warren of dark, insalubrious *caruggi* (narrow streets), frequented by sex workers and beggars, while the excessive shrewdness of the Genovese banking families earned them an infamy according to author Thomas Nugent, as 'a treacherous and over-reaching set of people'.

And yet with tourists and businesspeople arriving from around the world, Genoa was, and still is, a cosmopolitan place. The **Rolli Palaces**, a collection of grand mansions originally meant to host visiting popes, dignitaries and royalty, made Via Balbi and Strada Nuova (now Via Giuseppe Garibaldi) two of the most famous streets in Europe. Visit the finest of them, the **Palazzo Spinola** *(palazzospinola.cultura.gov.it)* and the **Palazzo Reale** *(palazzorealegenova.cultura.gov.it)*. Afterwards stop for sweets at **Pietro Romanengo fu Stefano** *(romanengo.com)*.

THE DRIVE: This 365km drive takes most of the day, so stop for lunch in Cremona. Although the drive is on the *autostrade*, endless fields of corn line the route. Take the A7 north out of Genoa and at Tortona exit onto the A21 around industrial Piacenza to Brescia. At Brescia, change again onto the A4 direct to Padua.

03 Padua

Bound for Venice (Venezia), Grand Tourists could hardly avoid visiting Padua (Padova), although by the 18th century international students no longer flocked to **Palazzo Bo** *(unipd.it/en/bo)*, the Venetian Republic's radical university where Copernicus and Galileo taught.

You can visit the university's claustrophobic, wooden anatomy theatre (the first in the world), although on the average tourist itinerary it's no longer de rigueur to witness dissections. Afterwards don't forget to pay your respects to the skulls of noble professors who donated themselves for dissection due to the difficulty involved in acquiring fresh corpses. Their skulls are lined up in the graduation hall.

Beyond the university the melancholy air of the city did little to detain visitors. Even Giotto's spectacular frescoes in the **Cappella degli Scrovegni** *(cappelladegli scrovegni.it)*, where advance reservations are essential, were of limited interest as medieval art was out of fashion, and only devout Catholics ventured to revere the strange relics of St Anthony in the **Basilica di Sant'Antonio** *(basilicadelsanto.org)*.

THE DRIVE: Barely 40km from Venice, the drive from Padua is through featureless areas of light industry along the A4 and then the A57.

04 Venice

Top of the itinerary, Venice at last! Then, as now, La Serenissima's watery landscape captured the imagination of travellers. At **Carnevale** *(carnevale.venezia.it)* in February numbers swelled to 30,000; now they number in the hundreds of thousands.

You cannot take your car onto the lagoon islands so leave it in a secure garage in Mestre, such as **Garage Europa Mestre** *(garageeuropamestre.com)*, and hop on the train to Venice Santa Lucia where water taxis connect to all the islands.

Aside from the mind-improving art in the **Gallerie dell'Accademia** *(gallerieaccademia.it)* and extraordinary architectural masterpieces such as the **Palazzo Ducale**, the **Campanile**, Longhena's **Chiesa**

Palazzo Bo

FEDELE FERRARA/SHUTTERSTOCK

di Santa Maria della Salute and the glittering domes of **Basilica di San Marco** *(basilicasanmarco.it)*, Venice was considered an exciting den of debauchery.

Venetian wives were notorious for keeping handsome escorts (*cicisbei*), and whole areas of town were given over to venality. One of Venice's best restaurants, **Antiche Carampane** *(antiche carampane.com)*, is located in what was once a den of vice, so called because of the notorious brothel at Palazzo Ca' Rampani.

Eighteenth-century tourists would inevitably have stopped for coffee at the newly opened **Caffè Florian** *(caffeflorian.com)* and paid a visit to the opera house, **Teatro La Fenice** *(teatrola fenice.it)*, to hear groundbreaking concerts now being revived by the **Venice Music Project** *(venice musicproject.it)*.

THE DRIVE: Retrace your steps to Padua on the A57 and A4 and navigate around the ring road in the direction of Bologna to pick up the A13 southwest for this two-hour drive. After Padua the *autostrada* dashes through wide-open farmland and crosses the Po river, which forms the southern border of the Veneto.

05 Bologna

Home to Europe's oldest university (established in 1088) and once the stomping ground of Dante, Boccaccio and Petrarch, Bologna had an enviable reputation for courtesy and culture. Its historic centre, complete with 20 soaring towers, is one of the best-preserved medieval cities in the world.

In the **Basilica di San Petronio** *(basilicadisanpetronio.org)*, originally intended to dwarf St Peter's in Rome, Giovanni Cassini's sundial (1655) proved the problems with the Julian calendar giving us the leap year. Meanwhile Bolognesi students advanced human knowledge in obstetrics, natural science, zoology and anthropology; you can peer at their strange model waxworks and studiously labelled collections in the **Palazzo Poggi** *(sma.unibo.it/it/il-sistema-museale/museo-di-palazzo-poggi)*.

In art as in science, the School of Bologna gave birth to the Carracci brothers Annibale and Agostino and their cousin Ludovico, who were among the founding fathers of Italian baroque and were deeply influenced by the Counter-Reformation.

See their emotionally charged blockbusters in the **Pinacoteca Nazionale** *(pinacoteca bologna.beniculturali.it)*.

THE DRIVE: Bologna sits at the intersection of the A1, A13 and A14. From the centre navigate west out of the city, across the river Reno, onto the A1. From here it's a straight shot into Florence for 100km, leaving the Po plains behind you and entering the low hills of Emilia-Romagna and the forested valleys of Tuscany.

☑ TOP TIP

JUMP THE QUEUE IN FLORENCE

In July, August and other busy periods such as Easter, long queues are a fact of life at Florence's key museums. Tickets to the Uffizi and Galleria dell'Accademia (where David lives) can be booked in advance. Book at uffizi.it and firenzemusei.it.

06 Florence

From Filippo Brunelleschi's red-tiled dome atop Florence's **Duomo** *(museumflorence.com)* to Michelangelo's and Botticelli's greatest hits, *David* and *The Birth of Venus*, in the **Galleria dell'Accademia** *(galleriaaccademiafirenze.it)* and the **Galleria degli Uffizi** *(uffizi.it)*, Florence, according to UNESCO, contains the highest number of artistic masterpieces in the world.

Whereas Rome and Milan have torn themselves down and been rebuilt many times, incorporating a multitude of architectural whims, central Florence looks much as it did in 1550, with stone towers and cypress-lined gardens.

THE DRIVE: The next 210km, continuing south along the A1, travels through some of Italy's most lovely scenery. Just southwest of Florence the vineyards of Greve in Chianti harbour some great farm stays, while Arezzo lies to the east. Exit at Orvieto and follow on the SR71 and SR2 for the final 45km into Viterbo.

07 Viterbo

From Florence the road to Rome crossed the dreaded and pestilential *campagna* (countryside), a swampy, mosquito-infested low-lying area. Unlike today, inns en route were uncomfortable and hazardous, so travellers hurried through Siena, stocking up on wine for the rough road ahead. They also stopped briefly in medieval Viterbo for a quick douse in the thermal springs at the **Terme dei Papi** *(termedei papi.it)*, and a tour of the High Renaissance gardens at Villa Lante.

THE DRIVE: Rejoin the A1 after a 28km drive along the rural SS675. For the next 40km the A1 descends through Lazio,

♥ WHY I LOVE THIS TRIP

DUNCAN GARWOOD, WRITER

Inspired by the 18th-century Grand Tour, this timeless route retraces the footsteps of the trailblazing tourists who set off for Italy in search of sun, culture and perhaps a little illicit adventure. Covering the country's show-stopping cities, it offers travellers a view of Italy's very best art, architecture and antiquities, while transporting them from snowcapped alpine peaks to sun-kissed southern shores.

criss-crossing the Tevere river and keeping the ridge of the Apennines to the left as it darts through tunnels. At Fiano Romano exit for Roma Nord and follow the A1dir and SS4 (Via Salaria) for the final 20km push into the capital.

08 Rome

In the 18th century, Rome, even in ruins, was still thought of as the august capital of the world.

Here more than anywhere the Grand Tourist was awakened to an interest in art and architecture – although the **Colosseum** *(colosseo.it)* was still filled with debris and the **Palatine Hill** *(colosseo.it/area/palatino)* was covered in gardens – its excavated treasures slowly accumulating in the world's oldest national museum, the **Capitoline Museums** *(museicapitolini.org)*.

Arriving through the Porta del Popolo, visitors first espied the dome of **St Peter's** *(www.basilicasanpietro.va)* before clattering along the *corso* to the customs house.

Once done, they headed to the **Piazza di Spagna** – the city's principal meeting place, where Keats penned his love poems and died of consumption – and nearby **Trevi Fountain**. Although the **Pantheon** *(pantheonroma.com)* and **Vatican Museums** *(museivaticani.va)* were a must, most travellers preferred to socialise in the grounds of the **Borghese Palace** *(galleria borghese.beniculturali.it)*.

Follow their example and mix the choicest sights with pleasures such as fine dining at **Aroma** *(aromarestaurant.it)* and souvenir shopping at antique perfumery **Officina Profumo Farmaceutica di Santa Maria Novella** *(smnovella.com)*.

THE DRIVE: Past Rome the landscape is hotter and drier, trees give way to Mediterranean shrubbery and the grass starts to yellow. Beyond the vineyards of Frascati, 20km south of Rome, the A1 runs 225km to Naples (Napoli), a two-hour drive that can take longer if there's heavy traffic.

PHOTO OPPORTUNITY

FLORENCE

Florence's multicoloured, marble duomo (cathedral).

09 Naples

Only the more adventurous Grand Tourists continued south to the salacious southern city of Naples.

At the time, Mt Vesuvius glowed menacingly on the bay, erupting no fewer than six times during the 18th century and eight times in the 19th century.

But Naples was the home of opera and commedia dell'arte (improvised comedic drama satirising stock social stereotypes), and singing lessons and seats at **Teatro San Carlo** were obligatory.

Then there were the myths of Virgil and Dante to explore at **Lago d'Averno** and the **Campi Flegrei** (Phlegrean Fields).

And, after the discovery of **Pompeii** *(pompeiisites.org)* in 1748, the unfolding drama of a Roman town in its death throes drew throngs of mawkish voyeurs. Then, as now, it was one of the most popular tourist sights in Italy and its priceless mosaics, frescoes and colossal sculptures fill Naples' **Museo Archeologico Nazionale** *(museoarcheologiconapoli.it/en)*.

TOP TIP

ROME INFO LINE

The Comune di Roma (Rome city council) runs a phone line (06 06 08) providing info on sights, events, transport and accommodation. You can also book theatre, concert, exhibition and museum tickets. Staff speak English, as well as French, Spanish, German and Japanese. Its website *(060608.it)* is also a good source of up-to-date information.

Trevi Fountain

TONI PALOMARES/SHUTTERSTOCK

02

EPIC TRIP: WORLD HERITAGE WONDERS

DURATION: 14 DAYS

DISTANCE: 870KM/540 MILES

GREAT FOR: HISTORY, FOOD AND DRINK

BEST TIME TO GO: APRIL, MAY AND SEPTEMBER FOR IDEAL WEATHER AND LOCAL PRODUCE.

BY DUNCAN GARWOOD

Topping the UNESCO charts with 61 World Heritage Sites, Italy offers the full gamut, ranging from historic city centres and human-made masterpieces to snowcapped mountains and areas of outstanding natural beauty. This trip through central and northern Italy touches on the country's unparalleled artistic and architectural legacy, taking in ancient Roman ruins, priceless Renaissance paintings, great cathedrals and, to cap it all off, Venice's unique canal-scape.

LINK YOUR TRIP

20 Etruscan Tuscany & Lazio
From Rome take the A12 *autostrada* up to Cerveteri and connect with this tour of ancient Etruscan treasures.

24 Tuscan Wine Tour
From Florence head south to Tuscany's Chianti wine country to indulge in some wine tasting at the area's historic vineyards.

01 Rome

An epic, monumental metropolis, Italy's capital is a city of thrilling beauty and high drama. Its historic centre, which according to UNESCO has some of antiquity's most important monuments, has been a World Heritage Site since 1980, and the Vatican, technically a separate state but in reality located within Rome's city limits, has been on the UNESCO list since 1984.

Of Rome's many ancient monuments, the most iconic is the **Colosseum** *(colosseo.it)*, the towering 1st-century-CE amphitheatre where gladiators met in mortal combat and condemned criminals fought off wild beasts. Nearby, the **Palatine Hill** *(colosseo.it/area/palatino)* was the ancient city's most exclusive neighbourhood, as well as its oldest – Romulus and Remus supposedly founded the city here in 753 BCE. From the Palatino, you can stroll down to the skeletal ruins of the **Roman Forum** *(colosseo.it/area/foro-romano)*, the

★ BEST FOR

ART & ARCHITECTURE

Florence's Galleria degli Uffizi.

OZEF / SHUTTERSTOCK

Galleria degli Uffizi, Florence (p22)

once-beating heart of the ancient city. All three sights are covered by a single ticket.

To complete your tour of classical wonders search out the **Pantheon** *(pantheonroma.com)*, the best preserved of Rome's ancient monuments. One of the most influential buildings in the world, this domed temple, now a church, is an extraordinary sight with its vast columned portico and soaring marble-clad interior.

THE DRIVE: The easiest route to Siena is the three-hour, 236km drive via the A1 *autostrada*. Join this from the Rome ring road, the GRA (Grande Raccordo Anulare), and head north, past Orvieto's dramatic clifftop cathedral, to the Valdichiano exit. Take this and follow signs onto the Raccordo Siena-Bettolle (E78) for the last leg into Siena.

02 Siena

Siena is one of Italy's most enchanting medieval towns. Its walled centre, a beautifully preserved warren of dark lanes, Gothic palazzi (mansions) and pretty piazzas, is centred on **Piazza del Campo** (known as Il Campo), the sloping shell-shaped square that stages the city's annual horse race, **Il Palio**, on 2 July and 16 August. On the piazza, the 102m-high **Torre del Mangia** *(museocivico.comune.siena.it)* soars above the Gothic **Palazzo Pubblico** (Palazzo Comunale), home to the city's finest art museum, the **Museo Civico**. Of Siena's churches, the one to see is the 13th-century **Duomo** (Cattedrale di Santa Maria Assunta; *operaduomo.siena.it*), one of Italy's greatest Gothic churches. Highlights include the remarkable white, green and red facade, and, inside, the magnificent inlaid marble floor that illustrates historical and biblical stories.

PHOTO OPPORTUNITY

ROME

The Roman Forum from the Palatino.

THE DRIVE: There are two alternatives to get to Florence. The quickest is the 76km, 1½ hour drive via the RA3 Siena–Firenze Raccordo. But if you have the time, we recommend the scenic 70km meander along the SR222, which snakes through the Chianti wine country, passing through quintessential hilltop towns and vine-laden slopes. Reckon on at least 2½ hours to properly appreciate this route.

DETOUR

San Gimignano

Start: 02 Siena

Dubbed the medieval Manhattan thanks to its 14 11th-century towers, San Gimignano is a classic hilltop town and an easy detour from Siena. From the car park next to **Porta San Giovanni**, it's a short walk up to Palazzo Comunale *(sangimignanomusei.it)*, which houses the town's art gallery, the **Pinacoteca**, and tallest tower, the **Torre Grossa**. Nearby, the Romanesque basilica, known as the **Collegiata** *(duomosangimignano.it)*, has some remarkable Ghirlandaio frescoes.

Before leaving, be sure to sample the local Vernaccia wine at the **Vernaccia di San Gimignano Wine Experience** (sangimignanomuseovernaccia.com) next to the **Rocca** (fortress).

San Gimignano is about 40km northwest of Siena. Head for Florence on the RA3 until Poggibonsi and then pick up the SS429.

03 Florence

Cradle of the Renaissance and home of Michelangelo, Machiavelli and the Medici, Florence (Firenze) is magnetic, romantic, unique and busy. A couple of days is not long here but enough for a breathless introduction to the city's top sights, many of which can be

ITALIAN ART & ARCHITECTURE

The Ancients

In pre-Roman times, the Greeks built theatres and proportionally perfect temples in their southern colonies at Agrigento, Syracuse and Paestum, while the Etruscans concentrated on funerary art, creating elaborate tombs at Tarquinia and Cerveteri. Coming in their wake, the Romans specialised in roads, aqueducts and monumental amphitheatres such as the Colosseum and Verona's Arena.

Romanesque

With the advent of Christianity in the 4th century, basilicas began to spring up, many with glittering Byzantine-style mosaics. The Romanesque period (c 1050–1200) saw the construction of fortified monasteries and robust, bulky churches such as Bari's Basilica di San Nicola and Modena's cathedral. Pisa's striking duomo (cathedral) displays a characteristic Tuscan variation on the style.

Gothic

Gothic architecture, epic in scale and typically embellished by gargoyles, pinnacles and statues, took on a more classical form in Italy. Assisi's Basilica di San Francesco is an outstanding early example, but for the full-blown Italian Gothic style check out the cathedrals in Florence, Venice, Siena and Orvieto.

Renaissance

From quiet beginnings in 14th-century Florence, the Renaissance erupted across Italy before spreading across Europe. In Italy, painters such as Giotto, Botticelli, da Vinci and Raphael led the way, while architects Brunelleschi and Bramante rewrote the rule books with their beautifully proportioned basilicas. All-rounder Michelangelo worked his way into immortality, producing masterpieces such as *David* and the Sistine Chapel frescoes.

Baroque

Dominating the 17th century, the extravagant baroque style found fertile soil in Italy. Witness the Roman works of Gian Lorenzo Bernini and Francesco Borromini, Lecce's flamboyant *centro storico* (historic centre) and the magical baroque towns of southeastern Sicily.

Neoclassicism

Signalling a return to sober classical lines, neoclassicism majored in the late-18th and early-19th centuries. Signature works include Caserta's Palazzo Reale and La Scala opera house in Milan. In artistic terms, the most famous Italian exponent was Antonio Canova.

Cappella degli Scrovegni, Padua (p33)

REDMASON/SHUTTERSTOCK

WHY I LOVE THIS TRIP

DUNCAN GARWOOD, WRITER

Every one of the towns and cities on this drive is special. The great treasures of Rome, Florence and Venice are amazing but, for me, it's the lesser-known highlights that make this such an incredible trip – Siena's Gothic Duomo, Modena's stunning Romanesque cathedral, the Cappella degli Scrovegni in Padua, and Verona's gorgeous medieval centre.

JOHN HARPER/GETTY IMAGES

The Leaning Tower, Pisa

WORLD HERITAGE SITES

With 61 World Heritage Sites, Italy has more than any other country. But what exactly is a World Heritage Site? It's anywhere that UNESCO's World Heritage Committee decides is of 'outstanding universal value' and inscribes on the World Heritage List. It could be a natural wonder such as the Great Barrier Reef in Australia or a human-made icon such as New York's Statue of Liberty, a historic city centre or a great work of art or architecture.

The list was set up in 1972 and has since grown to include over 1200 sites from 170 countries. Italy first got in on the act in 1979 when it successfully nominated its first entry – the prehistoric rock drawings of the Valcamonica valley in northeastern Lombardy.

The inscription process requires sites to be nominated by a country and then independently evaluated. If they pass scrutiny and meet at least one of 10 selection criteria, they get the green light at the World Heritage Committee's annual meeting. Once on the list, sites qualify for management support and access to the World Heritage Fund.

Italian nominations have generally fared well and since Rome's historic centre and the Chiesa di Santa Maria delle Grazie in Milan were inscribed in 1980, many of the nation's greatest attractions have made it onto the list – the historic centres of Florence, Naples, Siena and San Gimignano; the cities of Venice, Verona and Ferrara; the archaeological sites of Pompeii, Paestum and Agrigento; as well as natural beauties such as the Amalfi Coast, Aeolian Islands, Dolomites and Tuscany's Val d'Orcia.

enjoyed on foot. Towering above the medieval skyline, the **Duomo** (Cattedrale di Santa Maria del Fiore; *museumflorence.com*) dominates the city centre with its famous red-tiled dome and striking facade. A short hop away, **Piazza della Signoria** opens onto the sculpture-filled **Loggia dei Lanzi** and the **Torre d'Arnolfo** above **Palazzo Vecchio** *(musefirenze.it)*, Florence's lavish City Hall. Next to the palazzo, the **Galleria degli Uffizi** *(uffizi.it)* houses one of the world's great art collections, including works by Botticelli, Leonardo da Vinci, Michelangelo, Raphael and many other Renaissance maestros.

THE DRIVE: You can cover the 90km from Florence to Pisa in just over an hour along the A11 *autostrada*; alternatively, take the speedy, toll-free FI-PI-LI (SS67) linking the two cities. At the end of either route, follow signs to Pisa *centro*.

04 Pisa

Once a maritime republic to rival Genoa and Venice, Pisa now owes its fame to an architectural project gone horribly wrong. The **Leaning Tower** *(opapisa.it)* is an extraordinary sight and one of Italy's most photographed monuments. The tower, originally erected as a campanile (bell tower) in the late 12th century, is one of three Romanesque buildings on the immaculate lawns of **Piazza dei Miracoli** (also known as Campo dei Miracoli or Piazza del Duomo).

The candy-striped **Duomo** (Duomo di Santa Maria Assunta; *opapisa.it*), begun in 1063, has a graceful tiered facade and cavernous interior, while to its west, the cupcake-like **Battistero** *(opapisa.it)* is something of an architectural hybrid, with a Pisan-Romanesque lower section and a Gothic upper level and dome. End your Piazza dei Miracoli foray with a saunter atop the city's old medieval walls, **Mura di Pisa** *(muradipisa.it)*.

THE DRIVE: It's a 206km, 2½-hour trip up to Modena from Pisa. Head back towards Florence on the A11 and then pick up the A1 to Bologna. Continue as the road twists and falls through the wooded Apennines before flattening out near Bologna. Exit at Modena Sud (Modena South) and follow signs for the *centro*.

05 Modena

One of Italy's top foodie towns, Modena has a stunning medieval centre and a trio of UNESCO-listed sights. First up is the gorgeous **Duomo** (Cattedrale Metropolitana di Santa Maria Assunta e San Geminiano; *museideldAnd uomodimodena.it*), which is widely considered to be Italy's finest Romanesque church. Features to look out for include the Gothic rose window and a series of bas-reliefs depicting scenes from Genesis.

Nearby, the 13th-century **Torre Ghirlandina** *(visitmodena.it)*, an 87m-high tower topped by a Gothic spire, was named after Seville's Giralda bell tower by exiled Spanish Jews in the early 16th century. The last of the UNESCO threesome is **Piazza Grande**, just south of the cathedral. The city's focal square, this is flanked by the porticoed **Palazzo Comunale**, Modena's elegant town hall.

THE DRIVE: From Modena it's about 1¼ hours for the 105km drive to Verona, via the A22 and A4 *autostrade*. Follow the A22 as it traverses the flat Po valley plain, passing the medieval town of Mantua (Mantova; worth a quick break) before connecting with the A4. Turn off at Verona Sud and follow signs for the city centre.

06 Verona

A World Heritage Site since 2000, Verona's historic centre is a beautiful compilation of architectural styles and inspiring buildings. Chief among these is its stunning Roman amphitheatre, known as the **Arena**. Dating to the 1st century CE, this is Italy's third-largest amphitheatre after the Colosseum and Capua amphitheatre, and although it no longer seats 30,000, it still draws sizeable crowds for opera and concerts.

But Verona isn't simply a relic. A thriving city, it also hosts a fantastic modern art gallery, **Galleria d'Arte Moderna Achille Forti** *(gam.comune.verona.it)*, with a fabulous collection of under-appreciated modernists such as Felice Casorati and Angelo Zamboni. It's also packed with contemporary restaurants like **Locanda 4 Cuochi** *(locanda4cuochi.it)* and wine bars, such as **Antica Bottega del Vino** *(bottegavini.it)*.

THE DRIVE: The 90km jaunt from Verona to Padua takes about an hour on the A4 Venice *autostrada*. Exit at Padova Ovest (Padua West) and join the SP47 after the toll booth. Follow this until you see, after a road bridge, a turnoff signposted to the *centro*.

07 Padua

Travellers to Padua (Padova) usually make a beeline for the city's main attraction, the **Cappella degli Scrovegni** *(cappelladegliscrovegni.it)*, but there's more to Padua than Giotto frescoes and it's actually the **Orto Botanico** *(ortobotanico1545.it)* that represents Padua on UNESCO's list of World Heritage Sites. The oldest botanical garden in the world, this dates to 1545 when a group of medical students planted some rare plants in order to study their medicinal properties. Discover Padua's outsized contribution to science and, in particular, medicine at the fascinating **Museum of Medical History** *(musme.it)*, housed in what was ostensibly the world's first hospital where medical students learnt clinical practice at a patient's bedside.

THE DRIVE: Traffic permitting, it's about 45 minutes to cover the 40km to Venice along the A4. Pass through Mestre and over the Ponte della Libertà bridge to Interparking Venezia Tronchetto on the island of Tronchetto.

08 Venice

The end of the road, quite literally, is Venice (Venezia). Of the city's many must-sees the most famous are on **Piazza San Marco**, including the **Basilica di San Marco** *(basilicasanmarco.it)*, Venice's great showpiece church. Built to house the bones of St Mark, it's a truly awe-inspiring vision with its spangled spires, Byzantine domes, luminous mosaics and lavish marble. For a bird's-eye view, head to the **Campanile**.

Adjacent to the basilica, the **Palazzo Ducale** *(palazzoducale.visitmuve.it)* was the residence of Venice's doges (ruling dukes) from the 9th century. Inside, its lavishly decorated chambers harbour some seriously heavyweight art, including Tintoretto's gigantic **Il Paradiso** in the Sala del Maggiore Consiglio. Connecting the palace to the city dungeons, the **Ponte dei Sospiri** (Bridge of Sighs) was named after the sighs that prisoners (including Casanova) emitted en route from court to cell. If you're hungry, hit the streets on foot to get a real taste of the city.

SWITZERLAND
AUSTRIA
SLOVENIA
CROATIA
FRANCE
Bern
Rhein
Draw
VALLE D'AOSTA
PIEDMONT
LOMBARDY
LIGURIA
ALTO ADIGE (SÜDTIROL)
TRENTINO
VENETO
FRIULI VENEZIA GIULIA
EMILIA-ROMAGNA
TUSCANY
SAN MARINO
LE MARCHE
Adriatic Sea
Golfo di Genova (Gulf of Genoa)
Lago di Como
Lago d'Iseo
Lago di Garda
Po
Adige
Piave
Arno
Domodossola
Locarno
Cannobio
Verbania
Stresa
Varese
Como
Bellagio
Gravedona
Sondrio
Tirano
Bormio
Malè
Merano
Bolzano
Siusi
Bressanone (Brixen)
La Villa
Brunico (Bruneck)
Vigo di Fassa
Cortina d'Ampezzo
Sappada
Tolmezzo
Tarvisio
Cividale del Friuli
Udine
Cormons
Gorizia
Aquileia
Trieste
Pordenone
Belluno
Trento
Rovereto
Riva del Garda
Salò
Bassano del Grappa
Treviso
Vicenza
Mestre
Venice
Padua
Chioggia
Este
Verona
Desenzano del Garda
Brescia
Bergamo
Monza
Rho
Milan
Crema
Cremona
Mantua
Novara
Pavia
Piacenza
Turin
Issogne
Alessandria
Tortona
Asti
Alba
Bra
Racconigi
Cuneo
Limone Piemonte
Triora
Ventimiglia
San Remo
Imperia
Finale Ligure
Savona
Genoa
Camogli
Sestri Levante
La Spezia
Lerici
Pisa
Florence
Parma
Modena
Bologna
Ferrara
Ravenna
San Marino
Ancona
A8
E25
A26
E35
A4
A55
E70
A21
A6
E74
A1
A7
A10
A15
A12
A22
E45
A13
A14
SS14
03
04
05
06
07
08
09
10
11
12
0 50 km
0 25 miles

EVA PRUCHOVA/SHUTTERSTOCK

Cinque Terre (p54)

NORTHERN ITALY

EXPLORE

NORTHERN ITALY

From glacial lakes to vine-clad hills, coastal villages to cosmopolitan cities, northern Italy boasts natural wonders and cultural treasures. The area has been luring travellers since the days of the Grand Tour, and it's easy to see what draws them: art and architecture, an embarrassment of culinary riches, cult wines and a slew of sophisticated cities. Our trips reveal the area in all its diversity – coastal roads meander down the Italian Riviera, country lanes skirt lakes and prized vineyards, and high-speed highways lead to historic cities. Stunning scenery awaits on every route as you motor past flourishing wineries, royal palaces and romantic lakeside gardens.

Milan

Many trips to northern Italy pass through Milan, the area's historic powerhouse.

A fast-paced, forward-looking metropolis renowned for its fashion, design and high-end shopping, it's a city of trend-setters, start-ups and sharply dressed financiers.

Among its many banks and boutiques, it also harbours some celebrated masterpieces including its fairy-tale Gothic Duomo and Leonardo da Vinci's *The Last Supper*.

To reach the city you can fly to its two airports (Malpensa and Linate) or get a national or international train into Milano Centrale.

For drivers, autostradas strike out in all directions – the A4 is a principal artery, pushing east to cities such as Bergamo, Brescia, Verona and Venice.

To the north, lakes Maggiore and Como are accessible by train or car.

Venice

Italy's beguiling canal city is a magical place, a startling red-brick labyrinth punctuated by charming squares and romantic corners.

There are no roads in the historic centre, just working waterways flanked by Gothic palaces and domed basilicas.

Visitors swarm to headline sights such as Piazza San Marco and the Bridge of Sighs, but head into the backstreets and you can still escape the crowds.

WHEN TO GO

April to June is best for floral displays and balmy temperatures while September and October see the arrival of autumnal colours and the grape harvest. Summer means hot, humid weather and outdoor festival action. Winter also has its compensations. If you don't mind the cold, you'll find far fewer tourists and low-season prices from November to March.

Accommodation is plentiful and, while it's universally pricey, there's a good range to choose from.

Transport-wise, Venice is served by its own airport and a second one at Treviso, 40km to the north.

It's also well connected by rail with services to major cities and regional destinations like Padua, Vicenza and Verona.

Trieste, gateway to Italy's far northeast, is 160km to the east, accessible by train or the A4 autostrada.

Genoa

Genoa, Italy's largest Mediterranean port, is perfectly placed for trips to the Italian Riviera and, to the southeast, the Cinque Terre.

In the northwestern region of Liguria, it's a formidable city packed with history, charm and grit.

Grand aristocratic palaces testify to the wealth of its historic banking dynasties while its extensive old town is threaded with salty backstreets and fascinating corners.

Trattorias and restaurants pepper its streets, serving up classic city cuisine.

As a working port, it has good transport links: flights to Cristoforo Colombo Airport, regular year-round ferries, and trains to its two principal stations, Principe and Brignole.

Some 170km to the northwest, and easily accessible by train or car, Turin provides a gateway to the northwestern Alps and Piedmont's foodie towns.

TRANSPORT

You can fly to various destinations in northern Italy, including Milan, Bergamo, Venice and Bologna. From these cities you can continue on by train – the rail network is extensive and services are regular and efficient – or pick up a hire car and hit the road.

WHERE TO STAY

You'll have no trouble finding accommodation to suit your style and budget. The area offers everything from great-value B&Bs to opulent five-stars and swank design hotels.

Popular destinations fill quickly at peak times and for major events such as Carnevale in Venice, Milan's Salone Internazionale del Mobile and Verona's summer opera festival, so it pays to book ahead.

For a slice of life in the slow lane, apartment rentals are popular on the Cinque Terre and *agriturismi* (farm stays) are a great way of experiencing local cuisine in places like Piedmont's Langhe hills.

RESOURCES

- **Venezia Autentica**
  Promotes sustainable tourism, listing locally run shops, restaurants, bars and guided tours. *veneziaautentica.com*

- **Gestione Navigazione Laghi**
  Covers ferry services on lakes Maggiore, Como and Garda. The website includes timetables and pricing. *navigazionelaghi.it*

WHAT'S ON

- **La Biennale di Venezia**
  (labiennale.org) Europe's premier arts event sets up on the canal-side streets of Venice between May and November.

- **Verona Opera Festival**
  (arena.it) Verona's ancient Roman amphitheatre sets the stage for summer opera between late June and late August.

- **Barcolana Regatta**
  (barcolana.it) Thousands of boats take to Trieste's bay waters for the world's largest sailing regatta in early October.

03

NORTHERN ITALY

SAVOY PALACE CIRCUIT

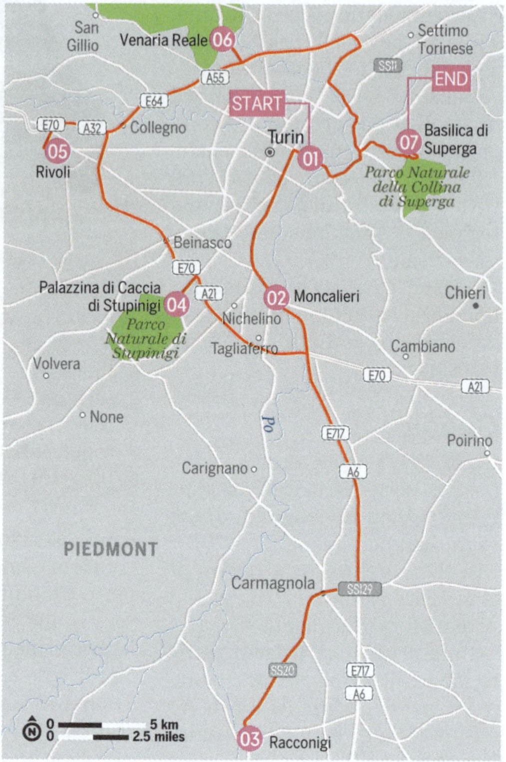

DURATION: 3–4 DAYS

DISTANCE: 152KM/94 MILES

GREAT FOR: HISTORY, FOOD AND DRINK

BEST TIME TO GO: APRIL TO OCTOBER, WHEN THE CASTLES ARE OPEN FOR VIEWING.

The Savoys abandoned their old capital of Chambéry in France in 1563 and set up home in Turin (Torino). To make themselves comfortable they spent the next 300 years building an array of princely palaces (many of them designed by Sicilian architect and stage-set designer Filippo Juvarra), country retreats and a grand mausoleum. They encircle Turin like an extravagant baroque garland and make for fascinating day trips or an easy long-weekend tour.

LINK YOUR TRIP

01 Grand Tour
From Italy's first capital to a Grand Tour of the peninsula, continue from Turin to Genoa (Genova) on the A21 and A7.

04 Gourmet Piedmont
Head south of Turin on the A6 to tour the rich culinary hinterland of the Langhe, Piedmont's jealously guarded larder.

01 Turin

Bisected by the Po and overshadowed by the Alps, Turin has an air of importance, adorned as it is with sumptuous Savoy palaces, grand hunting lodges and Napoleonic boulevards.

Piazza Castello served as the seat of dynastic power for the House of Savoy. It is dominated by **Palazzo Madama** *(palazzomadamatorino.it)*, a part-medieval, part-baroque castle built in the 13th century on the site of the old Roman gate and named after Madama Reale Maria Cristina (widow of Vittorio Amedeo I, also known as the Lion of Susa and nominally King of Cyprus and Jerusalem), who lived here in the 17th century.

Nearby statues of mythical twins Castor and Pollux guard the entrance to the **Palazzo Reale** *(museireali.beniculturali.it)*. Built for Carlo Emanuele II around 1646, its lavishly decorated rooms house an assortment of gilded furnishings and one of the greatest armouries

ALESSANDRO CRISTIANO/SHUTTERSTOCK

★ BEST FOR

HISTORY

Palazzo Carignano, where key events leading to Italian unification took place.

Palazzo Carignano

in Europe, the Armeria Reale. Also in the palace is the Galleria Sabauda, which contains the Savoy art collection.

'The road through Memphis and Thebes passes through Turin', trumpeted French hieroglyphic decoder Jean-François Champollion in the 19th century, and he wasn't far wrong. The Palazzo dell'Accademia delle Scienze houses the most important collection of Egyptian treasure outside Cairo in the **Museo Egizio** *(museoegizio.it)*.

Opposite, **Palazzo Carignano** is where Carlo Alberto (1798–1849) and the first King of Italy, Vittorio Emanuele II (1820–78), were born, and it provided the seat for Italy's first parliament. Now it houses the unmissable **Museo Nazionale del Risorgimento Italiano** *(museo risorgimentotorino.it)*, which charts the course of the modern nation state.

THE DRIVE: Drive south along Corso Unitá d'Italia. This busy dual carriageway turns into Corso Trieste and then Via Custoza. Take a right for Moncalieri, beneath the A6 and across the river Po on Via Martiri della Libertá. Turn right on Via Arduino and you'll arrive at the castle after about 9km.

02 Moncalieri

The 12th-century **Castello di Moncalieri**, the first fortress built by Thomas I of Savoy, is just south of the centre of Turin, commanding the southern access to the city. The family then moved to more splendid accommodation in the city centre.

Since 1921 it has been the HQ for the *carabinieri* (military police), the police corps created by Vittorio Emanuele I of Savoy in 1726 as a police force for the island of Sardinia (briefly within Savoy dominion) and which later became Italy's first police force following unification in 1861. While the royal apartments can only be visited on a prebooked guided tour, you can wander around the garden and enjoy the view from the belvedere.

THE DRIVE: Leave Moncalieri heading southeast, following signs saying *tutte le direzioni* (all directions) and then pick up the A6 southbound towards

Savona/Piacenza. Drive 15km on the autostrada, then exit for Carmagnola, which will put you first on the SP129 (as you skirt Carmagnola) and then on the SS20 towards Racconigi, a further 12km southwest.

03 Racconigi

South of Moncalieri, the enormous **Castello di Racconigi** *(museipiemonte.cultura.gov.it)* was another 12th-century fortress, guarding the contested borderlands around Turin. Originally the domain of the Marquis of Saluzzo, the castle came into Savoy possession through marriage and inheritance.

Inhabited by various branches of the family up until WWII, the castle was a favourite for summering royals, hosting Tsar Nicholas II of Russia in 1909. In 1904 the last king of Italy, Umberto II, was born in the castle and in 1925 the grand wedding of Philip of Hesse and Mafalda of Savoy was hosted here. Tragically, Mafalda later died in the concentration camp of Buchenwald during WWII. Now you can wander the strangely intimate apartments of kings and queens – full of elegant furnishings, family photos and personal objects – and enjoy the grand portrait gallery with its 1875 dynastic portraits.

THE DRIVE: The 38km drive north to Palazzina di Caccia di Stupinigi retraces much of the previous journey, first on the SS20 and then the A6. However, after 14km on the autostrada, before you reach Moncalieri, take the exit for the E70 (Tangenziale) towards Aosta. Now heading northwest, drive a further 8.5km and then take the exit for Stupinigi. The Viale Torino runs right up to the *palazzina* (hunting lodge).

04 Palazzina di Caccia di Stupinigi

The Savoy's finest hunting park, the **Palazzina di Caccia di Stupinigi** *(ordinemauriziano.it)* was cleverly acquired by the almost landless Emanuele Filiberto, Duke of Savoy from 1553 to 1580. Known as Testa di Ferro ('Ironhead') due to his military prowess, Emanuele was the only child of Charles III, Duke of Savoy, and Beatrice of Portugal, who left him little more than his title when they died. However, through diligent service in the armies of

Palazzina di Caccia di Stupinigi

MIKEDOTTA/SHUTTERSTOCK

the Austro-Hungarian Empire he slowly and surely reclaimed Savoyard lands, including the Stupinigi park and Turin, where he moved the family seat in 1563.

The fabulous *palazzina* came later, thanks to Vittorio Amadeo II, who set Filippo Juvarra to work in 1729. He enlisted decorators from Venice to attend to the interiors covering the 137 rooms and 17 galleries in *trompe l'œil* hunting scenes such as the *Triumph of Diana* in the main salon. Now the rooms accommodate the **Museo di Arte e Ammobiliamento**, a fabulous museum of arts and furnishings, many of them original to the lodge.

THE DRIVE: Continue on the Turin periphery (E70) heading further northwest towards Fréjus for the 21km drive to Rivoli. You'll be on the E70 for 11km before exiting at Rosta/Avigliana. From here it's a short 4km drive before exiting on the SS25 towards Rivoli. Brown signs direct you to the castle.

05 Rivoli

Works by Franz Ackermann, Gilbert and George, and Sophie Calle would have been beyond the wildest imagination of the Savoy family, who used the 17th-century **Castello di Rivoli** as one of their country retreats.

Since 1984, the cutting edge of Turin's contemporary art scene has been housed here in the **Museo d'Arte Contemporanea** *(castello dirivoli.org)*, creating shocking juxtapositions between the classical architecture and the art, such as the 1997 exhibition that showcased Maurizio Cattelan's taxidermy horse suspended from the rococo ceiling.

Rivoli's latest crown jewel is the **Villa Cerruti**, the former mansion-home of a reclusive art collector

PA IMAGES/GETTY IMAGES

Mafalda of Savoy

MAFALDA OF SAVOY (1902–44)

Mafalda of Savoy was the second of four daughters of King Vittorio Emanuele III of Italy and Elena of Montenegro. Known for her cultured, pious character, she made a grand marriage to Prince Philip, Landgrave of Hesse, grandson of German Emperor Frederick III and great-grandson of Queen Victoria of England. Affiliated with the German National Socialist (Nazi) movement, Philip, with his international connections, rose rapidly in the Nazi hierarchy, becoming a trusted member of the Reichstag and acting as an intermediary between Hitler and Mussolini. But Hitler distrusted the outspoken Mafalda and suspected her of working against the German war effort. When her father, Vittorio Emanuele, ordered the arrest of Mussolini in July 1943 and signed the armistice with the Allies, the Gestapo reacted by arresting Mafalda for subversive activities and transferring her to Buchenwald concentration camp. There she was wounded during an Allied attack on the camp's munitions factory in 1944; and she later died of her wounds, beseeching fellow prisoners to remember her not as an Italian princess, but an Italian sister.

who amassed over €600 million worth of artistic treasures. Shuttle buses (with separate tickets purchased online well in advance) from the castle whisk visitors out to the villa for a guided tour of the lavish antique-filled home filled with works by Modigliani, Kandinsky, Giacometti, Picasso, Klee, de Chirico and Magritte.

THE DRIVE: Return to the Tangenziale via the SS25 and continue northeast in the direction of Aosta/Mont Blanc/Milano. This puts you on the A55/E64 for 9km. Then take the exit for Venaria and at the traffic lights turn left onto Corso Giuseppe Garibaldi, from where you'll see the palace signposted.

06 Venaria Reale

The **Reggia di Venaria Reale** *(lavenaria.it)* is a UNESCO-listed palace complex built by Amedeo di Castellamonte for Carlo Emanuele II between 1667 and 1690. It's one of the biggest royal residences in the world and lengthy restoration works were concluded in 2010. The full trajectory of the buildings stretches 2km. Highlights include the **Galleria Grande**, the **Cappella di Sant'Uberto** and the **Juvarra stables**.

Outside, there's more: 17th-century grottoes, the **Fontana del Cervo** (Stag Fountain), the **Rose Garden** and the 17th-century **Potager Garden**, all of which took eight years to restore and required the replanting of 50,000 plants. It's all set against the 30-sq-km La Mandria park.

THE DRIVE: Return to the A55/E64 and continue northeast for 6km, then take the Falchera exit for Torino Nord. Follow the signs for Torino Centro and merge southwards onto the A4 for 2.5km. Before you hit the river Po, turn left onto Lungo Stura Lazio, which skirts the river before crossing over it. The next 5km are through a natural park until you reach the suburb of Sassi where you turn left onto the Strada Comunale Superga.

07 Basilica di Superga

In 1706 Vittorio Amedeo II promised to build a basilica to honour the Virgin Mary if Turin was saved from besieging French and Spanish armies. The city was saved, so Duke Amadeo once again commissioned Juvarra to build the **Basilica di Superga** *(basilicadisuperga.com)* on a hill across the Po river in 1717.

Magnificently sited as it is, with a crowning dome 65m high, it is visible for miles around and in due course it became the final resting place for 50 members of the Savoy family. Their lavish tombs make for interesting viewing. In their company, at the rear of the church, lies a tomb commemorating the Gran Torino football team, all of whom died in 1949 when their plane crashed into the basilica in thick fog.

THE DRIVE: To return to the city centre, descend down Strada Comunale Superga and take a left along Via Agudio for 3km. Cross the river eastwards over Ponte Sassi onto Corso Belgio. Drive to the end of the road and turn right onto Corso Regina Margherita. At the roundabout take a left through the Royal Gardens to Piazza Castello.

Basilica di Superga
CRYSTAL PROVENCHER/500PX

PHOTO OPPORTUNITY

The classical facade of the Basilica di Superga.

04

★ BEST FOR

OENOPHILES

Sampling glasses of Barolo for only €3 at Castello Falletti.

NORTHERN ITALY

GOURMET PIEDMONT

Castello Falletti (46)

DURATION: 6 DAYS

DISTANCE: 220KM/137 MILES

GREAT FOR: FOOD AND DRINK, NATURE

BEST TIME TO GO: SEPTEMBER TO NOVEMBER FOR AUTUMN FOOD FESTIVALS.

The hills, valleys and towns of Piedmont are northern Italy's specialist pantry, weighed down with sweet hazelnuts, rare white truffles, arborio rice and Nebbiolo grapes that metamorphose into Barolo and Barbaresco wines. Out here in the damp Po river basin they give out Michelin stars like overzealous schoolteachers give out house points, and with good reason. Trace a gourmet route, and counter the calorific overload with rural walks and bike rides.

LINK YOUR TRIP

05 Italian Riviera
From Bra continue south along the A6 to enjoy a tour of the olive groves and gardens along the Italian Riviera.

15 Valle d'Aosta
Cheese-lovers beware: the A5 from Turin takes you into the heart of the Valle d'Aosta, where days of hiking end with *fontina* fondues.

01 Turin

Turin gave the world its first saleable hard chocolate, is home to the Holy Shroud and played a key role in the creation of the Italian state. You can follow the epic story in the **Museo Nazionale del Risorgimento Italiano** *(museorisorgimentotorino.it)*. Aside from the national narrative and the intriguing Shroud of Turin, which you can learn all about in **Museo della Sindone** *(sindone.it)*, you've come to Turin for chocolate.

Planning your trip for November, when the **CioccolaTò** *(www.cioccola.to.it)* festival is in full swing, is a good start. Otherwise visit **Al Bicerin** *(bicerin.it)*, named after *bicerin*, a caffeine-charged hot drink of chocolate, coffee and cream. Then there's **Guido Gobino** *(guidogobino.com)*, one of Turin's favourite modern chocolatiers. Order a box of his tiny tile-like ganache chocolates or a bag of his classic *gianduiotto* (triangular chocolates made from *gianduja* –

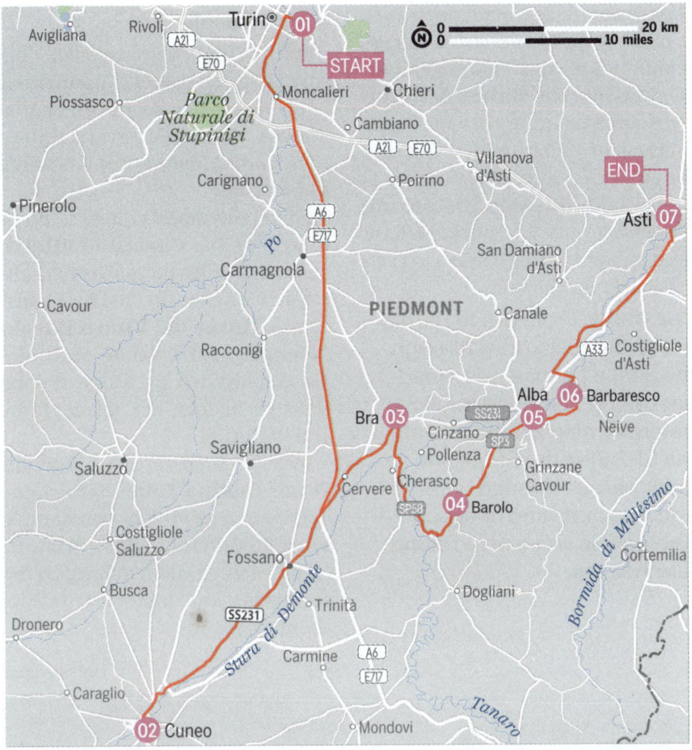

ANDERSPHOTO/SHUTTERSTOCK

SLOW FOOD

Slow Food *(slowfood.it)* was the 1980s brainchild of a group of disenchanted Italian journalists from the Piedmontese town of Bra who, united by their taste buds, successfully ignited a global crusade against the fast-food juggernaut whose tentacles were threatening to engulf Italy's gastronomic heritage. Their mantra was pleasure over speed and taste over convenience in a manifesto that promoted sustainability, local production and the protection of longstanding epicurean traditions. Today, Slow Food has over 100,000 members in 160 countries.

Turin's hazelnut paste). Beyond the chocolate, Turin is home to Slow Food's groundbreaking 'supermarket', **Eataly** *(eataly.net)*. Housed in a converted factory, it showcases a staggering array of sustainable food and beverages, and hosts regular tastings and cookery workshops.

THE DRIVE: Cuneo lies 100km south of Turin, virtually a straight shot down the A6 autostrada. Head out of Turin on Corso Unitá d'Italia and across the river Po. Then join the autostrada for 70km. Exit at Fossano and join the SS231 for the final 20km.

02 Cuneo

A condensed version of Turin, Cuneo is a genteel town with an impressive Renaissance square, the grand arcaded **Piazza Galimberti**, where market stalls set up every Tuesday. It's a good place for festivals, too, such as the **music festival** in June and the impressive **Chestnut Fair** in October, which fills the town. The city's signature rum-filled chocolates can be sampled year-round.

Cuneo also has some wonderfully dark and zealous churches. The oldest is the deconsecrated San Francisco convent and church, which today houses the **Museo Civico di Cuneo**, tracking the history of the town and province.

THE DRIVE: The 44km journey to Bra retraces much of the previous drive along the SS231. Head back to Fossano, but instead of reconnecting with the A6, take the periphery north and continue northeast through Cervere, where the countryside opens out into green fields.

03 Bra

Up on the 1st floor of a recessed courtyard, the little **Osteria del Boccondivino** *(boccondivino slow.it)*, lined with wine bottles, was the first restaurant to be opened by Slow Food in the 1980s. The food is predictably excellent, and the local Langhe menu changes daily. In the same courtyard you'll find the **Slow Food headquarters**, which includes a small bookshop selling guides to all of Italy's Slow Food–accredited restaurants and heritage producers.

Just outside Bra, in the village of Pollenzo, 4km southeast, is the Slow Food **Università di Scienze Gastronomiche** (University of

SNAILS, GLORIOUS SNAILS

Set within the Langhe's lush wine country, Cherasco, just south of Bra, is best known for *lumache* (snails). Snails in this neck of the woods are dished up *nudo* (shell-free). They can be pan-fried, roasted, dressed in an artichoke sauce or minced inside ravioli. Piedmontese specialities include *lumache al barbera* (snails simmered in Barbera wine and ground nuts) and *lumache alla Piemontese* (snails stewed with onions, nuts, anchovies and parsley in a tomato sauce). One traditional trattoria serving such dishes is Osteria della Rosa Rossa in Cherasco.

Gastronomic Sciences; *unisg.it*). It offers three-year courses in gastronomy and food management. Next door is the **Banca del Vino** *(bancadelvino.it)*, and a wine-cellar 'library' of Italian wines. Reserve for guided tastings. Also nearby is the acclaimed **Guido Ristorante** *(guidoristorante.it)* that people have been known to cross borders to visit, especially for the veal.

THE DRIVE: From Bra to Barolo is a lovely 20km drive through the gentle Langhe hills. Head east along the SS231 for 3km before turning southeast onto the SP7, then the SP58. The latter passes through orchards and vineyards and offers up photogenic views of old stone farmhouses.

04 Barolo

Wine lovers, rejoice! This tiny 18-sq-km parcel of undulating land immediately southwest of Alba knocks out the Ferrari of Italian reds, Barolo. Many argue it is Italy's finest wine.

The eponymous village is dominated by the **Castello Falletti**, once owned by the powerful Falletti banking family. Today it houses the **Museo del Vino a Barolo** *(wimubarolo.it)*, where multimedia displays tell the story of wine through history, art, music, films and literature.

Tucked behind the castle, **Agrilab Wine Tasting Tour** *(barolowine tastingtour.com)* lets you sample some 36 different wines (from €1 to €4 each) while listening to descriptions and historical tidbits about them.

Barbaresco

ESSEVU/SHUTTERSTOCK

THE DRIVE: The short 15km hop from Barolo to Alba is another pleasant drive through Barolo's vineyards as you head northeast along the SP3, which takes you all the way into the centre of Alba.

05 ALBA

Alba's fertile hinterland, the vine-striped Langhe Hills, radiates out from the town, an undulating vegetable garden replete with grapes, hazelnut groves and vineyards. Exploring them on foot or with two wheels is a rare pleasure.

Alba's **tourist office** *(langheroero.it)* can organise an astounding number of Langhe/Roero valley excursions, including a variety of cross-country walks through chestnut groves and vineyards, winery tours, cycling tours and truffle-hunting excursions (price depends on the group size).

In October and November the town hosts its renowned **truffle fair** (every weekend), and the equally ecstatic *vendemmia* (grape harvest).

THE DRIVE: Barbaresco sits in the hills just 10km northeast of Alba. Exit Alba along Viale Cherasca and then pick up the narrow, winding SP3 as it loops through the pretty residential suburb of Altavilla and out into the countryside.

PHOTO OPPORTUNITY

Endless vistas of vines in Barolo or Barbaresco.

06 Barbaresco

Only a few kilometres separate Barolo from Barbaresco, but a rainier microclimate and fewer ageing requirements have made the latter into a softer, more delicate red.

Sample it at the atmospheric **Enoteca Regionale del Barbaresco** *(enotecadelbarbaresco.it)*, housed inside a deconsecrated church. The *enoteca* (wine bar) also has information on walking trails in the vicinity.

If you haven't had your fill of wine yet, head a further 4km east to the pin-drop-quiet village of Neive, where you'll find the **Bottega dei Quattro Vini** *(bottegadei4vini.com)*. This two-room shop was set up by the local community to showcase the four 'DOC' wines (Dolcetto d'Alba, Barbaresco, Moscato and Barbera d'Alba) produced on Neive's hills.

THE DRIVE: The final 30km stretch to Asti leaves Barbaresco's vineyards behind on the SP3 and rejoins the A33 for an uninterrupted drive to Asti. Although it's a two-lane highway, it slices through more unspoilt farmland.

07 Asti

Asti and Alba were fierce medieval rivals ruled over by feuding royal families, who built Asti's legendary 150 towers. Of these, only 12 remain, and only the **Torre Troyana o Dell'Orologio** *(museidiasti.com)* can be climbed (if you make a reservation). Asti's rivalry with Alba is still recalled in the annual **Palio d'Asti**, a bareback horse race on the third Sunday of September that commemorates a victorious battle.

The 10-day **Douja d'Or** (a *douja* being a terracotta wine jug unique to Asti), in the first or second week in September, is complemented by the **Delle Sagre** food festival on the second Sunday of September. Otherwise you can sample some fine regional fare and beautiful wines among the bottle-lined shelves of **Enoteca Assetati** *(assetati.shop)*.

Like Alba, the countryside around Asti contains precious black and white truffles. Asti's truffle fair is in November.

05

NORTHERN ITALY

ITALIAN RIVIERA

★ BEST FOR

FINE DINING

Purple San Remo prawns on the terrace of San Giorgio.

DURATION: 4 DAYS

DISTANCE: 214KM/133 MILES

GREAT FOR: FOOD AND DRINK, FAMILIES

BEST TIME TO GO: APRIL, MAY AND JUNE FOR FLOWERS AND HIKING; OCTOBER FOR THE HARVEST.

Genoa

The Italian Riviera, backed by the Maritime Alps, curves west from Genoa to the French border at Ventimiglia. The contrast between sun-washed, sophisticated coastal towns and a mountainous hinterland full of heritage farms, olive oil producers and wineries gave rise to the Riviera's 19th-century fame, when European expatriates outnumbered locals. They amused themselves in lavish botanical gardens, gambled in the casino of San Remo and dined in style in fine art nouveau villas, much as you will on this tour.

LINK YOUR TRIP

04 Gourmet Piedmont
Up the A6 from food-town Savona is Slow Food HQ Bra and the start of a gourmet tour of the Langhe.

13 Meandering the Maritime Alps
From Ventimiglia slice through France on the D6204 to Limone Piemonte to start an adventure in the Maritime Alps.

01 Genoa

Like Dr Jekyll and Mr Hyde, Genoa is a city with a split personality. At its centre, medieval *caruggi* (narrow streets) untangle outwards to the **Porto Antico** and teem with hawkers, merchants and office workers. Along Via Garibaldi and Via XXV Aprile is another Genoa, one of UNESCO-sponsored palaces, smart shops and grand architectural gestures like **Piazza de Ferrari** with its monumental fountain, art nouveau **Palazzo Borsa** (once the city's stock exchange) and the neoclassical **Teatro Carlo Felice** *(operacarlofelicegenova.it)*.

Join the well-dressed haute bourgeoisie enjoying high-profile art exhibits in the grand Mannerist halls of the **Palazzo Ducale** *(palazzoducale.genova.it)*, then retire to sip a spritz amid 17th-century frescoes at **Les Rouges**.

THE DRIVE: Exit Genoa westward, through a tangle of

ANDREI ANTIPOV/SHUTTERSTOCK

flyovers and tunnels, to access the A10 for the 56km drive to Savona. Once out of the suburbs the forested slopes of the Maritime Alps rise to your right and sea views peep out from the left as you duck through tunnels.

02 Savona

Don't be put off by Savona's horrifying industrial sprawl; the Savonesi were a powerful maritime people and the town centre is unexpectedly graceful. Standing near the port are three of the many medieval towers that once studded the cityscape. Genoa's greatest rival, the town was savagely sacked in 1528, the castle dismantled and most of the population slaughtered, but somehow the **Fortezza del Priamàr** and the **Cattedrale di Nostra Signora Assunta** survived.

But you're not here for the architecture – you're here for the food. The **covered market** is crammed with fruit-and-veg stalls and fish stands stacked with salt cod. **Grigiomar** salts its own local anchovies. Then there are the local specialities like the addictive *farinata di grano* (wheat-flour flat bread) at **Vino e Farinata**.

THE DRIVE: Rejoin the A10 and leave the industrial chimneys of Savona behind you. For the first 13km the A10 continues with views of the sea, then at Spotorno it ducks inland for the final 15km to the Finale Ligure exit. Descend steeply for 3km to the Finale hamlets on the coast.

03 Finale Ligure

Finale Ligure comprises several seaside districts. The marina is narrow and charming, spreading along the sandy shore between two small rivers, the Porra and the Sciusa. A good place to pick up some picnic fare is **Salumeria Chiesa**, a delicatessen with a huge array of seafood salads, salamis, cheeses and gnocchi with pesto, of course.

Around 1.5km north of the seaside, **Finalborgo** is the old medieval centre. Its cobblestone streets are ripe for exploring, and you can stop for a meal or a pick-me-up at one of many charming restaurants with outdoor tables on the pavement. Each year in March, Finalborgo's cloisters are home to the **Salone dell'Agroalimentare**

Ligure, where local farmers hawk seasonal delicacies and vintages.

On Thursday it's worth driving 9km up the coast to picturesque **Noli** for the weekly outdoor market on Corso d'Italia.

THE DRIVE: Once again take the high road away from the coast and follow the A10 for a further 35km to Alassio. Near Albenga you'll cross the river Centa and the broad valley where dozens of hothouses dot the landscape.

04 Alassio

Less than 100km from the French border, Alassio's popularity among the 18th- and 19th-century jet set has left it with an elegant character.

Its pastel-hued villas range around a broad, sandy beach, which stretches all the way to **Laigueglia** (4km to the south). American presidents have holidayed here and Edward Elgar composed *In the South* inspired by his stay in 1904. **Il Muretto**, a ceramic-covered wall, records the names of 550 celebrities who've passed through. Follow the local lead and promenade along Via XX Settembre or the unspoilt waterfront.

Take coffee at **Antico Caffè Pasticceria Balzola** *(balzola1902.com)* and enjoy gelato on the beach beneath a stripy umbrella.

> **PHOTO OPPORTUNITY**
>
> Cascading terraces of exotic flowers at Giardini Botanici Hanbury in Ventimiglia.

THE DRIVE: If you have time take the scenic coast road, SS1 (Via Roma), from Alassio through Laigueglia and Marina di Andora to Imperia. It is a shorter and more scenic jaunt when traffic is light. The alternative, when traffic is heavy, is to head back to the A10.

05 Imperia

Imperia consists of two small seaside towns, Oneglia and Porto Maurizio, on either side of the Impero river.

Oneglia, birthplace of Admiral Doria, the Genoese Republic's greatest naval hero, is the less attractive of the two, though **Piazza Dante**, with its arcaded walkways, is a pleasant place to grab a coffee.

This is also where the great olive

San Remo

ZOYA STAFIENKO/GETTY IMAGES

oil dynasties made their name. Visit the **Museo dell'Olivo** *(www.museodellolivo.com)*, housed in an art nouveau mansion belonging to the heritage Fratelli Carli factory. The museum is surprisingly extensive and details the history of the Italian Riviera industry from the 2nd century BCE. Buy quality oil here or anywhere in town.

West of Oneglia is pirate haven **Porto Maurizio**, perched on a rocky spur that overlooks a yacht-filled harbour.

THE DRIVE: Rejoining the A10 at Imperia, the landscape begins to change. The olive terraces are dense, spear-like cypresses and umbrella pines shade the hillsides, and the fragrant maquis (herbal scrubland) is prolific. Loop inland around Taggia and then descend slowly into San Remo.

06 San Remo

San Remo, Italy's wannabe Monte Carlo, is a sun-dappled Mediterranean resort with a grand belle-époque **Sanremo Casino** and lashings of Riviera-style grandeur.

During the mid-19th century the city became a magnet for European exiles such as Czar Nicolas of Russia, who favoured the town's balmy winters.

They built an onion-domed **Russian Orthodox church** reminiscent of Moscow's St Basil's Cathedral, which still turns heads down by the seafront.

Swedish inventor Alfred Nobel also maintained a villa here, the **Villa Nobel**, which now houses a museum dedicated to him.

SAN GIORGIO

Cult restaurant **San Giorgio** *(sangiorgiocervo.it)* has been quietly wowing gourmets with its authentic Ligurian cooking since the 1950s when mother-and-son team Caterina and Alessandro opened the doors of their home in the *borgo* (medieval hamlet) of Cervo Alta. Dine out on the bougainvillea-draped terrace in summer, or in intimate dining rooms cluttered with family silverware and antiques in winter. Below the restaurant, in an old oil mill, is the less formal wine bar and deli San Giorgino.

Beyond the waterfront, San Remo hides a little-visited old town, a labyrinth of twisting lanes that cascade down the Italian Riviera hillside.

Curling around the base is the **Italian Cycling Riviera**, a path that tracks the coast as far as Imperia. For bike hire, enquire at the **tourist office** *(visitriviera.info)*.

THE DRIVE: For the final 17km stretch to Ventimiglia take the SS1 coastal road, which hugs the base of the mountains and offers uninterrupted sea views. In summer and at Easter, however, when traffic is heavy, your best bet is the A10.

07 Ventimiglia

Despite its enviable position between the glitter of San Remo and the Côte d'Azur, Ventimiglia is a soulful but disorderly border town, its Roman past still evident in its bridges, amphitheatre and ruined baths. Now it's the huge **Friday market** that draws the crowds.

If you can't find a souvenir here then consider one of the prized artisanal honeys produced by **Marco Ballestra**, which has hives in the hills above the Valle Roya. There are over a dozen different types.

To end the tour head over to the pretty western suburb of Ponte San Ludovico to the **Giardini Botanici Hanbury** *(giardinihanbury.com)*, the 18-hectare estate of English businessman Sir Thomas Hanbury; he planted it with an extravagant 5800 botanical species from five continents.

DETOUR

L'Entroterra

Start: 07 Ventimiglia

The designation 'Riviera' omits the pleated, mountainous interior – *l'entroterra* – that makes up nine-tenths of the Italian Riviera. Harried by invasions, coast-dwellers took to these vertical landscapes over 1000 years ago, hewing their perched villages from the rock face of the Maritime Alps. You'll want to set aside two extra days to drive the coiling roads that rise up from Ventimiglia to Dolceacqua, Apricale and Pigna. If you do make the effort, book into gorgeous boutique hotel *Apricus Locanda (apricuslocanda.com)*; it's worth it for the breakfast and dreamy mountain panoramas.

06

★ BEST FOR

HIKING

Any one of the Cinque Terre's sanctuary walks.

NORTHERN ITALY

CINEMATIC CINQUE TERRE

DURATION: 5-7 DAYS

DISTANCE: 173KM/107 MILES

GREAT FOR: NATURE, FAMILIES, FOOD AND DRINK

BEST TIME TO GO: BALMY DAYS IN APRIL AND OCTOBER ARE GREAT FOR HIKING AND SWIMMING.

Cinque Terre

From the Portofino peninsula, via the Cinque Terre's cliff-side villages to Portovenere, this trip exudes Riviera glamour. But amid billionaire motor yachts you'll find a hard-working community. Challenged by a mountainous landscape, Ligurian farmers have been reclaiming the Levante's wild slopes with neatly banded stone terraces for over 2000 years. Planted with olives, grapes, basil and garlic, they snake from sea level to crest gravity-defying precipices and are now protected as a UNESCO World Heritage Site.

LINK YOUR TRIP

07 Northern Cities
Swap the coastal scenery for the cultural cities of the Po plain by driving north to Milan (Milano) on the A7.

26 Foodie Emilia-Romagna
From Lerici, head up the A15 to Parma to sample the gourmet hams, cheese and pasta of Emilia-Romagna.

01 Camogli

Still an authentic fishing village with tall, *trompe l'œil* painted villas and a broad curving beach, Camogli's name is said to derive from *case delle mogli* (the wives' houses) for the women left behind by their fisherfolk husbands. In the 19th century it had the largest merchant fleet in the Mediterranean, but now it's a charming holiday spot for weekending Milanese who shop for supplies in the Wednesday **mercato** on Via XX Settembre. Fishing traditions also continue here, such as the *tonnara di Punta Chiappa,* a large, complex fishing net between Camogli and San Fruttuoso, which is used for the trapping of tuna between April and September. It's been here since the 1600s and during the season it's pulled up by hand once or twice a day. Boats leave from Via Garibaldi to the **Punta Chiappa**, where you can swim and sunbathe in summer.

MAURIZIO DE MATTEI/SHUTTERSTOCK

In May the village celebrates the **Sagra del Pesce** (Fish Festival) with a huge fry-up, when hundreds of fish are cooked in 3m-wide pans along the busy waterfront.

For the best views in town, take a short drive up to **San Rocco di Camogli**, a small hamlet wrapped in olive groves with panoramic views. Trailheads crossing **Monte di Portofino** start here.

THE DRIVE: Climb out of Camogli and pick up the SS1 in the direction of Santa Margherita Ligure. The cypress-lined road sweeps around the headland past gloriously grand villas. Just past San Lorenzo della Costa, exit right and descend steeply into Santa Margherita. When you hit the waterfront turn right on Corso Marconi (SP227), past Villa Durazzo, and follow the waterfront 5km to Portofino.

02 Portofino

With its striking setting and pastel-hued villas framed by the dense pine-covered slopes of the peninsula, Portofino ranks among the world's most famous fishing villages. A favourite destination of billionaires and celebrities, it has long been exclusive and expensive. In the late 16th century, aristocratic traveller Giambattista Confalonieri complained, 'You were charged not only for the room, but for the very air you breathed.'

Surprisingly, though, the best experience in Portofino is free: a hike along one of the 80km of trails that crisscross the **natural park** *(parcoportofino.it)*. Enquire at the tourist office for maps. You can walk the full 18km from Portofino to Camogli, via San Fruttuoso. Otherwise take the Salita San Giorgio stairs from the harbour, past the **Chiesa di San Giorgio**, to Portofino's unusual **Castello Brown** *(castellobrown.com)*. In 1867 it became the private home of British diplomat Montague Yeats Brown, who no doubt derived endless pleasure from the spectacular views from its garden.

THE DRIVE: This short 9km seafront drive is fantastically scenic. Taking the only road out of town (SP227), follow its path back to Santa Margherita, where you can take a quick stroll in the gorgeous gardens of Villa Durazzo. The rest of the journey wends its way through Santa Margherita, which merges almost seamlessly with Rapallo.

03 Rapallo

WB Yeats, Max Beerbohm and Ezra Pound all garnered inspiration in Rapallo and it's not difficult to see why. Set on a curving bay lined with striped umbrellas and palm trees, and backed by the 1900m Montallegro, Rapallo is the picture of Riviera living.

On Thursdays the historic centre comes alive when market stalls fill **Piazza Cile**. Otherwise stroll the gorgeous **Lungomare Vittorio Veneto**, explore exhibitions in the castle and take the 1934-vintage cable car up to the **Santuario Basilico di Montallegro** (612m), built on the spot where the Virgin Mary was reportedly sighted in 1557. Given the heavenly view, it's hardly surprising.

THE DRIVE: You can do the 25km drive from Rapallo to Sestri Levante all along the autostrada if you're pressed for time. Otherwise, it's worth taking the more scenic route out of Rapallo along the coast road (SS1) through Zoagli and rejoining the autostrada just before Chiavari (famous for its *farinata* flat bread). From here it's a further 13km to Sestri Levante.

04 Sestri Levante

Set in a broad flat valley with a long sandy beach and two sheltered bays, Sestri, as the locals call it, has something of a 1950s feel. This might have something to do with the striped umbrellas that dot the beach, the old-style refreshment kiosks, play areas and amusements along the waterfront and the meandering cycle paths where well-dressed ladies pedal with brightly coloured towels in their baskets. Many of the beachfront apartments are owned by Milanese and Genovese families, so you can be sure of a high standard of restaurants, cafes and ice-cream shops in the densely packed historic centre, which sits squeezed between the incredibly photogenic **Baia del Silenzio** (Bay of Silence) and the **Baia della Favola** (Fairy-Tale Bay), the latter named after fairy-tale author Hans Christian Andersen, who lived in Sestri in the early 19th century.

THE DRIVE: From Sestri head southeast onto the E80 autostrada for the 42km drive to Monterosso al Mare. The first 13km are uneventful, but once you exit onto the SS566dir to Monterosso you descend steeply through the forested mountains along an improbable mountain road. The views, across deep valleys to the sea, are superb. There are two car parks on either side of the village: Fegina and Loreto (€20-25 per day, depending on season).

05 Parco Nazionale delle Cinque Terre

Five dramatically perched seaside villages – **Monterosso al Mare**, **Vernazza**, **Corniglia**, **Manarola** and **Riomaggiore** – make up the five communities of the UNESCO-protected **Parco Nazionale delle Cinque Terre** *(parconazionale5terre.it)*. A site of genuine and marvellous beauty, it may not be the undiscovered Eden it was 100 years ago, yet it remains a world apart. Sinuous paths traverse seemingly impregnable cliffs, while a 19th-century railway line cuts through coastal tunnels linking village to village. Cars are banned, so park in Monterosso or Riomaggiore, and take to the hills on foot or skirt the spectacular cliffs by boat.

Rooted in antiquity, the Cinque Terre's five towns date from the early medieval period, and include several castles and a quintet of illustrious parish churches. Buildings aside, the Cinque Terre's most unique

CINQUE TERRE CARD

The best way to get around the Cinque Terre is with the Cinque Terre card (1/2 days €7.50/14.50, four-person family card €19.60), which gives you unlimited use of the Sentiero Azzurro trail and electric village buses, as well as free use of normally fee-charging toilets at park offices. With the addition of train travel, a one-/two-day card costs from €19.50/34 to €32.50/59, depending on the season. A four-person family card costs €49 with train travel. Cards are sold at all **Cinque Terre park information offices** *(parconazionale5terre.it)*, located in the village train stations. If you just want to hike, you can also purchase a one-day hiking pass at the Sentiero Azzurro trailheads.

Rapallo
GARSYA/SHUTTERSTOCK

feature is the steeply terraced cliffs banded by a complicated system of fields and gardens that have been chiselled, shaped and layered over the course of two millennia.

Since the 2011 floods, many of the Cinque Terre's walking paths have been in a delicate state. While most of the spectacular network of trails is open and you can plan some excellent village-to-village hikes along 30 numbered paths, only part of the iconic **Sentiero Azzurro** (Blue path, SVA on maps) is open. To hike this trail you must pay an admission charge (€7.50) or purchase a Cinque Terre card (p54). All other trails are free.

From late March to October, the **Consorzio Marittimo Turistico Cinque Terre Golfo dei Poeti** *(navigazionegolfodeipoeti.it)* runs daily shuttle boats between the villages.

PHOTO OPPORTUNITY

Views over pastel-coloured Camogli from San Rocco.

THE DRIVE: If the roads are busy take the longer, 67km autostrada route via the A12 and A15. However, if you have more time you can take the more scenic, but winding, SP51 and SS370 through the mountains of the Cinque Terre National Park until you hit the coast just south of La Spezia. From here turn southwards on the SS530 for the final 12km coastal drive into Portovenere.

06 Portovenere

If the Cinque Terre had to pick an honorary sixth member, Portovenere would surely be it. Perched on the western promontory of the Gulf of Poets (Shelley and Byron were regulars here), the village's seven-storey houses form a citadel around **Castello Doria**. No one knows the origins of the castle, although Portus Veneris was a Roman base en route from Gaul to Spain. The current structure dates from the 16th century and offers wonderful views from its terraced gardens. Just off the promontory you'll spy the tiny islands of Palmaria, Tino and Tinetto.

The wave-lashed **Chiesa di San Pietro** sits atop a Roman temple dedicated to the goddess Venus

Chiesa di San Pietro

MASSIMO PARISI/SHUTTERSTOCK

(born from the foam of the sea) from whom Portovenere takes its name. At the end of the quay a Cinque Terre panorama unfolds from the **Grotta Arpaia**. This is better known as the Grotto di Byron, as it was a favourite spot of Lord Byron, who once swam across the gulf to Lerici to visit his fellow romantic, Shelley.

THE DRIVE: Head north to La Spezia via the SS530 and cross through town to exit eastwards on the SP331. Driving along waterfront boulevards lined with umbrella pines you'll pass La Spezia's marina, then go through suburbs such as San Terenzo, until at Pugliola you turn right onto the SP28 and climb up the villa-lined road into Lerici.

07 Lerici

Magnolia, yew and cedar trees grow in the 1930s public gardens at Lerici, an exclusive retreat of handsome villas that cling to the cliffs along its beach. In another age Byron and Shelley sought inspiration here and gave the Gulf of Poets its name. The Shelleys stayed at the waterfront **Villa Magni** (closed to visitors) in the early 1820s but sadly Percy drowned here when his boat sank off the coast in 1822.

From Lerici, you can head into the hillsides for a scenic 6km stroll passing high above the magnificent bay of **Fiascherino**, through abandoned villages like **Barbazzano** and **Portesone** (deserted during a medieval plague epidemic). You'll descend at **Tellaro**, a fishing hamlet with pink-and-orange houses cluttered about narrow lanes and tiny squares. Sit on the rocks at the **Chiesa San Giorgio** and imagine an octopus ringing the church bells – which, according to legend, it did to warn the villagers of a Saracen attack.

MBVI/SHUTTERSTOCK

Vineyards, Cinque Terre

SANCTUARY WALKS

Each of Cinque Terre's villages is associated with a sanctuary perched high on the cliff sides. Reaching these religious retreats used to be an act of penance, but these days the walks are for pure pleasure.

Monterosso to Santuario della Madonna di Soviore Follow trail No 509 up through forest to the Italian Riviera's oldest sanctuary.

Vernazza to Santuario della Madonna di Reggio Follow trail No 508 past 14 sculpted Stations of the Cross to this 11th-century chapel with a Romanesque facade.

Corniglia to Santuario della Madonna delle Grazie Ascend the spectacular Sella di Comeneco on trail No 587 to this church with its adored image of the Madonna and Child.

Manarola to Santuario della Madonna delle Salute The pick of all the sanctuary walks is this breathtaking traverse (trail No 506) through Cinque Terre's finest vineyards.

Riomaggiore to Santuario della Madonna di Montenero Trail No 593V ascends to this frescoed 18th-century chapel that sits atop an astounding viewpoint.

07

★ BEST FOR

ART LOVERS

The little-known treasures in Bergamo's Accademia Carrara.

NORTHERN ITALY

NORTHERN CITIES

DURATION: 7–10 DAYS

DISTANCE: 395KM/245 MILES

GREAT FOR: HISTORY, FOOD AND DRINK

BEST TIME TO GO: SEPTEMBER TO MAY TO AVOID THE CROWDS.

Duomo, Milan

The Po valley, with its waving cornfields and verdant rice paddies, hosts some of Italy's most prosperous towns, from the handsome walls of Bergamo to the romantic canals of Venice. Make your way through the farmlands from the Lombard powerhouse of Milan to Roman Brescia, the Gonzaga stronghold of Mantua and the serene Republic of Venice. This is a land of legends spun by Virgil, Dante and Shakespeare, where grand dynasties fought for power and patronised some of the world's finest art.

LINK YOUR TRIP

09 A Weekend at Lago di Garda
Got an urge for the outdoors? Jump off the A4 before Verona to Desenzano del Garda and mess around Lago di Garda for a weekend.

02 World Heritage Wonders
Further the tour of artistic and architectural blockbusters by continuing on the A22 from Mantua to Modena.

01 Milan

From Charlemagne to Napoleon, and even Silvio Berlusconi, mercantile Milan (Milano) has always attracted the moneyed and the Machiavellian. Follow the city's changing fortunes through the frescoed halls of the **Castello Sforzesco** *(milanocastello.it)*, some of them decorated by Leonardo da Vinci, where exquisite sculptures, paintings and weapons tell the turbulent tale of the city. From its ramparts, look out over the **Parco Sempione** and spy the pearly pinnacles of the **Duomo** *(duomomilano.it)*. Begun in 1387, it took six centuries to build, and was rushed to completion in the 19th century so that Napoleon could crown himself King of Italy in its cavernous interior.

True to Milan's spirit of free enterprise, one of the city's finest art collections is the private collection of **Museo Poldi Pezzoli** *(museopoldi pezzoli.it)*, where priceless Bellinis

JAN CATTANEO/SHUTTERSTOCK

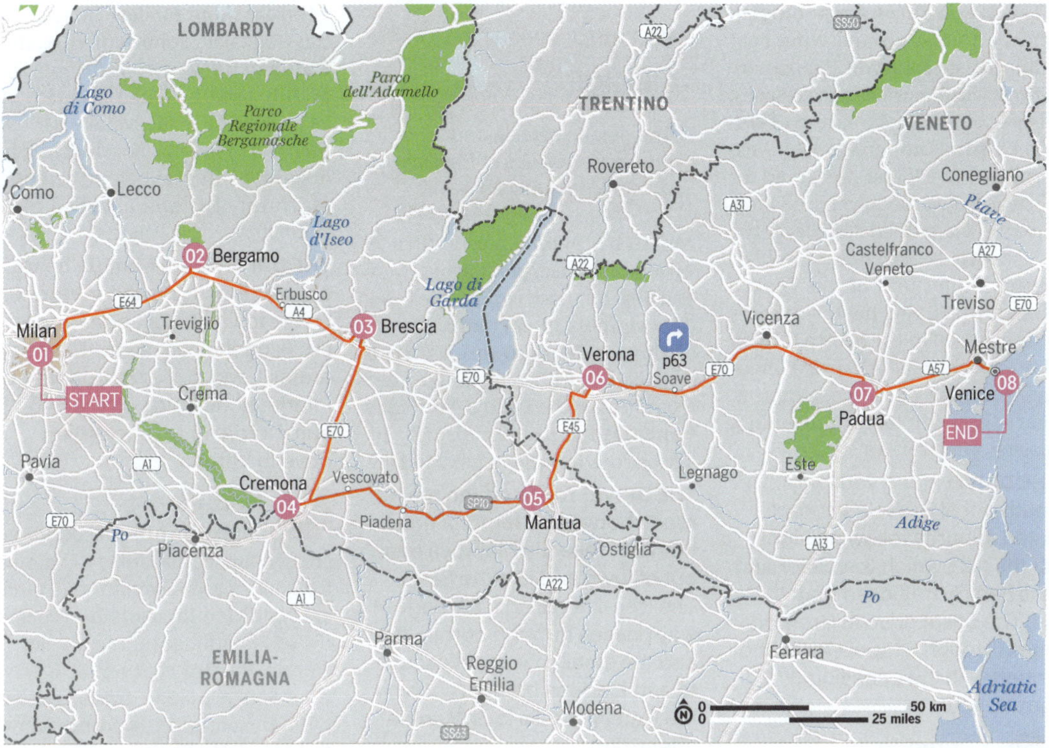

and Botticellis hang in Pezzoli's 19th-century *palazzo* (mansion). From here walk around the city's nearby 'Golden Quadrangle' of designer shops.

THE DRIVE: Head northeast out of town along Corso Venezia, or via the ring road, depending on where you're staying in town. Merge with the A4 Milan–Brescia autostrada for an uneventful 56km drive to Bergamo.

02 Bergamo

Beautiful Bergamo, its domes and towers piled on a promontory at the foot of the Alps, is one of the most arresting urban views in Italy. Le Corbusier admired the incredible beauty of **Piazza Vecchia**, its magnificent ensemble of medieval and Renaissance buildings much influenced by Venetian fashions, with the Lion of St Marks emblazoned on the **Palazzo della Ragione**. The city's **Venetian walls** were recognised by UNESCO in 2017 for their historical value, and you can walk around them in a long morning gazing on hazy views of the *città bassa* (lower city) and the Lombard plains beyond.

Back in the centre, look through the arches of the Palazzo della Ragione for a glimpse of a second square, the **Piazza Duomo**, fronted by the extraordinary polychromatic marble facade of the **Cappella Colleoni**, the mausoleum-chapel of Venice's most famous mercenary commander, Bartolomeo Colleoni (1696–1770).

THE DRIVE: Leave Bergamo via the *città bassa* southwards and rejoin the A4 in the direction of Brescia. Surprisingly, this 55km stretch is relatively scenic, especially as you drive through the wine region of Franciacorta.

03 Brescia

Despite its seedy urban periphery, Brescia's old town contains the most important Roman ruins in Lombardy and an extraordinary, circular Roman church, the **Duomo Vecchio** (Old Cathedral), built over the ancient Roman baths.

From here the Via dei Musei, the ancient *decumanus maximus* (east–west main street), leads to the heart of Brixia, the best-preserved Roman remains in northern Italy.

The **Brixia Parco Archeologico** offers an underground wing containing a 1st-century-BCE sanctuary with rescued mosaics and frescoes. They sit alongside the alfresco **Tempio Capitolino**, erected by Vespasian in 73 CE and preserved for posterity by a medieval mudslide. Next to the ruined temple is the unexcavated *cavea* (semi-circular, tiered auditorium) of the **Teatro Romano**. If you have time, it's worth a peep in the **Santa Giulia** *(bresciamusei.com),* a vast monastery complex and museum that charts Brescian history, including more Roman remains.

THE DRIVE: Wend your way south out of Brescia's complicated suburbs following signs for the A21, which is smaller and less heavily trafficked than the A4. The 53km drive to Cremona goes through unspoilt farmland dotted with the occasional farmhouse.

04 Cremona

Famous for its violins, nougat and the tallest bell tower in Italy (111m), Cremona is a charming stopover. The stout-hearted can climb the 502 steps to the top of the **Torrazzo**, perusing a 'vertical museum' dedicated to astronomy and clocks on the way. The **Duomo** *(cattedraledicremona.it)* next door is one of the most exuberant expressions of Lombard Romanesque architecture.

Aside from the views, Cremona made a name for itself as the violin capital of Europe, after Andrea Amati discovered in 1566 that with a bit of adjustment his old medieval fiddle could be made to sing the sweetest tunes. By the 18th century Andrea's son, Nicolò Amati, his pupil Antonio Stradivarius and Giuseppe Guarneri were crafting the best violins ever. See the originals in Cremona's state-of-the-art **Museo del Violino** *(museodelviolino.org)*. To hear them, head to the **Teatro Amilcare Ponchielli** *(teatroponchielli.it)*; its season runs from September to May.

PHOTO OPPORTUNITY

VENICE

The golden domes and precious mosaics of Basilica di San Marco in Venice.

THE DRIVE: You're off the main roads between Cremona and Mantua. Take Via Mantova east out of town and join the SP10. The tree-lined single carriageway passes through cornfields and the small towns of Vescovato and Piadena before reaching the watery outskirts of Mantua after 67km.

05 Mantua

The Latin poet Virgil was born just outside Mantua (Mantova) in 70 BCE, and the modern town preserves its antique timeline in its art and architecture. Ruled by the Gonzaga dynasty for three centuries, the court attracted artists of the highest calibre, including Pisanello, Rubens and, more famously, Andrea Mantegna, who was court painter from 1460 until his death in 1506. It's their dazzling frescoes that decorate the **Palazzo Ducale** *(mantovaducale.beniculturali.it)*. During busy periods you may have to book to see the biggest draw – Mantegna's 15th-century frescoes in the **Camera degli Sposi** (Bridal Chamber).

Hardly more modest in scale is the Gonzaga's suburban villa, the **Palazzo Te** *(centropalazzote.it)*. Mainly used by Duke Federico II as a place of rendezvous with his mistress, Isabella Boschetti, it is decorated in playboy style with playful motifs and encoded love symbols.

THE DRIVE: From Mantua head almost directly north for Verona. Leave town on Via Legnago, crossing the causeway that separates Lago di Mezzo from Lago Inferiore, then pick up the E45 autostrada for an easy 40km drive to Verona.

06 Verona

Shakespeare placed star-crossed Romeo and Juliet in Verona for good reason: romance, drama and fatal family feuds have been the city's hallmark for centuries.

From the 3rd century BCE, Verona was a Roman trade centre, with ancient gates, a forum (now **Piazza delle Erbe**) and a grand Roman **Arena**, which still hosts summer opera performances. But Shakespearean tragedy came with the territory.

After Mastino della Scala (aka Scaligeri) lost re-election to Verona's comune in 1262, he claimed absolute control, until murdered by his rivals. On the north side of **Piazza dei Signori** stands the early-Renaissance **Loggia del Consiglio**, the 15th-century city council. Through the archway you'll find the Arche Scaligere – elaborate Gothic tombs of the Scaligeri family, where murderers are interred next to the relatives they killed.

Paranoid for good reason, the fratricidal Cangrande II (1351–59)

Basilica di San Marco (p63)
PAOLO GALLO/SHUTTERSTOCK

THE ORIGINAL GHETTO

In medieval times, the Cannaregio island of Ghetto Nuovo housed a *getto* (foundry) – but its role as Venice's designated Jewish quarter from the 16th to 18th centuries gave the word its current meaning.

In accordance with the Venetian Republic's 1516 decree, Jewish lenders, doctors and clothing merchants were allowed to attend to Venice's commercial interests by day, while at night and on Christian holidays, most were restricted to the gated island of Ghetto Nuovo.

When Jewish merchants fled the Spanish Inquisition for Venice in 1541, there was no place to go in the Ghetto but up: around Campo del Ghetto Nuovo, upper storeys housed new arrivals, synagogues and publishing houses.

Despite a 10-year censorship order issued by the church in Rome in 1553, Jewish Venetian publishers contributed hundreds of titles popularising new Renaissance ideas on religion, humanist philosophy and medicine.

built the **Castelvecchio** *(museodicastelvecchio.comune.verona.it)* to guard the river Adige, which snakes through town. Now it houses Verona's main museum with works by Tiepolo, Carpaccio and Veronese.

To get an alternative view of the castle and the city, cast off on the river with **Adige Rafting** *(adigerafting.it)* for a thrilling two-hour Raft & Wine ride beneath a dozen bridges with pit stops for prosecco and plates of mountain cheese and prosciutto.

THE DRIVE: The 95km drive from Verona to Padua is once again along the E70. This stretch of road is heavily trafficked by heavy-goods vehicles. The only rewards are glimpses of Soave's crenellated castle to your left and the tall church spire of Monteforte d'Alpone. You could extend your trip with a stop to take in the World Heritage architecture of Vicenza.

DETOUR

Soave

Start: 06 Verona

East of Verona, Soave serves its namesake DOC white wine in a storybook setting. Built by Verona's fratricidal Scaligeri family, the **Castello di Soave** *(castellodisoave.it)* encompasses an early-Renaissance villa, grassy courtyards and the Mastio, a defensive tower. More inviting is 1898 **Cantina di Soave** *(cantinasoave.it)*, a cooperative of 2000 Soave producers upholding the lemony, zesty DOC Soave Classico quality standards.

07 Padua

Dante, da Vinci, Boccaccio and Vasari all honour Giotto as the artist who officially ended the Dark Ages. Giotto's startlingly humanist approach not only changed how people saw the heavenly company, it changed how they saw themselves; not as lowly vassals but as vessels for the divine, however flawed.

This humanising approach was especially well suited to the **Cappella degli Scrovegni** *(cappelladegliscrovegni.it)*, the chapel in Padua (Padova) that Enrico Scrovegni commissioned in memory of his father, who as a moneylender was denied a Christian burial.

Afterwards, tour the **Musei Civici agli Eremitani** for pre-Roman Padua downstairs and a pantheon of Veneto artists upstairs.

THE DRIVE: The 40km drive from Padua to Venice is through a tangle of suburban neighbourhoods and featureless areas of light industry along the A4 and then the A57.

08 Venice

Like its signature landmark, the **Basilica di San Marco** (St Mark's Basilica; *basilicasanmarco.it*), the Venetian empire was dazzlingly cosmopolitan. Armenians, Turks, Greeks and Germans were neighbours along the Grand Canal, and Jewish communities persecuted elsewhere in Europe founded publishing houses and banks here. By the mid-15th century, Venice (Venezia) was swathed in golden mosaics, imported silks and clouds of incense.

Underneath the lacy pink cladding, the **Palazzo Ducale** *(palazzoducale.visitmuve.it)* ran an uncompromising dictatorship. Discover state secrets on the Itinerari Segreti **tour**, which takes you to the sinister Trial Chamber and Interrogation Room.

Centuries later, Napoleon took some of Venice's finest heirlooms to France. But the biggest treasure in the **Museo Correr** *(correr.visitmuve.it)* couldn't be lifted: Jacopo Sansovino's **Libreria Nazionale Marciana**, covered with larger-than-life philosophers by Veronese, Titian and Tintoretto.

For more visual commentary on Venetian high life, head for the **Gallerie dell'Accademia** *(gallerieaccademia.it)*, whose hallowed halls contain more murderous intrigue and forbidden romance than most Venetian parties. Alternatively, immerse yourself in the lagoon larder by walking around the city's markets and bars.

Palazzo Ducale

JOSHUA RAIF/SHUTTERSTOCK

STAY AWHILE

PARCO NAZIONALE DELLE CINQUE TERRE

BY GREGOR CLARK

Perched precipitously above the Ligurian Sea, the five pastel-coloured villages of the Cinque Terre – Riomaggiore, Vernazza, Corniglia, Manarola and Monterosso al Mare – offer a rare glimpse of traffic-free Italian life. Accessible only on foot, by train or by boat, they invite visitors to leave the car behind and embrace a more languid lifestyle. A network of several dozen numbered walking trails connects the villages and surrounding hillsides, threading through steeply terraced vineyards, olive orchards and lemon groves demarcated by ancient dry stone walls.

In the four decades since I first visited and fell in love with this spot, the Cinque Terre have been incorporated into a **national park** *(parconazionale5terre.it)*, with a corresponding influx of tourism, yet the region's underlying appeal remains intact. The most popular trail connecting the five villages, the **Sentiero Verde Azzurro**, runs for 12km and can be walked in a single, rather strenuous day, but you'll get much more out of the experience if you spend a night or two within the park's boundaries and allow some time for leisurely exploration.

My favourite villages are the two in the middle, Corniglia and Vernazza. Vernazza's brightly hued assemblage of houses hugs the edge of a harbour that's home to a dwindling fishing fleet and a small sandy beach, backed by the ruined Castello Doria. Tiny Corniglia, highest of the five villages, straddles a steep promontory reachable only by a 377-step staircase or a shuttle bus, and this relative inaccessibility makes it the most peaceful place to stay. For even more vertiginous views, climb to the neighbouring village of Volastra, where **Cantina Capellini** *(cantinacapellini.it)* offers tastes of the Cinque Terre's prized Sciacchetrà wine at the source.

LINK YOUR TRIP

The national park is a great base to take on the **6 Cinematic Cinque Terre** road trip.

FROM LEFT: SASHA64F/SHUTTERSTOCK, JULIA LAV/SHUTTERSTOCK

Left & right: Cinque Terre National Park

PLACES TO STAY

- **Punto Zero**
  Large, quiet apartments with kitchenette and sea views in tranquil Corniglia. *(puntozerocorniglia.it)*

- **Hotel Gianni Franzi**
  Smallish rooms loaded with an atmospheric mix of antique furniture and simple traditional architecture in Vernazza. Spectacular breakfasts are served on a shared terrace. *(giannifranzi.it)*

- **Hotel Locanda del Sole**
  This super-friendly establishment at the top end of Riomaggiore offers hearty breakfasts, simple but clean rooms and a pretty patio. *(locandadelsole.net)*

- **La Malà**
  Four charming rooms in a typical Ligurian house in the cliff-side heights of Vernazza. Fitted out with a clean-lined contemporary aesthetic, they provide lazy comfort and fabulous sea views. *(lamala.it)*

08

★ BEST FOR

GLAMOUR

Touring Bellagio's headland in a mahogany cigarette boat.

NORTHERN ITALY

THE GRACEFUL ITALIAN LAKES

DURATION: 5–7 DAYS

DISTANCE: 213KM/132 MILES

GREAT FOR: HISTORY, FOOD AND DRINK, NATURE

BEST TIME TO GO: APRIL TO JUNE, WHEN THE CAMELLIAS ARE IN FULL BLOOM.

Lago Maggiore

Writers from Goethe to Hemingway have lavished praise on the Italian Lakes. They have an enduring natural beauty, dramatically ringed by snow-powdered mountains and garlanded by grand villas and exotic, tropical flora. At Lago Maggiore the palaces of the Borromean Islands lie like a fleet of fine vessels in the gulf, while the siren call of Lago di Como draws Arabian sheikhs and James Bond location scouts to its discreet forested slopes.

LINK YOUR TRIP

01 Grand Tour
From Stresa take the A8 to Milan (Milano), from where you can commence your own Grand Tour of Italy.

14 Roof of Italy
From Como take the SS340 to Gravedona, from where you plunge eastwards into the Valtellina vineyards and over the Alps to Merano.

01 Stresa

More than Como and Garda, Lago Maggiore has retained the belle-époque air of its early tourist heyday. Attracted by the mild climate and the easy access the new 1855 railway provided, the European *haute bourgeoisie* flocked to buy and build grand lakeside villas. The best of them are paraded in the small but select lakeside town of Stresa.

From here it's a short punt to the palace-punctuated Borromean Islands (Isole Borromee; *terreborromeo.it*), Maggiore's star attractions. **Isola Bella** took the name of Carlo III's wife, the bella Isabella, in the 17th century, when its centrepiece, **Palazzo Borromeo**, was built. Construction of the villa and gardens was thought out in such a way that the island would have the appearance of a vessel, with the villa at the prow and the gardens dripping down 10 tiered terraces at the rear. Inside, you'll find the work of countless old masters. By contrast, Isola Madre eschews ostentation for a

MASTER1305/SHUTTERSTOCK

more romantic, familial atmosphere. The 16th- to 18th-century **Palazzo Madre** includes a 'horror' theatre with a cast of devilish marionettes, while Chinese pheasants stalk the English gardens.

THE DRIVE: Leave Stresa westwards on the Via Sempione (SS33), skirting the edge of the lake for this short 14km drive. Pass through Baveno and round the western edge of the gulf through the greenery of the Fondo Toce natural reserve. When you reach the junction with the SS34, turn right for Verbania.

DETOUR

Lago d'Orta

Start: 01 Stresa

Separated from Lago Maggiore by Monte Mottarone (1492m) and enveloped by thick, dark-green woodlands, Lago d'Orta would make a perfect elopers' getaway. At 13.4km long by 2.5km wide you can drive around the lake in a day. The focal point is the captivating medieval village of **Orta San Giulio**, which sits across from Isola San Giulio, where you'll spy the frescoed, 12th-century **Basilica di San Giulio**. Come during the week and you'll have the place largely to yourself.

PHOTO OPPORTUNITY

The cascading gardens of Palazzo Borromeo.

02 Verbania

There are two Verbanias: Pallanza, a waterside maze of serpentine streets that serves as an embarkation point for the Borromean Islands, and Intra, the broader, newer ferry port. Between them sits the late-19th-century **Villa Taranto** *(villataranto.it)*. In 1931, royal archer and Scottish captain Neil McEacharn bought the villa from the Savoy family and started to plant some 20,000 species. With its rolling hillsides of purple rhododendrons and camellias, acres of tulip flowers and hothouses full of equatorial lilies, it is considered one of Europe's finest botanical gardens. During the last week in April, **Settimana del Tulipano** takes place, when tens of thousands of tulips erupt in magnificent multicoloured blooms.

The Drive: Pick up the SS34 again, continuing in a northeasterly direction out of Verbania, through the suburbs of Intra and Pallanza. Once you've cleared the town the 20km to Cannobio are the prettiest on the tour, shadowing the lakeshore the entire way with views across the water.

03 Cannobio

Sheltered by a high mountain and sitting at the foot of the Cannobina valley, the medieval hamlet of Cannobio is located 5km from the Swiss border. It is a dreamy place. **Piazza di Vittorio Emanuele III**, lined with pastel-hued houses, is the location of a huge Sunday market that attracts visitors from Switzerland.

You can hire SUP boards, canoes and small sailing boats from **Tomaso Surf & Sail** next to the town *lido* (beach). A good boat excursion is to the ruined **Castelli della Malpaga**, located on two rocky islets to the south of Cannobio. In summer it is a favourite picnic spot.

Alternatively, explore the wild beauty of the **Valle Cannobina**. Trails begin in town and snake alongside the surging Torrente Cannobino stream into the heavily wooded hillsides to **Malesco**. Just 2.5km along the valley, in Sant'Anna, the torrent forces its way powerfully through a narrow gorge known as the **Orrido di Sant'Anna**, crossed at its narrowest part by a Romanesque bridge.

The Drive: The next part of the journey involves retracing the previous 22km drive to Verbania-Intra to board the cross-lake ferry to Laveno. Ferries run every 20 minutes. Once in Laveno pick up the SP394dir and then the SP1var and SS394 for the 23km drive to Varese.

04 Varese

Spread out to the south of the Campo dei Fiori hills, Varese is a prosperous provincial capital. From the 17th century onwards, Milanese nobles began to build second residences here, the most sumptuous being the **Palazzo Estense**, completed in 1771 for Francesco III d'Este, the governor of the Duchy of Milan. Although you cannot visit the palace, you are free to wander the vast Italianate gardens (open 8am to dusk).

To the north of the city sits another great villa, **Villa Panza** *(fondo ambiente.it)*, donated to the state in 1996. Part of the donation was 150 contemporary canvases collected by Giuseppe Panza di Biumo, mostly by post-WWII American artists. One of the finest rooms is the 1830 **Salone Impero** (Empire Hall), with heavy chandeliers and four canvases by David Simpson (b 1928).

The Drive: The 28km drive from Varese to Como isn't terribly exciting, passing through a string of small towns and suburbs nestled in the wooded hills. The single-lane SS342 passes through Malnate, Solbiate and Olgiate Comasco before reaching Como.

05 Como

Built on the wealth of its silk industry, Como is an elegant town and remains Europe's most important producer of silk products. The **Museo della Seta** *(Silk Museum; museosetacomo.com)* unravels the town's industrial history, with early dyeing and printing equipment on display. At **A Picci** you can buy top-quality scarves, ties and fabrics.

After wandering the medieval alleys of the historic centre, take a stroll along **Passeggiata Lino Gelpi**, where you pass a series of waterfront mansions, finally arriving at **Villa Olmo**. Set grandly facing the lake, this Como landmark was built in 1728 by the Odescalchi family, related to Pope Innocent XI, and now hosts blockbuster art shows. On Sundays you can continue your walk through the gardens of **Villa del Grumello** and the **Villa Sucota** on the so-called Chilometro della Conoscenza (Kilometre of Knowledge).

On the other side of Como's marina, the **Funicolare Como–Brunate** *(funicolarecomo.it)* whisks you uphill to the quiet village of Brunate for splendid views across the lake.

The Drive: The 32km drive from Como to Bellagio along the SS583 is spectacular. The narrow road swoops and twists around the lakeshore the entire way and rises up out of Como giving panoramic views over the lake. There are plenty of spots en route where you can pull over for photographs.

06 Bellagio

It's impossible not to be charmed by Bellagio's waterfront of bobbing boats, its maze of stone staircases, cypress groves and showy gardens.

Bellagio is a place best absorbed slowly on your own. You can pick up three self-guided walking tour brochures from the **tourist office** *(bellagiolakecomo.com)*. The longest three-hour walk takes in neighbouring villages, including **Pescallo**, a small one-time fishing port about 1km from the centre, and **Loppia**, with the 11th-century Chiesa di Santa

TOP TIP

LAGO MAGGIORE EXPRESS

The Lago Maggiore Express *(lagomaggioreexpress.com)* is a picturesque day trip you can do without the car. It includes train travel from Arona or Stresa to Domodossola, from where you get the charming Centovalli train, crossing 100 valleys, to Locarno in Switzerland and a ferry back to Stresa. The two-day version is perhaps better value if you have the time.

Palazzo Estense

NATALIA MACHEDA/SHUTTERSTOCK

Maria, which is only visitable from the outside.

The walk to one of Como's finest mansions, **Villa Melzi d'Eril** *(giardinidivillamelzi.it)*, heads south along the lakeshore from the Bellagio ferry jetties, revealing views of ranks of gracious residences stacked up on the waterside hills. The grounds of the neoclassical Villa Melzi run right down to the lake and are adorned with classical statues couched in blushing azaleas.

For on-the-lake frolics, **Barindelli** *(barindellitaxiboats.it)* operates slick, mahogany cigarette boats in which you can tool around the headland on a sunset tour.

The Drive: The best way to reach Tremezzo, without driving all the way around the bottom of the lake, is to take the ferry from Piazza Mazzini. The journey takes 10 minutes, but for sightseeing you may want to consider the one-day central lake ticket, covering Bellagio, Varenna, Tremezzo and Cadenabbia.

SEAPLANES ON THE LAKE

For a touch of Hollywood glamour, check out **Aero Club Como** *(aeroclubcomo.com)*, which has been sending seaplanes out over the lakes since 1930. A 30-minute panoramic tour from Como to Bellagio and back starts from €480 for two people. Longer excursions over Lago Maggiore are also possible. In summer you need to reserve at least three days in advance.

07 Tremezzo

Tremezzo is high on everyone's list for a visit to the 17th-century **Villa Carlotta** *(villacarlotta.it)*, whose botanic gardens are filled with orange trees knitted into pergolas and some of Europe's finest rhododendrons, azaleas and camellias.

The villa, which is strung with paintings and fine alabaster-white sculptures (especially lovely are those by Antonio Canova), takes its name from the Prussian princess who was given the palace in 1847 as a wedding present from her mother.

Varenna

CLAUDIA GORI/LONELY PLANET

The Drive: As with the trip to Tremezzo, the best way to travel to Varenna is by passenger ferry either from Cadenabbia (1.3km north of Tremezzo's boat dock) or Bellagio.

08 Varenna

A mirror image of Bellagio across the water, Varenna is a beguiling village bursting with florid plantlife, narrow lanes and pastel-coloured houses stacked up on mountain slopes that defy the laws of physics.

You can wander the flower-laden pathway from Piazzale Martiri della Libertà to the gardens of **Villa Cipressi** *(hotelvillacipressi.it)*, now a luxury hotel, or undertake a 40-minute walk up to the 13th-century **Castello di Vezio** *(castellodivezio.it)*, high above the terracotta rooftops of Varenna.

The castle was once part of a chain of early-warning medieval watchtowers. These days it hosts alfresco temporary exhibitions of avant-garde art – daily except Tuesdays and Fridays. There's also a small cafe.

The Drive: Departing Bellagio, pick up the SS583, but this time head southeast towards Lecco down the other 'leg' of Lago di Como. As with the stretch from Como to Bellagio, the road hugs the lake, offering spectacular views along the whole 20km to Lecco. Once you reach Lecco head south out of town down Via Industriale and pick up the SS342 for the final 40km to Bergamo.

09 Bergamo

Although Milan's skyscrapers are visible on a clear day, historically Bergamo was more closely associated with Venice. The Venetian-style architecture can be seen in **Piazza Vecchia** and, more stridently, in the **City Walls** that were included as part of a UNESCO World Heritage Site in 2017.

Behind this secular core sits the **Piazza del Duomo** with its modest baroque cathedral. A great deal more interesting is the **Basilica di Santa Maria Maggiore** next door. To its whirl of frescoed, Romanesque apses, begun in 1137, Gothic touches were added, as was the Renaissance **Cappella Colleoni**, the mausoleum-chapel of the famous mercenary commander, Bartolomeo Colleoni (1696–1770). Demolishing an entire apse of the basilica, he commissioned Giovanni Antonio Amadeo to create a tomb that is now considered a masterpiece of Lombard art.

Also like Venice, Bergamo has a grand art academy. The seminal **Accademia Carrara** *(lacarrara.it)* is both school and museum, its stunning collection of 1800 Renaissance paintings amassed by local scholar Count Giacomo Carrara (1714–96).

♥ WHY I LOVE THIS TRIP

BRENDAN SALISBURY, WRITER

Maggiore has always been my favourite Italian lake, where you can escape into the quiet woods of the Valle Cannobina and convalesce afterwards in a history-evoking belle-époque cafe in Stresa. And who doesn't have a soft spot for Como, where history buffs can vicariously become Napoleon, or James Bond, in a gilded lakeside villa? Away from the water, Bergamo continues the classic theme, but with a little less pretension.

09

NORTHERN ITALY

A WEEKEND AT LAGO DI GARDA

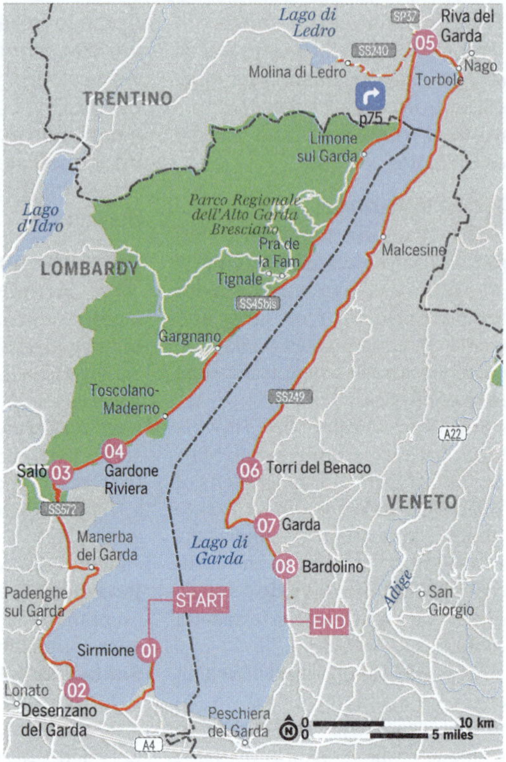

DURATION: 4 DAYS

DISTANCE: 135KM/84 MILES

GREAT FOR: FAMILIES, NATURE

BEST TIME TO GO: JULY FOR LAKE SWIMMING AND OCTOBER FOR BARDOLINO'S WINE FESTIVAL.

Lago di Garda is the largest of the Italian lakes, straddling the border between Lombardy and the Veneto. Vineyards, olive groves and citrus orchards range up the slopes and ensure the tables of Garda's trattorias are well stocked with fine products. Boats buzz across the water and paragliders utilise the thermals that caress Monte Baldo. All you need now is a vintage Fiat 500 (or its modern electric counterpart) to blend in like an Italian.

LINK YOUR TRIP

07 Northern Cities
A 30-minute drive down the A22 and A4 from Bardolino brings you to Verona and the culture-heavy Northern Cities tour.

14 Roof of Italy
Climb out of the lake basin on the SS240 from Riva del Garda to Rovereto for a dose of modern art and an epic drive across Europe's highest pass.

01 Sirmione

Over the centuries impossibly pretty Sirmione has drawn the likes of Catullus and Maria Callas to its banks. The village sits astride a slender peninsula that juts out into the lake and is occupied in large part by the **Grotte di Catullo** *(musei lombardia.cultura.gov.it)*, a misnomer for the ruins of an extensive Roman villa now comprising teetering stone arches and tumbledown walls. There's no evidence that Catullus actually lived here, but who cares? The wraparound lake views from its terraced hillside are legendary. **Rocca Scaligera** is an enormous square-cut castle at the entrance to old Sirmione.

In true Roman style, there's an offshore thermal spring that pumps out water at a natural 37°C. Wallow lakeside in the contemporary outdoor pool at **Terme di Sirmione** *(termedisirmione.com)*.

The Drive: The first 7km from Sirmione to Desenzano del Garda is on the SS572 lake road.

ESSEVU/SHUTTERSTOCK

★ BEST FOR

FAMILIES

Night swimming off pontoons floating along Riva's waterfront.

Sirmione

Exit Sirmione past the Garda Village campground and at the first major roundabout turn right towards Desenzano; total distance 11km.

02 Desenzano del Garda

Known as the *porta del lago* (gateway to the lake), Desenzano may not be as pretty as other lakeside towns, but its ancient harbour, broad promenades and vibrant **Piazza Matteotti** make for pleasant wanderings. It is also a hub for summer nightlife.

Best of all are the mosaics in Desenzano's **Roman Villa**. Wooden walkways lead directly over vivid scenes of chariot-riding, grape-gathering cherubs. Stretching north of Desenzano, the rolling hills of the Valtenesi are etched with vine trellises and olive groves. **Frantoio Montecroce** *(frantoiomontecroce.it)* offers tutored oil tastings.

The Drive: From Desenzano return to the SS572 and start to meander north right by the lakeshore. The first 6km to Padenghe sul Garda are some of the most scenic on the lake, lined with cypresses and umbrella pines with clear views over the water. Total distance to Salò is 19km.

03 Salò

Sedate and refined as Salò is today, in 1943 it was named the capital of the Social Republic of Italy as part of Mussolini's last-ditch efforts to organise Italian fascism in the face of advancing Allied forces. This episode, known as the Republic of Salò, saw more than 16 buildings turned into Mussolini's ministries and offices. You can fill in more gaps in Salò's history at the **Museo di Salò** *(museodisalo.it)*. Exhibits include objects relating to Mussolini, along with a collection of violins in honour of local-born luthier Gasparo di Salò (1542–1609), one of the world's earliest violin-makers.

The Drive: Exit the medieval centre of Salò uphill on Via Umberto I and pick up the SS45bis heading north to Gardone. It's barely 7km along the narrow single carriageway, past old stone walls hiding lemon-coloured villas surrounded by luxuriant flora.

04 Gardone Riviera

In Gardone tour the home of Italy's most controversial poet, Gabriele d'Annunzio. Poet, soldier, hypochondriac and proto-fascist, d'Annunzio's home **Il Vittoriale degli Italiani** *(vittoriale.it)* is as bombastic and extravagant as it is unsettling, and a perfect reflection of the man's enigmatic personality. He retreated to Gardone in 1922, claiming that he wanted to escape the world that made him sick.

For something less oppressive visit the flower-filled oasis of **Giardino Botanico Fondazione André Heller** *(hellergarden.com)*. Hidden among the greenery are 30 pieces of contemporary sculpture.

The Drive: Exit Gardone northeast on Corso Zanardelli for a long, scenic 43km drive north. At Tignale and Limone sul Garda you'll pass the stone pillars of Garda's lemon houses. The final 12km from Limone to Riva del Garda are extraordinary, passing through dynamite-blasted tunnels dramatic enough to make this the location for the opening chase scene in *Casino Royale* (2006).

PHOTO OPPORTUNITY

Lakeside towns backed by mountains from aboard a boat.

05 Riva del Garda

Even on a lake blessed by dramatic scenery, Riva del Garda still comes out on top. Encircled by towering rock faces and a looping landscaped waterfront, its appealing centre is a medley of grand architecture and wide squares. The town's strategic position was fought over for centuries and exhibits in the **Museo Alto Garda** *(museoaltogarda.it)* reflect this turbulent past. Riva makes a natural starting point for walks and bike rides, including trails around **Monte Rocchetta** (1575m), which looms over the northern end of the lake. Just south of town **La Strada del Ponale** (ponale.eu) is a walking path that ascends gently for 2.6km to **Ponale Alto Belvedere**, a bar-restaurant where a couple of waterfalls are visible from the deck.

The Drive: From Riva pick up the SS240 around Torbole and then turn south on the SS249. Lake views abound through columned 'windows' as you

Giardino Botanico Fondazione André Heller

KYNA STUDIO/SHUTTERSTOCK

pass through mountain tunnels, and to the left Monte Baldo rises above the lake. A cable car runs to the summit from Malcesine. The total distance from Riva to Torri del Benaco is 38km.

DETOUR

Lago di Ledro

Start: 05 Riva del Garda

FROM RIVA take the SP37 and then the SS240 west into the mountains, past olive groves and vine-lined terraces. After 11km the road flattens and Lago di Ledro *(valledilendro.com)* comes into view. Only 2.5km long and 2km wide, this diminutive lake sits at an altitude of 650m and is set in a gorgeous valley beneath tree-covered mountains. **Molina di Ledro** is at the lake's eastern end, where thatched huts line up beside beaches and boat-hire pontoons.

06 Torri del Benaco

Picturesque Torri del Benaco is one of the most appealing stops on the eastern bank. The 14th-century **Castello Scaligero** overlooks a pint-sized harbour and packs a wealth of history into dozens of rooms, including exhibits on the lake's traditional industries of fishing, olive-oil production and lemon growing.

TOP TIP

LAKE CRUISING

Fleets of ferries link many Lago di Garda communities, providing a series of scenic mini-cruises. They're run by **Navigazione sul Lago** di Garda *(navigazionelaghi.it)*, which publishes English-language timetables online. Car ferries cross year-round from Toscolano-Maderno on the west bank to Torri del Benaco on the east bank.

The Drive: From the waterfront at Torri del Benaco it's a short 7km drive to Garda, around the secluded Punta San Viglio headland. En route low stone walls or railings are all that stand between you and the water, while cypresses line front lawns to your left.

07 Garda

The bustling town of Garda lacks obvious charms, but it does possess the leafy headland of Punta San Vigilio, a gorgeous crescent bay backed by olive trees 3km to the north.

The privately owned **Parco Baia delle Sirene** has sunloungers and picnic tables beneath the trees.

The tiny headland is also the location of **Locanda San Vigilio** *(locanda-sanvigilio.it)*, with its excellent harbourside taverna, the perfect perch for Lago di Garda sunsets.

The Drive: The final 4km drive to Bardolino, continuing on the SS249, gives you your last fill of big views. Over the short distance the road rises up, giving you lofty views over the water before dropping down amid olive groves into Bardolino.

08 Bardolino

More than 70 vineyards and wine cellars grace the gentle hills that roll east from Bardolino's shores. They produce an impressive array of pink Chiaretto, ruby Classico, dry Superiore and young Novello.

One of the most atmospheric ways to savour their flavours is a tutored tasting (€5 per person) at the **Museo del Vino** *(museodelvino.it)*, which is housed within the **Zeni Winery**. Zeni has been crafting quality wines from Bardolino's morainic hills since 1870.

After this proverbial 'warm up', head into town (with designated driver) and hit the Amarone and Valpolicella varietals at **La Bottega del Vino**.

10

NORTHERN ITALY

A VENETIAN SOJOURN

DURATION: 5-6 DAYS

DISTANCE: 283KM/176 MILES

GREAT FOR: HISTORY, FOOD AND DRINK

BEST TIME TO GO: APRIL TO JUNE FOR SPRINGTIME SPLENDOR AT THE VENETO'S VILLAS; SEPTEMBER FOR THE GRAPE HARVEST.

★ BEST FOR

ART

From the avant-garde in Venice to Tiepolo frescoes in Palladian villas.

Grand Canal

Artistic and cultural enticements abound in Venice and the surrounding Veneto region – waft of fresh espresso from Piazza San Marco's 250-year-old cafes, faded villas on the Brenta Riviera and masterpieces everywhere: Titians in Venice, Palladios in Vicenza and Giottos in Padua. This calls for a toast with bubbly local prosecco – so raise your glass to *la bea vita* (the good life).

LINK YOUR TRIP

12 Trieste to Sappada
Look eastwards down the A4 to Trieste and the borderlands with Slovenia, as many Venetians have done before you.

02 World Heritage Wonders
From the wonders of Venice to UNESCO's list of World Heritage Sites, continue down the A4 from Vicenza to Verona.

01 Venice

Take the No 1 *vaporetto* (passenger ferry) down the **Grand Canal** for scene-stealing backdrops featured in four James Bond films. It starts with controversy at the **Ponte della Costituzione** (Ponte di Calatrava), a luminous glass-and-steel bridge opened in 2008 and that cost triple the original €4 million estimate. Ahead are castle-like **Fondaco dei Turchi**, the historic Turkish trading house, and **Ca' d'Oro** *(cadoro.org)*, a 1430 filigree Gothic marvel. Points of Venetian pride include the **Pescaria**, where fishmongers have been slinging lagoon crab for 700 years, before the marble marvel of the **Ponte di Rialto**. If you're feeling peckish, jump ashore for a gourmet food tour.

The next two canal bends could cause architectural whiplash, with Renaissance **Palazzo Grimani** *(palazzogrimani.org)*, followed by **Palazzo Grassi** *(cultura.gov.it/luogo/museo-di-palazzo-grimani)*, site of contemporary-art sensations

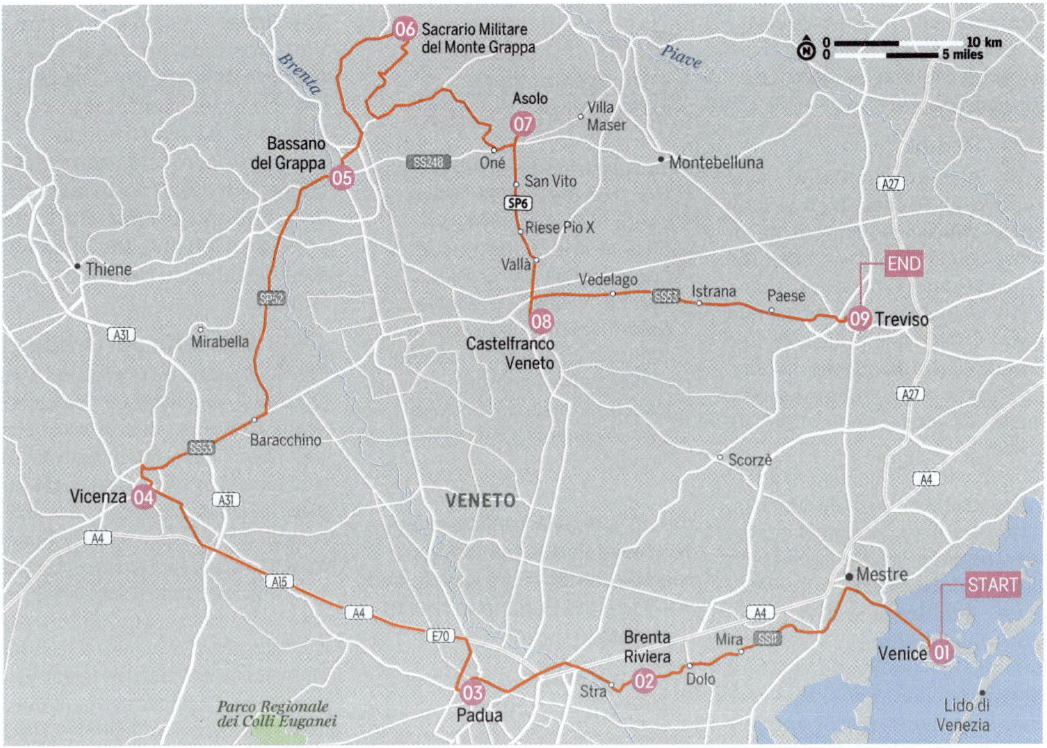

CANADASTOCK/SHUTTERSTOCK

between Biennales, and Baldassare Longhena's baroque jewel box **Ca' Rezzonico** (Museum of 18th-Century Venice; *carezzonico.visitmuve.it*).

Finally, stone lions flank the **Peggy Guggenheim Collection** (*guggenheim-venice.it*), where the American heiress collected ideas, lovers and art. It's situated just before the dramatic dome of Longhena's **Basilica di Santa Maria della Salute** (Our Lady of Health Basilica; *basilicasalutevenezia.it*) comes into view.

The Drive: Ironically, the first 15km of the drive, from Venice to the Brenta Canal's most romantic villa, is the least attractive part of this route, which takes you through the industrial wastelands of Mestre along the SS11. For Villa Pisani and Villa Foscarini Rossi continue a further 19km on the gradually more scenic Via Nazionale through Mira and Dolo.

02 Brenta Riviera

Every 13 June for 300 years, summer officially kicked off with a traffic jam along the Grand Canal, as a flotilla of fashionable Venetians headed to their villas along the Brenta Riviera. Eighty villas still strike elegant poses, although private ownership and privacy hedges leave much to the imagination. Just four of them are open to the public as museums.

The most romantic of the four is the Palladio-designed, 1555–60 **Villa Foscari** (*lamalcontenta.com*), also known as 'La Malcontenta' for the grande dame of the Foscari clan allegedly exiled here for adultery. Further downriver, at Stra, **Villa Pisani Nazionale** (*villapisani.beniculturali.it*) strikes a Versailles-like pose with its 114 rooms, vast gardens and reflecting pools.

Well-heeled Venetians wouldn't dream of decamping to the Brenta without their favourite cobblers, sparking a local tradition of high-end shoemaking. Their art is commemorated with a Shoemakers' Museum in **Villa Foscarini Rossi** (*museodellacalzatura.it*).

The Drive: From Stra it's a short 13km drive through the Padovan periphery into Padua. Leave Stra northwest on Via Venezia, cross beneath the A4 autostrada and follow the road round to merge with the Tangenziale Nord into Padua.

03 Padua

The Brenta Canal once ran through Padua, 40km west of Venice, which was convenient for Padua-bound Venetians when the city came under Venetian dominion in 1405. Venetian governors set up house in the triple-decker, Gothic **Palazzo della Ragione**, its vast main hall frescoed by Giotto acolytes Giusto de' Menabuoi and Nicolò Mireto.

One illustrious Venetian, general Erasmo da Narni (aka Gattamelata, or 'Honeyed Cat'), is commemorated with the 1453 bronze equestrian **Gattamelata statue** in front of the epic **Basilica di Sant'Antonio** *(basilicadelsanto.org)*. Not far from Gattamelata is the **Oratorio di San Giorgio** *(santantonio.org)*, where Titian's 1511 portrait of St Anthony shows him calmly reattaching his own foot.

Padua holds a distinguished place in the history of art. The presence of the university at **Palazzo Bo** *(unipd.it/en/bo)* attracted big names such as Giotto, Fra Filippo Lippi, Donatello and even Mantegna. Padua was also the birthplace of Palladio, and Antonio Canova sculpted his first marble here for the **Prato della Valle** square. See the original in the **Musei Civici agli Eremitani**, along with Giotto's heavenly vision in the **Cappella degli Scrovegni** *(cappelladegliscrovegni.it)*.

The Drive: Leave Padua following signs for Verona and the A4 autostrada for the 42km drive northwest to Vicenza. Although the A4 is heavily trafficked, as you leave Padua behind the road becomes more scenic and you'll spy the Euganean hills to the south.

TOP TIP

CRUISING THE VENETIAN RIVIERA

Travel the length of the Brenta Canal on *Il Burchiello*, a luxury barge that lets you watch 50 villas drift by from velvet couches. Full-day cruises leave from Venice's Pontile della Pietà pier on Riva degli Schiavoni (Tuesday, Thursday and Saturday) or from Padua's Pontile del Portello pier (Wednesday, Friday and Sunday).

04 Vicenza

When Andrea Palladio moved from Padua to Vicenza he began to produce some extraordinary buildings, marrying sophistication and rustic simplicity, reverent classicism and bold innovation. Go for a walk while you're here to see some of his finest works. His showstopper, **La Rotonda** *(villalarotonda.it)*, sits on a hill overlooking the city, its namesake dome and identical colonnaded facades giving it the ultimate classical proportions.

Walk up the narrow path opposite to **Villa Valmarana 'ai Nani'** *(villavalmarana.com)*, which is nicknamed for the 17 *nani* (dwarfs) who guard the garden walls. In 1757 the entire interior was redecorated with frescoes by Italian painter Giambattista Tiepolo and his son Giandomenico.

The Drive: Pushing away from the autostrada, northwards towards Bassano del Grappa, the scenery becomes decidedly rural, passing through vineyards, cornfields and small towns. Drive 7km northeast on the SS53 and just past Baracchino turn left onto the SP52 for the final 20km to Bassano del Grappa.

05 Bassano del Grappa

Bassano del Grappa sits with charming simplicity on the banks of the river Brenta as it winds its way free of the Alpine foothills. It is broached by the **Ponte degli Alpini**, Palladio's 1569 covered bridge. Fragile as it seems, it is designed to withstand the rush of spring meltwaters from Monte Grappa. It's always been critical in times of war: Napoleon bivouacked here for many months and in the Great War hundreds of soldiers were stationed here. Now the charming walled town is full of smart shops and restaurants and the largest collection of Dürer prints in the world, which can be seen at **Museo Civico** and **Palazzo Sturm** *(museibassano.it)*.

The town is also famous for its after-dinner firewater, grappa, which was invented here. Sample it at **Poli Museo della Grappa** *(poligrappa.com)*.

The Drive: Head out of Bassano on the SP59, crossing the Brenta river eastwards. Then pick up the northbound SS47 before turning right onto the SP148. Once you leave the city limits you'll start the awesome climb up Monte Grappa via hairpin bends, enjoying ever more spectacular views.

The Descent of the Holy Ghost by Titian, Basilica diSanta Maria della Salute (p77)

RENATA SEDMAKOVA/SHUTTERSTOCK

♥ WHY I LOVE THIS TRIP

PAULA HARDY, WRITER

This trip is a fantastic combination of grand-slam sites and delightful out-of-the-way surprises. Venice's marble palaces and Giotto's ground-breaking frescoes in the Scrovegni Chapel are understandably world famous, but who knows about the 1500 pairs of historic shoes in Villa Foscarini Rossi or the floor-to-ceiling frescoes at Villa Valmarana and Villa Maser? These places are quite wonderful, and what's more you'll often have them all to yourself.

06 Sacrario Militare del Monte Grappa

No battle defines Italy's struggle in the Great War better than the 1917–18 battle of Monte Grappa (1776m). Despite being severely weakened after the battles of Caporetto and Isonzo, Italian Alpine brigades mounted a heroic stand atop this barren mountain and finally brought a halt to the Austro-Hungarian advance. The savage conflict claimed the lives of 22,910 troops, who are now entombed in this **mausoleum**, which caps the summit in a monumental modernist ziggurat and is studded with bronze plaques commemorating the deceased.

The Drive: The 39km south to Asolo is one of the most stunning drives in the itinerary. The drive down the SP140 descends through tight hairpin bends with sweeping views of the plains. At the bottom, pick up the SP26 eastwards and meander through the country to Asolo.

07 Asolo

East of Bassano rises Asolo, known as the 'town of 100 vistas' for its panoramic hillside location. It was once the haunt of the Romans and a personal gift from Venice to Caterina, 15th-century queen of Cyprus, in exchange for her abdication. A hit with writers, poet Robert Browning bought a house here and named his last work *Asolando* (1889).

Beneath Asolo's forested hilltop, Palladio and Veronese conspired to create the Veneto's finest monument to *la bea vita* at **Villa di Maser** *(villadimaser.it)*. Palladio set the arcaded villa into a verdant hillside, while inside Veronese imagined an Arcadian idyll in floor-to-ceiling *trompe l'œil* frescoes.

> PHOTO OPPORTUNITY
>
> The magical views of folding hillsides from Asolo.

The Drive: Descend from Asolo's sylvan heights and zigzag across the SS248 onto the SP6 towards Castelfranco Veneto for a 15km drive south through the small towns of San Vito, Riese Pio X and Vallà.

08 Castelfranco Veneto

Giorgio Barbarelli da Castelfranco (aka Giorgione) was one of the masters of the High Renaissance, and one of its most mysterious.

Born in Castelfranco, he was a contemporary of Titian, but an early death from the plague in 1510 left an adoring public with just six acclaimed canvases.

Like Titian, he is credited with revolutionising Renaissance painting, using a refined chiaroscuro technique called *sfumato* ('smokey') to blur lines and enhance the emotional quality of colour, light and perspective.

Luckily for Castelfranco, one of his few surviving works, an altarpiece known as Castelfranco Madonna, still hangs in the Cappella Costanza in the **Duomo** *(chiesacastelfranco.it)*. More of the Giorgione school of work can be viewed in the **Casa di Giorgione** *(museocasagiorgione.it)*.

The Drive: At Castelfranco Veneto you're back on the SS53 again, this time heading 27km further east towards Treviso. Pass through Vedelago and on through flat, flat fields of corn to Istrana, Paese and then Treviso.

09 Treviso

Totally outdone by supermodel La Serenissima (Venice), Treviso seems becalmed beyond the tourist mayhem, its quiet canals, weeping willows and frescoed facades the backdrop to another mid-sized Italian town. So why drop in? Well, Treviso has made a handsome contribution to human happiness, giving us DēLonghi appliances, **Pinarello bicycles** *(pinarello.com)*, *radicchio Trevisano* (red radicchio, in season from December through February) and Italy's favourite dessert, tiramisù.

Settle down to sample Treviso's culinary treats in vintage trattoria **Toni del Spin**, where staff serve you risotto with white asparagus, sprinkled with wildflowers.

Afterwards, wander Treviso's pretty canals and visit the excellent modern-art museum, **Luigi Bailo** *(museicivicitreviso.it)*, or enjoy Italy's foremost graphic poster collection at the **Museo Collezione Salce** *(www.collezionesalce.beniculturali.it)*.

Asolo

LEOKS/SHUTTERSTOCK

11

★ BEST FOR

OENOPHILES

A glass of Quintarelli's rich, red Amarone.

NORTHERN ITALY

VALPOLICELLA WINE COUNTRY

DURATION: 4 DAYS

DISTANCE: 70KM/43 MILES

GREAT FOR: FOOD AND DRINK, HISTORY

BEST TIME TO GO: APRIL AND MAY FOR WALKING; AUTUMN FOR THE HARVEST.

Vineyards, Valpolicella

The vineyards of Valpolicella are within easy reach of sunny Lago di Garda and romantic Verona. The 'valley of many cellars' has been in the wine business since the ancient Greeks introduced their *passito* technique (using partially dried grapes) to create the blockbuster flavours still enjoyed in the region's Amarone and Recioto wines. Spread across 240 sq km, the valleys are dotted with villas and ancient hamlets, and harbour as much heritage and culture as they do wine.

LINK YOUR TRIP

09 A Weekend at Lago di Garda
From Bardolino continue on the SR249 and circumnavigate Lago di Garda for a spot of boating and wild swimming.

10 A Venetian Sojourn
From Verona head down the A4 to Vicenza for a dose of high-octane culture in the Venetian countryside.

01 Verona

Strategically situated at the foot of the Italian-Austrian Alps, Verona has been a successful trade centre since Roman times. Its ancient gates, busy forum (now **Piazza delle Erbe**) and grand Roman **Arena**, which still serves as one of the world's great opera venues, are testament to its prosperity – as is the city's handsome profile, which combines Renaissance gardens with the grand Gothic architecture of showcase churches, such as the **Basilica di Sant'Anastasia** *(chieseverona.it)*.

In summer people flock here to listen to opera beneath the stars, but in spring, food and wine professionals descend on the city for Italy's most important national wine fair, **Vinitaly** *(vinitaly.com)*. Unsurprisingly, Verona is also big on *aperitivo* culture. **Antica Bottega del Vino** *(bottegavini.it)* is an oenophile institution, its 19th-century cellars filled with over 4000 labels.

PHOTOFRA/SHUTTERSTOCK

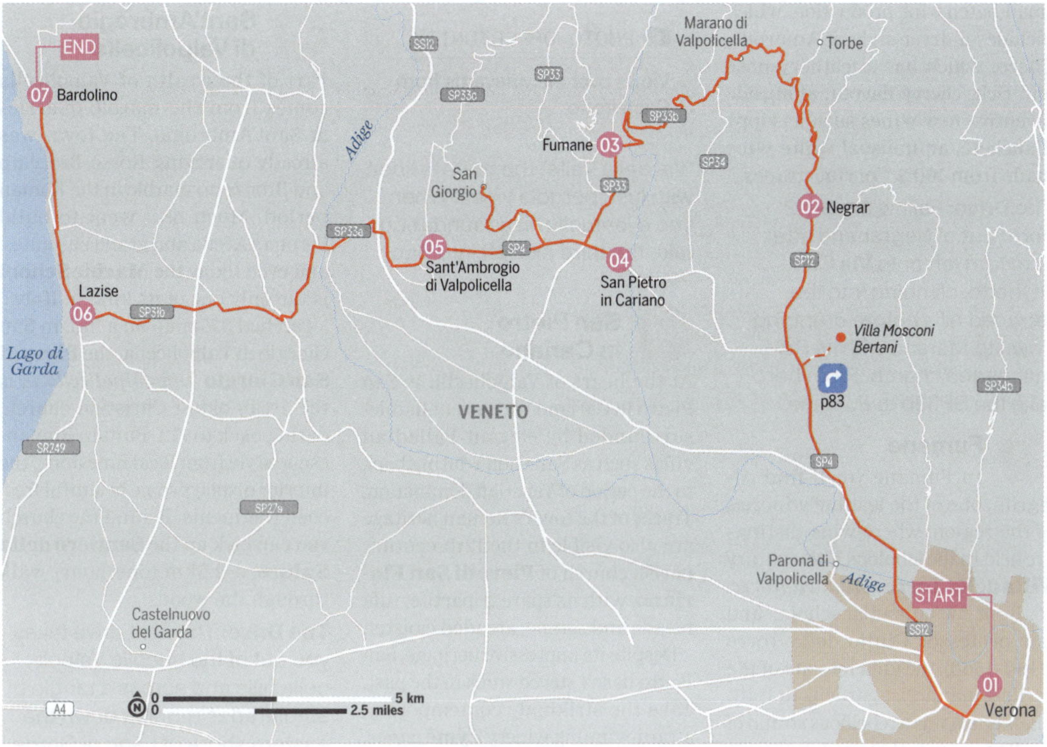

The Drive: Head northwest out of Verona on the SS12 crossing the river Adige before turning left onto the SP1. After 2.5km take the Arbizzano exit right onto the SP4, gradually leaving the suburbs behind and heading into the hills. At Arbizzano continue straight onto the SP12 towards Negrar.

DETOUR

Villa Mosconi Bertani

Start: 01 Verona

Before you reach Negrar take a quick 1.5km detour off the SP4 down Via Novare to the **Villa Mosconi Bertani** *(mosconi bertani.it)* in Arbizzano. Arguably one of the most beautifully sited villas in Valpolicella, this winery is one of the oldest continuously operating wine businesses in Italy. What's more, the lovely neo classical residence, completed in 1769, with a phalanx of Greek gods perched on the facade and a grand, frescoed **Chamber of the Muses** designed for small operatic performances, is a listed historic landmark and is well worth a tour. Beyond the house are 8 hectares of English-style romantic gardens, lakes, orchards and Guyot vineyards to explore. Tours and tastings run regularly between April and October, but require prebooking.

02 Negrar

Five communities compose the DOC quality-controlled heart of Valpolicella: Negrar, Marano di Valpolicella, San Pietro in Cariano, Fumane and Sant'Ambrogio di Valpolicella. Tiny Negrar, the so-called 'city of wine', is the largest and is set amid a patchwork of pergola vineyards, crisscrossed by lines of *marogne* (dry-stone walls) typical of the region. Amarone acolytes flock to the iconic **Giuseppe Quintarelli** estate, which, despite its modest appearance, produces one of the biggest, richest red wines this side of Porto.

Innovators, such as the fifth-generation vintners at **Damoli** *(damoli vini.com)*, are meticulous in their small-batch wine production, which includes a dryer style of Amarone, Checo, which has a leathery nose and rich, cherry flavour, alongside inventive new wines such as zippy Biancheté, an unusual white wine made from 100% Corvina grapes.

The Drive: Follow the SP12 north out of Negrar and after 3km turn left onto Via Ca' Righetto, climbing into the terraced hills before dropping down to Marano with its Romanesque church. From here take the SP33b to Fumane.

03 Fumane

In Fumane you'll find Allegrini, one of the leading wineries of the region, where wine tastings are held in the fabulous 16th-century **Villa della Torre** *(villadellatorre.it)*. Built for humanist scholar and law professor Giulio della Torre (1480–1563), the villa has one of the earliest mannerist gardens in Italy. Mannerism was a rebellious strand of the Renaissance that produced some of the most intriguing interiors and garden landscapes of the period. The Italian word *maniera* means 'style' and mannerist art and architecture is highly stylised and fantastical.

On its surface the Villa della Torre and its garden appear to present a regular Renaissance scene, but look closer and you'll find grotesque masks spitting water at promenaders, fireplaces that look like roaring monsters and a grotto that resembles a snarling hell's mouth. All of it together wittily suggests the veneer of civilisation is fragile, and despite humankind's best efforts, the primitive forces of nature are always lurking just beneath the surface.

The Drive: Head south on the SP33 from Fumane for the short 6km drive to San Pietro in Cariano. Otherwise known as the 'Via della Valle', the route is lined with lush pergola vines. When you eventually hit a roundabout, take the third exit left into San Pietro.

> PHOTO OPPORTUNITY
>
> Views over the vineyards from Castelrotto.

04 San Pietro in Cariano

At the heart of Valpolicella is San Pietro in Cariano, an ancient hamlet surrounded by elegant Palladian villas such as San Giona dating back to the period of Venetian domination. Traces of the town's Roman heritage are also visible in the 12th-century parish church of **Pieve di San Floriano**, with its spare tripartite, tufa facade and serene, arcaded cloister.

Despite its impressive heritage, San Pietro hasn't stayed stuck in the past. Take the strikingly contemporary, award-winning winery **Zýmē** *(zyme.it)*, designed by architect Moreno Zurlo. It has a reputation for bold, big-blend wines, the most famous of which is Harlequin, a thrilling IGP wine made using 15 local grape varieties. In town, you can sample Amarone at **Montecariano Cellars** *(montecariano.it)*, just off central Piazza San Giuseppe.

The Drive: A short 10km hop gets you from San Pietro in Cariano to Sant'Ambrogio via San Giorgio, a fraction (subdivision) of Sant'Ambrogio. Pick up the SP4 and head west out of San Pietro. After 2km turn right on Via Case Sparse Conca d'Oro, which leads uphill to San Giorgio. Then retrace your steps to the SP4 and continue west to Sant'Ambrogio.

05 Sant'Ambrogio di Valpolicella

Part of the wealth of Valpolicella comes from the marble quarries at Sant'Ambrogio. The town was already quarrying Rosso Broccato and Bronzetto marble in the Roman period. Much of it went to build Verona's Arena and grand city gates, and even today the **Marble School** is the only one of its kind in Italy.

Perched 375m up on a hill, in San Giorgio di Valpolicella, the **Pieve di San Giorgio** *(infovalpolicella.it)* is the area's oldest Christian church, dating back to 712. Built in Romanesque style from local limestone, the interior displays some beautiful frescoed fragments. Behind the church you can pick up the **Sentiero della Salute**, a 2.5km (one hour) walk through the woods.

The Drive: The next drive takes you out of the bucolic Valpolicella hills and across a tangle of autostradas running down the eastern shore of Lago di Garda. Exit Sant'Ambrogio west on the SP4 and then dog leg across the SS12 onto the SP33a. Wend your way along here, merging with the SP27a and SP31b to Lazise, 11km away.

06 Lazise

Sitting at the foot of the gentle hills of Valpolicella on the shores of Lago di Garda is Lazise. Dominated for centuries by the powerful and murderous Scaligeri clan from Verona, the town retains its impressive, turreted **castle** (privately owned) and encircling walls. Look out for the huge hole in the north wall of the main tower, made by a cannon during the 15th-century wars between Venice and Milan.

As an important medieval customs point, Lazise is surrounded by numerous grand villas such as

IMAGESEF/SHUTTERSTOCK

Marano di Valpolicella (p83)

Villa dei Cedri, set back from the waterfront in Colà. These days it is home to the fabulous **Parco Termale del Garda** *(villadei cedri.it)*, a 5.2-hectare natural spa with a couple of enormous thermal lakes fed by underground hot springs pumping out water at a balmy 33°C.

The Drive: A short, lovely 6km lakeside drive takes you north up the SR249 from Lazise to Bardolino. To your left the large, blue expanse of the lake stretches out lazily, while to your right ranks of olives and cypresses line the hillsides.

07 Bardolino

Prosperous Bardolino is a town in love with the grape. More than 70 vineyards grace the surrounding morainic hills interspersed with silvery olive groves, dark cypresses and cheerful pink oleanders.

The **tourist office** has a map of local wine producers on the **Strada del Vino** *(bardolino-stradadelvino.it)*.

The **Museo del Vino** *(museo delvino.it)* is set within the **Zeni Winery** *(zeni.it)* and offers a good insight into local production methods and grape varieties, coupled with free tastings and smell tests in a special Galleria Olfattiva. Wines to sample are the local Chiaretto and the young Novello, which rarely make it out of Italy.

If you happen to be visiting in May, October or November, you can probably catch one of the town's numerous **wine festivals**, when the waterfront fills up with food and wine stands, as well as musicians and dancers.

Otherwise, plan to visit on a Thursday in order to catch the **weekly market**.

12

★ BEST FOR

CULTURE

A true borderland: multilingual, multicultural and historically fascinating.

NORTHERN ITALY

TRIESTE TO SAPPADA

DURATION: 7 DAYS

DISTANCE: 224KM/139 MILES

GREAT FOR: HISTORY, FOOD AND DRINK, NATURE

BEST TIME TO GO: MAY TO OCTOBER FOR FINE WEATHER AND THE GRAPE HARVEST.

Castello di Miramare

Meandering the borderlands of northeastern Italy, a tour through Friuli Venezia Giulia reveals a place with a unique multicultural heritage, influenced through the centuries by its Austrian and Slavic neighbours. Starting in Trieste, the home of Habsburg princes and once Austria's seaside salon, climb the steep plateau to Cividale, the city of Julius Caesar, visit Europe's only school of mosaic in Spilimbergo, drink Hungarian-style Tocai in Collio and end in the linguistic mountain island of Sappada.

LINK YOUR TRIP

16 Grande Strada delle Dolomiti
From Sappada it's a super-scenic 57km drive, via the SR355, SS52 and SR48, through the mountains to Cortina d'Ampezzo.

10 A Venetian Sojourn
From Aquileia hop onto the A4 for a fast ride down to the Venetian lagoon, where golden domes and frescoed palaces await.

01 Trieste

From as long ago as the 1300s, Trieste has faced east. It flourished under Habsburg patronage between 1382 and 1918, attracting writers and philosophers such as Thomas Mann and James Joyce to the busy cafes on **Piazza dell'Unità d'Italia**. There they enjoyed the city's fluid character where Latin, Slavic, Jewish and Germanic culture intermingled. The neighbourhood of **Borgo Teresiano** reflects this cultural melange and on Via San Francesco d'Assisi you can tour Trieste's nationally important **Synagogue** *(triestebraica.it)* and the stunning Serbian Orthodox **Chiesa di Santo Spiridione** *(comunitaserba.org)*.

Seven kilometres from the city centre, **Castello di Miramare** *(miramare.cultura.gov.it)* is Trieste's bookend to Austrian rule, the fanciful neo-Gothic home of Archduke Maximilian, commander in chief of Austria's Imperial Navy, who came to Trieste as an ambitious young aristocrat in the 1850s and

was shot by firing squad in Mexico in 1867. The house is a reflection of his eccentric wanderlust.

The Drive: Head northwest out of Trieste along Viale Miramare (SS14), where you'll keep sea views to your left for almost 20km. At Sistiana join the A4 (towards Venice) for 18km to Redipuglia, where you can visit Italy's largest war memorial. Then exit southwest towards Papariano and Aquileia for the final 16km run.

02 Aquileia

Colonised by Rome in 181 BCE, Aquileia was one of the largest and richest cities of the empire. Levelled by Attila's Huns in 452 CE, the city's inhabitants fled south and west where they founded Grado and then Venice. A smaller town rose in its place in the early Middle Ages with the construction of the present **basilica** *(basilicadiaquileia.it)*, which is carpeted with one of the largest and most spectacular Roman-era mosaics in the world.

Beyond the basilica explore the scattered ruins of the **Porto Fluviale**, the old river port, and the standing columns of the ancient **Forum** on Via Giulia Augusta. Then visit the **Museo Archeologico Nazionale** *(museoarcheologico aquileia.cultura.gov.it)* for one of Italy's most important collections of Roman artefacts.

The Drive: A short 30km drive takes you to the Collio. Exit Aquileia north on the SS352 and after 3km veer off northeast onto the SS351 through open farmland towards Gradisca d'Isonzo. At Sagrado turn left onto the SR305 and head towards Borgnano where you'll turn right onto a small country road (SP16) that leads through vineyards to Cormòns.

> **PHOTO OPPORTUNITY**
>
> Mosaic sea monsters and songbirds at Aquileia.

03 Il Collio

Famed for its winemakers and country restaurants, the Collio produces some of the finest, mineral-rich white wines in Italy from local varietals such as Friulano, Malvasia Istriana and Ribolla Gialla. The area's vineyards are arranged like a quilt around the town of Cormòns, where the local wine shop, **Enoteca di Cormòns** *(enoteca dicormons.com)*, offers tastings with platters of Montasio cheese.

Even in high season, it is easy to drop in to dozens of family-run wineries and taste rare vintages with vintners such as **Renato Keber** *(renatokeber.com)*. Larger vineyards, offering international export, are **Venica & Venica** *(venica.it)*.

If you feel peckish, drop into **La Subida** *(lasubida.it)* or Michelin-starred **L'Argine a Vencò** *(larginea venco.it)* where farm-to-table ingredients bring the landscape to the plate.

The Drive: The next 18km to Cividale del Friuli are the most scenic on the trip. Rolling northwards from Cormòns on a country lane through the vineyards on the SS356, you'll pass through small villages such as Como di Rozzano, where Perusini offers tastings.

04 Cividale del Friuli

Founded by Julius Caesar in 50 BCE as Forum de Lulii (ultimately 'Friuli'), Cividale's picturesque stone streets are worth a morning's quiet contemplation. Splitting the town in two is the **Ponte del Diavolo** (Devil's Bridge), its central arch supported by a huge rock said to have been thrown into the river by the devil.

Cividale's most important sight is the **Tempietto Longobardo** *(tempiettolongobardo.it)*. Dating from the 8th century CE, its frescoes and ancient Lombard woodwork are both unusual and extremely moving. Afterwards head to the **Museo Cristiano** in the cathedral, where you can see the 8th-century stone Altar of Ratchis.

The Drive: Wend your way out of Cividale across the Natisone river on Via Fiore dei Liberi. To your right you'll get a great view of the Ponte del Diavolo. Then take a hard left onto Viale Udine, which becomes the SS54 and carries you 18km to Udine.

05 Udine

While reluctantly ceding its premier status to Trieste in the 1950s, Udine remains the spiritual, and gastronomic, capital of Friuli. At the heart of its walled medieval centre sits the **Piazza della Libertà**, dubbed the most beautiful Venetian square on the mainland.

Other Venetian echoes can be seen in the shimmering Tiepolo frescoes in the **cathedral** *(www.cattedraleudine.it)* and the **Oratorio della Purità**, open for guided tours only. The *Assumption* on the ceiling was one of Giambattista's very first commissions, while the eight biblical scenes in chiaroscuro are by his son Giandomenico. For more Tiepolos and rare views of the city framed by the Alps beyond, walk up the hill to the **castle** *(civicimuseiudine.it)*. Local legend has it that when Attila the Hun plundered Aquileia in 452 CE, he ordered his soldiers to build the hill from where he could witness its destruction. Today it houses the **Galleria d'Arte Antica**.

The Drive: A 22km meander down small provincial roads through charming towns like Martignacco and Fagagna. Leave Udine westward on the SR464. At Ciconicco turn right (north) onto the SP10 then the SP116 to San Daniele which sits on a gentle hill overlooking the broad Tagliamento river.

Sappada

HIGH FLIERS/SHUTTERSTOCK

06 San Daniele del Friuli

San Daniele del Friuli sits atop a rounded hill with a stunning view of the gently undulating surrounding landscape. Its 8000 inhabitants prepare Friuli's greatest gastronomic export, the dark, exquisitely sweet Prosciutto di San Daniele. Salt is the only method of preservation allowed and the 27 *prosciuttifici* (ham-curing plants) in the town are safeguarded by EU regulations. Learn the secrets of production and sample the ham at artisanal producer **La Casa del Prosciutto** *(lacasadelprosciutto.com)*.

In August, the town holds the **Aria di Festa** *(ariadisandaniele.it)*, a four-day festival of open-house tours and tastings. For a list of *prosciuttifici* that are open year-round, visit the **tourist office**.

The Drive: This 83km drive is the longest on the itinerary. Head northeast out of San Daniele on the SR463. Join the A23 at Osoppo and exit 20km later at Amaro onto the SS52. Follow the Tagliamento river to Villa Santina and then turn right onto the SR355, which then climbs slowly for 37km up to Sappada.

DETOUR

Spilimbergo

Start: 01 San Daniele del Friuli

The mosaic school, **Scuola Mosaicisti del Friuli** *(scuola mosaicistifriuli.it)*, in Spilimbergo is one of the most fascinating places in Friuli. Although established in 1922 in a postwar effort to provide vocational skills for the poverty-stricken area, the mosaic tradition in Spilimbergo is centuries old. Artisans from this school decorated much of Renaissance Venice and have created some of the world's most celebrated mosaics, including those in the Foro Italico in Rome, the Church of the Holy Sepulchre in Jerusalem and in the subway station at Ground Zero in New York.

Prebooked tours take you through classrooms explaining the different styles of mosaic taught: Roman, Byzantine and some stunning free-form modern mosaics. What's more, the school itself forms a canvas with every floor, staircase, bathroom, wall and pillar covered in different styles of mosaic. As such, it represents a unique record of 20th-century mosaic work and wows at every turn.

07 Sappada

Voted one of the most beautiful villages in Italy and the winner of a sustainability award in 2019, Sappada (Plodn in dialect) is a picture-postcard alpine village set on a sunny slope surrounded by dramatic Dolomitic peaks.

It's right on the border of the Veneto, Carnia and Carinthia (Austria) and was settled by families from East Tyrol.

It remains a unique linguistic island and the inhabitants proudly maintain their unique culture and traditions.

Chief among these is **Plodar Vosenocht**, the annual masked Carnival held in February or March, and September's **SappaMukky**, when the cattle are brought down from the high mountain pastures.

Otherwise, people in the know flock here for the fine-dining restaurants, the pristine mountain hikes and the excellent skiing facilities in winter, making it a perfect place to end the tour.

AUSTRIA
LIECHTENSTEIN
SWITZERLAND
FRANCE
Bern
Lausanne
Lake Geneva
Rhein
A8
ALTO ADIGE (SÜDTIROL)
TRENTINO
VENETO
LOMBARDY
PIEDMONT
VALLE D'AOSTA
LIGURIA
EMILIA-ROMAGNA
TUSCANY
13
14
15
16
17
Brunico (Bruneck)
Bressanone (Brixen)
Merano
La Villa
Siusi
Bolzano
Cortina d'Ampezzo
Vigo di Fassa
Bormio
Malè
Belluno
Tirano
Sondrio
Gravedona
Lago di Como
Trento
E45
Riva del Garda
Rovereto
Bassano del Grappa
Piave
Treviso
Lago d'Iseo
Bellagio
Como
Locarno
Domodossola
Cannobio
Verbania
Stresa
Varese
Aosta
E25
Issogne
Biella
A26
E35
Bergamo
Monza
Rho
A4
Milan
Novara
Ivrea
A55
Crema
Brescia
Salò
Lago di Garda
Desenzano del Garda
Verona
Vicenza
Padua
Mestre
Venice
Este
Chioggia
Adige
Po
A13
Susa
E70
Turin
Pavia
A1
Cremona
Mantua
A21
Piacenza
Pinerolo
Asti
Alessandria
Tortona
A6
E74
Racconigi
Bra
Alba
Savigliano
A7
A22
Ferrara
Parma
Modena
Bologna
Ravenna
A15
A14
Cuneo
Limone Piemonte
Genoa
Camogli
Savona
Sestri Levante
La Spezia
Lerici
Finale Ligure
A10
Golfo di Genova (Gulf of Genoa)
0 50 km
0 25 miles

IPICS/SHUTTERSTOCK

Dolomites (p106)

THE ITALIAN ALPS

EXPLORE

THE ITALIAN ALPS

Rising like a giant rock wall along Italy's northern borders, the Alps are an electrifying prospect. Roads snake across the mountainous terrain, traversing the country from Mont Blanc (Monte Bianco) in the far northwest to the saw-toothed steeples of the Dolomites in the east. Everywhere you go, the scenery is superb and the sports invigorating: superlative skiing and snowboarding in winter and hiking, climbing and mountain biking in the warmer months. Our trips take in the area's most thrilling landscapes, leading over hair-raising alpine passes to fairy-tale villages, spas and super-chic ski resorts.

Turin

Turin, Italy's original capital and now its fourth-largest city, makes an excellent starting point for the northwestern Alps.

Situated in the Piedmont region, it's easy to get to – by air to Caselle airport or by train from Rome, Milan, and other key cities – and is well positioned for onward road travel: the A32 autostrada runs west to Susa, Sestriere and the popular Via Lattea (Milky Way) ski area while the A5 leads north to Aosta and Mont Blanc on the French border.

The city itself is well worth a couple of days of your time, offering everything from high culture and chic dining to contemporary art and culinary experimentation.

You can explore royal palaces and world-class museums, hip galleries and baroque piazzas.

Historic cafes serve silky coffee and lavish evening aperitivi.

To stock up on provisions, there's Porta Palazzo, Europe's largest produce market, or the Eataly food emporium.

And for accommodation, take your pick from eco-friendly hostels, B&Bs, boutique suites and business hotels.

Bolzano

In the Trentino Alto-Adige region, the South Tyrolean city of Bolzano is considered the gateway to the Dolomites.

It's not a huge place – its population is around 106,600 – but it's well connected and has everything you'll need.

WHEN TO GO

If winter sports are your thing, the ski season runs from December to March. The Christmas period is particularly popular, with many towns staging Yuletide markets. Note, however, that many high-altitude passes close over winter, typically from October to May. For hikers and outdoor enthusiasts, the best months are June, July and September when the snow has largely melted and trails are open.

It's on the A22 autostrada, which runs from Verona to Austria, and is served by regular trains to/from Trento, Verona and Bologna. Regional buses run to towns and cities in the province and beyond.

A decent selection of guesthouses and hotels provide pleasant lodgings while traditional wood-panelled restaurants showcase the region's hearty local cuisine.

Before leaving town, a visit to the Messner Mountain Museum will get you in the mood for the mountains with its castle setting, mesh walkways and mountain-inspired art.

Cortina d'Ampezzo

One of Italy's most glamorous ski resorts, Cortina d'Ampezzo looks the part with its church spires and cascading piazzas framed by magnificent Dolomite peaks.

In the winter high season, it heaves with skiers and sharply dressed visitors, while summer sees climbers, hikers and mountain bikers move in. Its facilities are world-class and accommodation is plentiful, if pricey. To get here by road, take the north–south SS51 or east–west SS48. By public transport, your best bet is the Cortina Express or ATVO bus from Venice airport or Mestre train station.

TRANSPORT

Flights serve airports across the area, including Turin (for Aosta and the Maritime Alps), Verona and Venice (for the Dolomites and northeastern ranges). Alternatively, you can get trains to these cities from Milan, Rome and other major hubs. Once in the area, buses are generally more useful than trains, but you'll be better off with your own wheels.

WHERE TO STAY

You'll find no shortage of accommodation in The Italian Alps, with options ranging from family-friendly hotels to spa resorts, design hotels and romantic chalets. Many places are in the area's ski resorts, which heave in winter and do brisk business in the summer holiday season.

Higher up in the mountains, you can bunk down in mountain huts *(rifugi)*, which offer basic rooms sleeping anything from two to a dozen or more people. Many also supply hot meals and/or basic cooking facilities. They're generally open from June to late September and popular ones fill quickly, so try to book ahead.

RESOURCES

- **Dolomiti Skipass**
  For up-to-date information on skiing and summer activities in the Dolomites. *dolomitisuperski.com*
- **Via Lattea**
  Has everything you need to know about the Via Lattea ski area west of Turin. *vialattea.it*
- **CAI**
  Official website of the Club Alpino Italiano with lists of mountain refuges offering accommodation. *rifugi.cai.it*

WHAT'S ON

- **Mercatini di Natale**
  Get into the festive spirit at the twinkling Christmas markets held in Bolzano, Merano and Bressanone.
- **Merano Grape Festival**
  Locals in traditional Tyrolean costume parade around Merano in the third week of October to celebrate the annual grape harvest.
- **CioccolaTò**
  (www.cioccola.to.it) One for chocoholics, Turin revels in chocolate for 10 days in October/November with tastings, presentations and hands-on fun.

13

THE ITALIAN ALPS

MEANDERING THE MARITIME ALPS

DURATION: 7 DAYS

DISTANCE: 277KM/172 MILES

GREAT FOR: FAMILIES, NATURE

BEST TIME TO GO: OCTOBER TO JANUARY FOR FOOD FAIRS, HIKING AND SKIING.

Shoehorned between the rice-growing plains of Piedmont and the sparkling coastline of Liguria lie the brooding Maritime Alps – a unique pocket of dramatically sculpted mountains that rise like a stony-faced border guard along the frontier of Italy and France. Traverse their valleys and peaks to gaze in mirror-like lakes, ski the spotless Via Lattea (Milky Way) and hike amid forests rich with chestnuts.

LINK YOUR TRIP

03 Savoy Palace Circuit
For more bombastic Savoy palaces and castles, continue from Rivoli on a circuit around Turin on the Tangenziale.

05 Italian Riviera
From Cuneo cut across eastwards along the A33 and then down the A6 to Savona for a cruise along the Italian Riviera.

01 Turin

In 2008 Turin (Torino) held the title of European Capital of Design, and no wonder; the city's architecture mirrors its trajectory from the baroque elegance of the **Palazzo Reale** *(museireali.beniculturali.it)*, seat of the monarchic House of Savoy, to the futuristic steel-and-glass **Mole Antonelliana**, symbol of the city's industrial rebirth and now the repository for the **Museo Nazionale del Cinema** *(museocinema.it)*. Take the lift to the roof terrace for 360-degree views. From the Mole you may just be able to spy **Lingotto**, Turin's former Fiat factory, redesigned by Renzo Piano into an exhibition centre.

It also houses the 'treasure chest' rooftop gallery **Pinacoteca Giovanni e Marella Agnelli** *(pinacoteca-agnelli.it)*, with masterpieces by Canaletto, Manet, Matisse and Picasso.

Equally dazzling are the stalls in the famous Slow Food supermarket, **Eataly** *(eataly.net)* next door.

ENRICOALIBERTI ITALYPHOTO/SHUTTERSTOCK

★ BEST FOR

SKIING

The 400 spotless kilometres of skiing in the Via Lattea.

Via Lattea (p96)

The Drive: Leave Turin westwards along Corso Vittorio Emanuele II following signs for the A32/E70 to Bardonecchia/Fréjus. Join the autostrada for 11km and then take exit 2, Avigliana Est. Follow the road for 4km. At the roundabout turn right up the Via Sacra (SP188) to San Michele.

DETOUR

Rivoli

Start: 01 Turin

Works by Franz Ackermann, Gilbert and George, and Frank Gehry now sit amid the splendour of **Castello di Rivoli**, once the home of Savoy princes and now the venue for the **Museo d'Arte Contemporanea** *(castellodirivoli.org)*. The startling contrasts between the historic house and the avant-garde art are worth the trip.

02 Sacra di San Michele

Brooding above the A32, once a key stretch of the Via Francigena pilgrim path from Canterbury through Rome to Monte Sant'Angelo in Puglia, is the **Sacra di San Michele** *(sacradisanmichele.com)*. This Gothic-Romanesque abbey has kept sentry atop Monte Pirchiriano (962m) since the 10th century and exerted enormous power over abbeys throughout Italy, France and Spain, including Mont St Michel in France. It looks familiar because Umberto Eco used it as the basis for the abbey in *The Name of the Rose*. Approach as pilgrims would up the **Scalone dei Morti** (Stairway of the Dead), flanked by arches that would once have held the skeletons of dead monks. At the top enter through the whimsical, 12th-century Zodiac Door.

Within the walls, the complex houses a frescoed church and the remnants of the monastery, crowned by the **Torre della Bell'Alda** (Tower of Beautiful Alda). More beautiful though are the views down the Susa valley.

The Drive: Return to the A32 down the Via Sacra (SP188) for the 40km drive to Susa. Although you're on the autostrada the entire way, the journey passes through dense forests with snowcapped peaks slowly rising ahead of you. Just after Bussoleno, exit for Susa Est.

03 Susa

The Romans marched up the **Val di Susa** and crossed the Alps to secure a passage to the French ports of Nice and Marseille.

They enjoyed the thermal baths in Belvédère across the border in France, and grabbed Susa from the Gauls, thus securing the high passes of the Cottian Alps.

You'll find evidence of them all over town, including the remnants of an aqueduct, a still-used amphitheatre and the triumphal **Arco d'Augusto**, dating from 9 BCE.

Susa stands at the gateway to the Val di Susa, cut through by the Dora di Bardonecchia river and littered with stone towns such as **Exilles**, with its forbidding **Forte di Exilles**, said to be the keep of the Man in the Iron Mask between 1681 and 1687.

PHOTO OPPORTUNITY

The red-tiled rooftops of Saluzzo from the Torre Civica.

The Drive: The 46km from Susa to Sestriere is a scenic mountain drive. Rejoin the A32, heading for Fréjus, for 20km (you'll pass the exit for Exilles after 12km). Exit at Oulx Est onto the SS24 and follow the gushing torrent of Dora-Riparia to Cesana Torinese (alternatively you can head uphill and base yourself in Sauze d'Oulx). When the road forks, veer left onto the SS23 for the final winding ascent to Sestriere.

04 Sestriere

Developed in the 1930s by the Agnelli clan of Fiat, Sestriere ranks among Europe's most glamorous ski resorts due to its enviable location in the eastern realms of the **Via Lattea** *(www.vialattea.it)* ski area.

This picturesque region nestled among mountain slopes incorporates some 400km of piste and seven interlinked ski resorts: Sestriere (2035m), Sauze d'Oulx (1509m), Sansicario (1700m), Cesana Torinese (1350m), Pragelato (1524m) and Claviere (1760m) in Italy; and Montgenèvre (1850m) in neighbouring France.

Outside of ski season the **tourist office** *(turismotorino.org)* has information on every conceivable summer activity, including golfing on Europe's highest golf course, walking, free climbing and mountain biking.

Sacra di San Michele (p95)

FEDERICO CAPPONE/SHUTTERSTOCK

The Drive: The longest journey on this tour is the 86km out of the mountains to Saluzzo. Continue on the winding SS23 through mountain towns for 33km and descend southeast to Pinerolo. Then take the ramp to the SS589 (towards Cuneo), which brings you to Saluzzo after 29km.

MARGUAREIS CIRCUIT

The Marguareis Circuit is a 35km, two-day hike that starts in Limone Piemonte and tracks up across the mountain passes and ridges to the **Rifugio Garelli** *(rifugiogarelli.com)*. The peaks of the Argentera and Cime du Gélas massifs are clearly visible from the summit of Punta Marguareis (2651m), the highest point in the park. On day two, 4km of the trek passes through a mountainous nodule of France before swinging back round into Italy.

05 Saluzzo

Situated at the foot of Monte Viso, Saluzzo was once a powerful marquisate that lasted four centuries until the Savoys won it in a 1601 treaty with France.

Its historic significance – although diminished – has left a stirring legacy in its old centre.

The imposing castle, otherwise known as the **Castiglia di Saluzzo**, overlooks the cobbled alleys and Gothic and Renaissance mansions of the old town, which cluster around the **Salita al Castello**, literally 'the ascent to the castle'.

Nearby are the town hall and the **Torre Civica**, which you can climb for views over the burnt-red-tiled rooftops.

The Drive: It's a scenic 54km drive from Saluzzo to Cuneo, first on the SP161 and then on the SP25 after Villafalleto. Dropping from mountains into low-lying plains and up again, the road passes through vineyards and orchards and across mountain torrents.

06 Cuneo

Sitting on a promontory between the Gesso and Stura di Demonte rivers, Cuneo enjoys excellent alpine views framed by the high pyramid-shaped peak of Monte Viso (3841m). To the southwest lie the Maritime Alps, a rugged outdoor-adventure playground. After a hard day out hiking, you'll be thankful for the heart-warming buzz of a *cuneese al rhum* – a large, rum-laced praline, which you can lay your hands on at 1920s-vintage chocolatier **Arione** *(arionecuneo.it)*, located in magnificent **Piazza Galimberti**.

Cuneo also has some wonderful churches. The oldest is the deconsecrated San Francisco convent and church, which today houses the **Museo Civico di Cuneo**, tracking the history of the town and province.

The Drive: The final 28km to Limone Piemonte provide another picturesque mountain road. Leave Cuneo heading southwest on the SS20 to Borgo San Dalmazzo, where you veer left (keeping on the SS20) across the Torrente Gesso and up into the mountains.

07 Limone Piemonte

To the southwest of Cuneo lies the **Parco Naturale Alpi Marittime** *(parcoalpimarittime.it)*. Despite their diminutive size, there's a palpable wilderness feel to be found among these Maritime peaks.

The park is a walker's paradise, home to ibex, chamois and whistling marmots, which scurry around rocky crags covered in mist above a well-marked network of mountain trails, some of them old salt routes, others supply lines left over from two World Wars.

The best-equipped town for access to the park is picturesque **Limone Piemonte** *(limonepiemonte.it)*.

One of the oldest alpine ski stations, Limone has been in operation since 1907 and maintains 15 lifts and 80km of runs.

14

THE ITALIAN ALPS

ROOF OF ITALY

★ BEST FOR

WELLBEING

Dipping in Merano's hot and cold spa pools surrounded by soaring mountain peaks.

Terme Merano (p100)

DURATION: 6 DAYS

DISTANCE: 324KM/201 MILES

GREAT FOR: FAMILIES, NATURE

BEST TIME TO GO: JUNE TO SEPTEMBER, WHEN THE PASSO DELLO STELVIO IS OPEN.

Tracing the foothills of the Orobie Alps and the high passes of Parco Nazionale dello Stelvio, the borderlands of northern Italy offer up stunning wildernesses, stupendous scenery and warm welcomes in wooden farmhouses. Vineyards and orchards cloak the valleys of the Valtellina and Adige, while the region's historic cities – Merano, Trento and Rovereto – combine Austrian and Italian influences, creating a unique cultural and culinary melange.

LINK YOUR TRIP

62 The Graceful Italian Lakes
Take the scenic SS340dir to Tremezzo to tour Como's luxuriant gardens and Maggiore's Borromean palaces.

16 Grande Strada delle Dolomiti
Descend into Bolzano from Castello Firmiano on the SS42 and head east into the Dolomites for mountain hikes and gourmet dinners.

01 Alto Lario

The towns of **Dongo**, **Gravedona** and **Sorico** once formed the independent republic of the Tre Pievi (Three Parishes) and were a hotbed of Cathar heresy. Now they're more popular with watersports enthusiasts than Inquisitors. Lake Lario is another name for Lago di Como (Lake Como), so the area takes its name from being at the top *(alto)* of the lake. Gravedona, the largest of the three towns, sits on a gently curved bay with views across to Monte Legnone. Up on the plateau at Peglio, **Chiesa di Sant'Eusebio** offers lake views and masterly frescoes by Como painter Giovan Mauro della Rovere, better known as Il Fiammenghino (Little Fleming). He sought refuge here after murdering a man and did penance painting the vivid *Last Judgement*.

Sorico, the most northerly of the three towns, guards the mouth of the river Mera, which flows into shallow **Lago di Mezzola**, a bird-breeding nature reserve.

DROZDIN VLADIMIR/SHUTTERSTOCK

The Drive: From Sorico take the SS340dir north. Cross over the waterway that connects Lago di Como and Lago di Mezzola and continue until you hit a T-junction. Turn right, and at the roundabout turn left onto the SS38 towards Morbengo. Continue for a further 36km, chasing the Adda river all the way to Sondrio.

02 The Valtellina

The Valtellina cuts a broad swath down the Adda valley, where villages and vineyards hang precariously on the slopes of the Orobie Alps. The steep northern flank is carpeted by Nebbiolo grapes, which yield a light-red wine. Both body and alcohol content improve with altitude, so generations of Valtellinesi built upwards, carrying the soil in woven baskets to high mountain terraces. Their rewards: a DOC classification for Valtellina Superiore since 1968. In **Sondrio**, it's possible, by appointment, to visit the cellars of **Arpepe** *(arpepe.com)*, and in **Chiuro**, **Nino Negri** *(ninonegri.it)*.

The prettiest town in the valley is **Tirano**, the departure point for the **Trenino Rosso del Bernina** *(treninorosso.it)*. This gravity-defying rail track traverses 196 bridges, crests the Bernina Pass (2253m) and crosses the Morteratsch glacier on the way to St Moritz in Switzerland.

The Drive: From Tirano it is 37 scenic kilometres to the heady heights of Bormio. Continue northeast on the SS38, still tracking the Adda river and rising up through the terraces, past small hamlets such as Grosio and Sondalo and into the snowcapped mountains.

03 Bormio

Splendidly sited in a mountain basin at 1225m, Bormio was once the heart of a region dubbed Magnifica Terra. Most of the region's magnificent territory now lies within northern Italy's largest national park, the **Parco Nazionale dello Stelvio** *(stelviopark.it)*, an icy land of 100 glaciers that includes one of Europe's largest, the **Ghiacciaio dei Forni**. The park is largely the preserve of walkers, who come for the network of well-organised mountain huts and marked trails – but there are a couple of well-serviced ski runs at **Solda** and the **Passo dello Stelvio** (2757m), both of which offer year-round skiing.

Back in Bormio's medieval centre, the **Bagni di Bormio** *(qcterme.com)* were much loved by the likes of Pliny the Elder and Leonardo da Vinci. Hotel stays include unlimited spa access, but day passes are also available.

The Drive: The most difficult, and awe-inspiring, 96km is the road from Bormio to Merano, which crosses the cloud-covered Passo dello Stelvio, 25km from Bormio. Approaching along the SS38, the road rises through a series of switchbacks, some with very steep gradients, and descends via alarming hairpin bends to quaint Trafoi on the other side. From Trafoi continue on the SS38 to Merano. When the pass is closed, take the more circuitous 140km route through Switzerland via the SS301, Swiss route 28, SS41 and SS38.

DETOUR

Malles & Marienberg
Start: 03 Bormio

A short detour north off the main Bormio-to-Merano route via the scenic SS40 brings you to the old customs point of **Malles**. Aside from its handsome Gothic churches and historic centre, it's a convenient jumping-off point for nearby **Marienberg** *(marienberg.it)*, the highest Benedictine monastery in Europe. In the crypt are a series of superb Byzantine-Romanesque frescoes, which were only discovered in 1980.

PHOTO OPPORTUNITY

Cloud-busting views on the Passo dello Stelvio.

Their almost pristine condition makes them unique.

04 Merano

Merano is where 19th-century Mitteleuropeans came to soothe their weary bones, do a 'grape' cure and, perhaps, embark on a dalliance or two. The Hapsburg-era spa was the hot destination of its day and the city's therapeutic traditions have served it well in the new millennium, with the striking modern redevelopment of the **Terme Merano** *(termemerano.it)*. Swim through the sluice towards 12 outdoor pools in summer and be met by a vision of palm-studded gardens and snow-topped mountains.

You could also give over an entire day to the botanical gardens at **Castel Trauttmansdorff** *(trauttmansdorff.it)*, where exotic cacti and palms, and beds of lilies, irises and tulips, all cascade down the hillside surrounding a castle where Sissi (Empress Elisabeth) spent the summer.

The Drive: From Merano to Bolzano and the Castello Firmiano, the SS38 becomes a dual-lane autostrada, so the next 30km are easy motorway driving as you leave the high mountains behind you.

05 Castello Firmiano

Known as the 'Crown of Sigismund', the expansive walls and battlements of Castello Firmiano encircle the hilltop overlooking Bolzano and Appiano just like a princely coronet.

Fought over for 1000 years, it has long been a symbol of Tyrolean independence and now houses the **Messner Mountain Museum** *(messner-mountain-museum.it)*, named after celebrated mountaineer Reinhold Messner.

Exhibits explore humanity's relationship with the mountains, while the inspiring design suggests shifting altitudes and uneven mountain terrain.

South of the castle stretches the **Südtiroler Weinstrasse** *(suedtiroler-weinstrasse.it)*, a wine road winding through the Adige valley along the SP14 all the way to Trento. Producers line the route, although the hub of the region is **Caldaro**.

The Drive: South of Bolzano the autostrada carves a straight line through the midst of the Adige valley. It's a fast, scenic route with the mountains overlapping in descending order in front of you. If you have more time, however, the preferred route is to pick up the SP14 from the castle to Caldaro and follow the wine route all the way to Magrè, where you can stop and taste some of the prized Adige wines.

06 Trento

During the tumultuous years of the Counter-Reformation, the Council of Trent convened here, dishing out far-reaching condemnations to uppity Protestants. Modern Trento is less preachy: quietly confident and easy to like. Frescoed streets fan out from the **Duomo** (*Cattedrale di San Vigilio; cattedralesanvigilio.it*), which sits above a 6th-century temple and a paleo-Christian archaeological area.

On the opposite side of the square is what was once the bishop's residence, now the **Museo Diocesano Tridentino** *(museodiocesanotridentino.it)*, where illuminated manuscripts and paintings depict the Council of Trent.

Above it all, the mighty **Castello del Buonconsiglio** *(buonconsiglio.it)* is a reminder of the bloody history of these borderlands.

The Drive: The final 30km drive south on the A22 leaves most of the majestic scenery behind, and the broad valley tapers out towards Rovereto.

07 Rovereto

In the winter of 1769, Leopold Mozart and his soon-to-be-famous son visited Rovereto.

Those on a musical pilgrimage come to visit the **Chiesa di San Marco**, where the 13-year-old Wolfgang wowed the Roveretini, and for the annual festival of classical music, **Festival Settenovecento** *(settenovecento.it)*.

The town that Mozart knew still has its tightly coiled streets, but it's the shock of the new that lures most to the **Museo di Arte Moderna e Contemporanea** *(mart.tn.it)*, one of Italy's best 20th-century art museums.

Designed by Ticinese architect Mario Botta, it is a fitting home for some huge 20th-century works, including Warhol's *Four Marilyns* (1962), several Picassos and a clutch of contemporary art stars.

MY GOLDEN LIFE/SHUTTERSTOCK

PASSO DELLO STELVIO

The high and hair-raising Passo dello Stelvio *(stelvio.net)* is only open from June to early October, and is always subject to closures dependent on early or late snow falls. For the rest of the year, you'll need to skirt around the pass to get to Merano by taking the SS301 to Livigno and then route 28 through Switzerland to Tubre and then on to Merano via the SS41 and SS38.

15

THE ITALIAN ALPS

VALLE D'AOSTA

★ BEST FOR

SKIING

Courmayeur's slopes in the shadow of Mont Blanc.

DURATION: 5 DAYS

DISTANCE: 126KM/78 MILES

GREAT FOR: FAMILIES, NATURE

BEST TIME TO GO: JANUARY TO MARCH FOR SKIING; SEPTEMBER FOR HIKING.

Mont Blanc (p105)

The Valle d'Aosta carves a deep path through the Alps to Mont Blanc (Monte Bianco), and touring its castle-tipped peaks and glacial valley makes for one of Italy's most scenic drives. Courmayeur's fashion-parade of skiers hits the high slopes of Mont Blanc, while Valdostan farmers make alpine wines and *fontina* cheese in the pastures below. When the snow melts, hiking in the Gran Paradiso park and along Aosta's high-altitude trails is even more sublime.

LINK YOUR TRIP

03 Savoy Palace Circuit
The Gran Paradiso was the hunting preserve of the Dukes of Savoy; pick up their trail in Turin, down the A5 from Issogne.

08 The Graceful Italian Lakes
From alpine peaks to a Mediterranean microclimate, take the A5 and A4 from Issogne to Lago d'Orta.

01 Issogne

The Valle d'Aosta's peaks are crowned with castles, each within view of the next, so messages could be transferred up and down the valley via flag signals. Although many were little more than fortified barracks, as time progressed so their lordly inhabitants became more mindful of appearances. The **Castello di Issogne** *(lovevda.it)*, for example, sitting on the right bank of the Dora Baltea river and located on one of the only navigable routes over the Alps, is more of a signorial Renaissance residence, the interior decorated with rare alpine frescoes. It looks quite different to the dour **Castello di Verrès** *(lovevda.it)*, located on the opposite bank, with which it was in constant conflict.

The Drive: From Issogne it's a 26km drive along the A5 autostrada to Fénis. The peaks of the lower Alps are already visible and frame your route. After Montjovet duck through a series of tunnels as you sweep

westwards into the valley. Take the exit for Nus and follow signs for the castle.

02 Fénis

The finest castle in the Valle d'Aosta is without a doubt the magnificently restored **Castello di Fénis** *(lovevda.it)*, owned by the powerful Challant clan from 1242 onwards. It features rich frescoes, including an impressive etching of St George slaying a fiery dragon. The castle is laid out in a pentagonal shape with square and cylindrical turrets lording it over the lush chestnut forests. It was never really used as a defensive post, but served as a plush residence for the Challants until 1716. The on-site museum allows access to a weaponry display, the kitchens, the battlements, the former residential quarters and the frescoed chapel.

The Drive: Aosta is just 16km from the Castello di Fénis. Rejoin the A5/E25 for 8km through pretty mountainous forests. Then exit towards Aosta Est onto the E27 for 1.2km, and after you pass through the toll booths follow signs for Aosta Centro, which is a further 4km.

03 Aosta

Jagged alpine peaks rise like marble cathedrals above the town of Aosta, a once-important Roman settlement that has sprawled rather untidily across the valley floor since the opening of the Mont Blanc tunnel in the 1960s. But its 2000-year-old centre still harbours Roman relics, such as the **Arco di Augusto**, the **Roman bridge**, spanning the Buthier river since the 1st century, and the **Porta Praetoria**, the main gate to the Roman city. Even the **Roman Theatre** remains in use as a venue for summer concerts.

Elsewhere, more Challant-commissioned artworks can be seen in the **Chiesa di Sant'Orso**, which dates back to the 10th century.

For skiing and hiking on the slopes above, ascend the **Aosta-Pila cable car** to the 1800m-high resort of **Pila**.

The Drive: Leave Aosta heading westwards for the next scenic 26km to Cogne. You'll pick up the Viale Piccolo San Bernardino first for a couple of kilometres and then merge with the SS26. After about 3km turn left onto the SR47 and start the beautiful, mountain-hugging ascent into the Gran Paradiso.

DETOUR

Valpelline

Start: 03 Aosta

Aosta's signature cheese is made from the full-cream, unpasteurised milk of Valdostan cows that have grazed on pastures up to 2700m above sea level, before being matured for three months in underground rock tunnels. You can learn more about the history, 'terroir' and production of Aostan cheeses at the **Valpelline Visitors Centre** *(fontinacoop.it)*. Follow the SR28 for 7km north to the Valpelline valley, turn east towards Ollomont and after 1.5km turn west along a mountain road to Frissonière, where the centre is located.

PHOTO OPPORTUNITY

Top-of-the-world views from the Funivie Monte Bianco.

04 Parco Nazionale del Gran Paradiso

Italy's oldest national park, the **Parco Nazionale del Gran Paradiso** *(pngp.it)*, is aptly named. Originally it was the Savoy's own private hunting reserve until Vittorio Emanuele II made nice and gave it to the state in 1922 to ensure the protection of the endangered ibex.

The main stepping stone into the park is **Cogne** (1534m), famous for its lace-making, samples of which you can buy at **Le Marché Aux Puces**. Easy walks in the park are possible, such as the 3km stroll to the village of **Lillaz** on trail 23, where there is a geological park and a waterfall that drops 150m. Trails 22 and 23 will get you to the village of **Valnontey**, where you can visit the **Giardino Alpino Paradisia**, an alpine garden displaying mountain flora and rare butterflies.

The Drive: The longest drive on the tour is the 42km to Morgex and La Salle. The first 20km involve retracing your route down the SR47 out of the mountains. When you reach the bottom, follow signs to rejoin the A5/E25 autostrada in the direction of

Fénis (p103)

D-VISIONS/SHUTTERSTOCK

Mont Blanc. From here it's 18km to Morgex through the forested valley.

05 Morgex & La Salle

The ruined towers of **Châtelard**, which guard the road over the Piccolo San Bernardo pass, also cast a shadow over Europe's highest vineyards strung out between the two communes of Morgex and La Salle. The wines from these alpine vines, produced almost exclusively from the Prié Blanc grape grown between 900m and 1200m, is light and fruity with overtones of mountain herbs and freshly cut hay.

Given the extremes of temperature at this altitude (some vines run almost to the snow line), vintners employ a unique system of cultivation called *pergola bassa* (low-level arbours), where vines are planted low to the ground to protect them. Since 1983 the Aostan government has sought to preserve these ancient traditions by setting up the cooperative **Cave Mont Blanc de Morgex et La Salle** *(cavemontblanc.com)*, which processes the grapes from the 90 or so local smallholdings. Aosta's **tourist office** *(lovevda.it)* has an English-language booklet with information on individual cellars and the cooperative.

The Drive: From either La Salle or Morgex descend through the vineyards and rejoin the SS26 for the short 7km drive to Pré-Saint Didier. The road passes under the A5 and then wriggles alongside the river Thuile all the way to Pré.

SKIING MONT BLANC

Courmayeur offers some extraordinary skiing in the shadow of Mont Blanc. The two main ski areas – the Plan Chécrouit and Pré de Pascal – are interlinked by 100km of runs. Three lifts leave from the valley floor: one from Courmayeur itself, one from the village of Dolonne and one from nearby Val Veny.

They are run by **Funivie Courmayeur Mont Blanc** *(courmayeur-montblanc.com)*.

06 Pré-Saint Didier

Bubbling at a natural 37°C from the mountains' depths, where the river Thuile forces its way through a narrow gorge into the Dora valley, the thermal waters at **Terme di Pré-Saint-Didier** *(qcterme.com)* have been a source of therapeutic treatment since the bath-loving Romans were in town. In addition to saunas, whirlpools and toning waterfalls there's an indoor-outdoor thermal pool.

It's lit by candles and torches on Saturday nights, when it is spectacular amid the snow and stars.

The Drive: The scenic drive to Courmayeur is on the SS26dir. Cross over the river Thuile in Pré and head westwards with the towering snowcapped peaks of the high passes in front of you. They're an awesome sight, especially in spring when they're framed by the deepest green conifers.

07 Courmayeur

Flush up against France and linked by a dramatic cable-car ride to its cross-border cousin in Chamonix, Courmayeur has grafted upmarket ski facilities onto an ancient Roman base. Its pièce de résistance is lofty **Mont Blanc**, western Europe's highest mountain, 4810m of solid rock and ice that rises like an impregnable wall above the Valle d'Aosta. Ride the **Funivie Monte Bianco** *(montebianco.com)* for transglacial views that will take your breath away.

First stop is the 2173m-high mid-station **Pavillon du Mt Fréty**, where there's a restaurant and the **Mt Fréty Nature Oasis**. At the top of the ridge is **Punta Helbronner** (3462m).

From Punta Helbronner another cable car (late May to late September) takes you on a spectacular 5km ride across the Italian border to the **Aiguille du Midi** (3842m) in France, from where the world's highest cable car transports you into Chamonix.

The journey from Courmayeur to Chamonix costs €80 and the journey back to Courmayeur by bus is €15. It's pricey but spectacular.

16

THE ITALIAN ALPS

★ BEST FOR

OUTDOORS

The villages of Alta Badia and the beautiful Lago di Braies.

GRANDE STRADA DELLE DOLOMITI

DURATION: 7–10 DAYS

DISTANCE: 299KM/186 MILES

GREAT FOR: NATURE, FOOD AND DRINK, FAMILIES

BEST TIME TO GO: DECEMBER FOR CHRISTMAS MARKETS AND SKIING; JUNE FOR SPRING FLOWERS.

Lago di Braies (p108)

The Dolomites (Dolomiti) are one of the most beautiful mountain ranges in the world. Ranging across the South Tyrol, Alto Adige and Veneto, the area combines Austrian and Italian influences with the local Ladin culture. On this grand road trip *(grande strada)* your hosts may wear lederhosen, cure ham in their chimneys and use sleighs to travel. More recently a new generation of eco-chic hotels, cutting-edge spas and Michelin-starred restaurants has started grabbing the headlines, but overall these peaks remain low-key.

LINK YOUR TRIP

09 A Weekend at Lago di Garda
Tool down the A22 to Lago di Garda and visit the vineyards and olive groves around its shores.

10 A Venetian Sojourn
Drop down from Cortina d'Ampezzo on the SS51 and A27 for a tour of Venetian palaces and frescoes.

01 Bolzano

Once a stop on the coach route between Italy and the flourishing Austro-Hungarian Empire, Bolzano has been a long-time conduit between cultures. The city's fine museums include the **Museo Archeologico dell'Alto Adige** *(iceman.it)*, where the mummified remains of the 5300-year-old iceman, Ötzi, are on display. He was found 3200m up the melting glacier on Hauslabjoch Pass in 1991, but how he got there remains a matter of some debate.

At the other end of the spectrum, the city's contemporary art museum, **Museion** *(museion.it)*, is housed in a huge multifaceted glass cube, a surprising architectural assertion that beautifully vignettes the old-town rooftops and surrounding mountains from within. There's an impressive permanent collection, and temporary shows highlight the local art scene's ongoing dialogue with Austria and Germany.

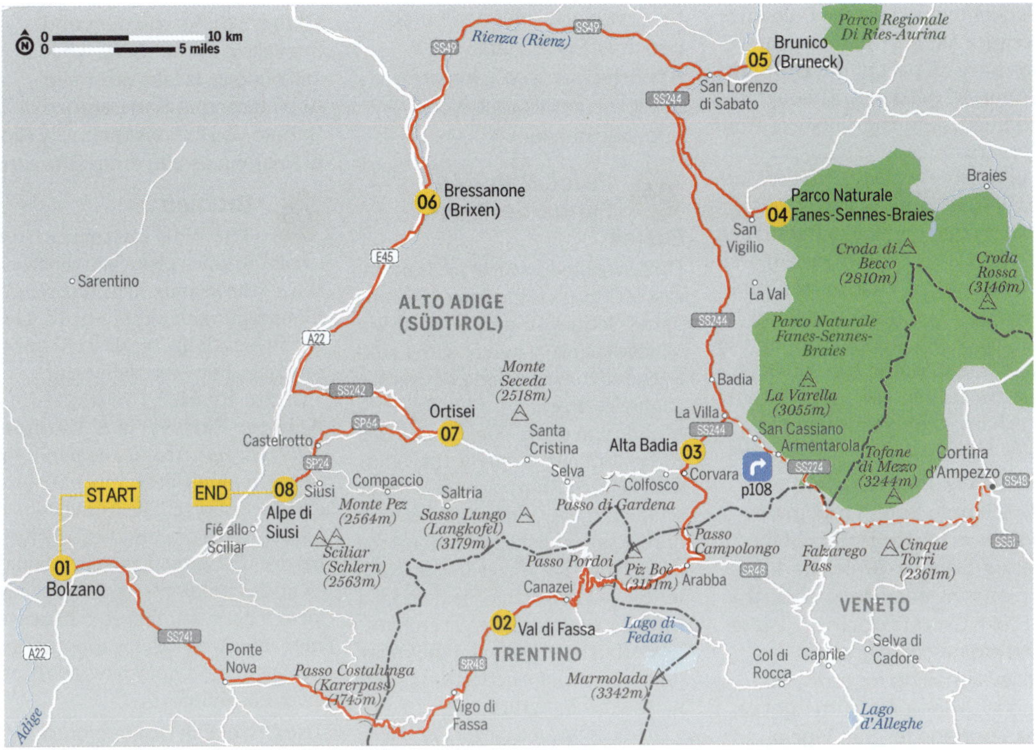

PETR TRAN/SHUTTERSTOCK

The Drive: Exit Bolzano on the SS241 to the Val di Fassa. The road is the start of a long ascent, the first section through a steep-sided canyon. At Ponte Nova the first peaks of the Dolomites come into view, and after 26km Lago di Carezza is visible on your right.

02 Val Di Fassa

Framed by the stirring peaks of the Gruppo del Sella to the north, the Catinaccio to the west and the Marmolada (3342m) to the southeast, the Fassa valley is a beautiful introduction to the rising mountain ranges. Amid the forests, the iridescent blue-green **Lago di Carezza** is known locally as *de lec ergobando* ('the lake of the rainbow'), as legend tells of a sorcerer who, trying to win the favour of the resident nymph, created a beautiful rainbow over the lake. Alas, the fearful nymph fled and in his fury the sorcerer shattered the rainbow in the lake, forever giving it its luminous colour.

The hub of the valley is the beautifully sited, but verging on over-developed, **Canazei** and, to a lesser extent, the riverside village of **Moena**. To access the **Gruppo del Sella** mountain range ascend to **Passo Pordoi** (2239m), where a cable car carries you to the **Sasso Pordoi** (2950m).

The Drive: From Lago di Carezza it's 38km up a series of rapid switchbacks to Passo Pordoi. From the lofty summit, you'll have a view over the 33 hairpin bends that you'll be descending on the SR48. It's only 7km, but it's slow going and the views over meadows and villages are superb. At Arabba bear left on the SS244 for Corvara.

03 Alta Badia

The area of Alta Badia *(altabadia.org)* is spectacularly located on the Sella Ronda massif, embraced by the peaks of Pelmo (3168m), Civetta (3218m) and the Marmolada.

In the valleys below, the villages of **Corvara** (1568m), **Colfosco** (1645m), **La Villa** (1433m), **Badia** (1324m), **San Cassiano** (1537m) and **La Val** (1348m) connect 130km of slopes over four mountain passes.

Undoubtedly one of the Dolomites' premier ski destinations, the villages are all part of the **Dolomiti Superski network**, although the best access to the slopes is from Corvara.

In summer a cable car ascends into the Parco Naturale Fanes-Sennes-Braies from the **Passo Falzarego** (2105m). Alternatively, pick up trail No 12, near La Villa, or trail No 11, which joins the Alta Via pathway No 1 at the Capanna Alpina. Either will take you up to the Alpe di Fanes.

Horseriding, mountain biking and hang-gliding are other popular valley activities.

The Drive: From Corvara the 27km to San Vigilio, the unofficial headquarters of the Fanes-Sennes-Braies park, is a pleasant, easy drive down the SS244. Chalets dot the hillsides and alpine cows graze in the valleys, making for an idyllic scene. After 23km turn right on Via Longega for San Vigilio.

DETOUR

Cortina d'Ampezzo

Start: 03 Alta Badia

Thirty-four winding kilometres in the shadow of Tofane di Mezzo (3244m) from La Villa lies pricey, icy Cortina d'Ampezzo, the Italian supermodel of ski resorts. Sitting in a crescent-shaped glacial valley surrounded by wooded slopes, Cortina is undeniably beautiful, gaining international fame in the '60s and '70s when Elizabeth Taylor and Henry Fonda came to town to film *Ash Wednesday*. Unapologetically Italian in feel, ladies in fur coats enjoy a *passeggiata* (stroll) along the Corso with their pampered pooches. Book a table at **SanBrite** *(sanbrite.it)* for farm-to-table specialities in a cool, upcycled interior.

04 Parco Naturale Fanes-Sennes-Braies

Hidden behind a wall of rocks northeast of Corvara is the Parco Naturale Fanes-Sennes-Braies, a 99-sq-km windswept plain, potent with Ladin legends that have resonated over the centuries, inspiring JRR Tolkien's Middle Earth in *The Lord of the Rings*. Not surprisingly, the valley and the high Fanes plateau, with its sculpted ridges and buttress towers of rock, are considered among the most evocative places in the Dolomites. Wordsworth considered it a heavenly environment and architect Le Corbusier envisioned the rocky pinnacles as a form of spectacular natural architecture.

For those up for a longer excursion, east down the Val Pusteria is the mystical **Lago di Braies**, a glassy lake set within an amphitheatre of stone. Crouched at its southern edge is 'Gate Mountain', **Sas dla Porta**, once thought to hide a gateway to the underworld.

The Drive: Head back down the hill from San Vigilio to the SS244 and take a right for Brunico, 17km north. As you descend the valley, the scenery, while still bucolic, is less dramatic. At picturesque San Lorenzo di Sabato you'll cross the milky Rio di Pusteria as you enter Brunico.

TOP TIP

SKI PASS

The **Dolomiti Superski** *(dolomitisuperski.com)* ski pass gives access to more than 1200km of pistes and 450 lifts spread over 12 resorts.

05 Brunico

The Val Pusteria's big smoke, Brunico gets a bad rap from those who've only driven through its unremarkable main drag. The quintessentially Tyrolean historic centre is, however, delightful.

Right by the town gate is **Acherer Patisserie & Blumen** *(acherer.com)*, creator and purveyor of the region's best apple strudel and Sachertorte. The young owner reopened his grandfather's former bakery after apprenticing in Vienna.

On the outskirts of town, visit local wool manufacturer **Moessmer** *(moessmer.it)* for top-quality cashmere and Tyrolean tweeds from its outlet shop.

The Drive: Exit Brunico onto the main SS49/E66 autostrada and follow the winding Rio di Pusteria river down the valley to Bressanone. After 21km you'll pass the frescoed Castello di Rodengo high up on your left, before dropping down through the vineyards of Varna into Bressanone.

06 Bressanone

Beautiful Bressanone (Brixen), with its palace of the prince-bishops and illustrious history, is the artistic and cultural capital of the Val Pusteria.

The first **cathedral** was built here in the 10th century by the Bishop of Säben. Though rebuilt in the 18th century along baroque lines, it retains its fabulous 12th-century

Marmolada
DANIEL PRUDEK/SHUTTERSTOCK

PHOTO OPPORTUNITY

The humpbacked Marmolada with a foreground of mountain flowers.

♥ WHY I LOVE THIS TRIP

PAULA HARDY, WRITER

It's hard to overstate the incredible natural beauty of the Dolomites, whose shapes, colours and contours are endlessly varied. Walking the *alte vie* (high ways) you honestly feel like Heidi. I'll never forget sitting down at Gostner Schwaige, a mountain hut near Castelrotto, and being presented with a creamy soup served in a bowl made of bread that was sitting on a hay base sprinkled with still-fragrant wildflowers.

cloister, the cross-vaults decorated with superb 15th-century frescoes. Bressanone's prince-bishops obviously had an eye for art, and their Renaissance palace, the Hofburg – which now houses the **Museo Diocesano** *(hofburg.it)* – was similarly decorated in lavish style. Amid the noble apartments you'll find treasures from the Middle Ages and a collection of *presepi* (wooden nativity scenes).

The Drive: From Bressanone you'll rejoin the main A22 autostrada south towards Modena. It winds through forested valleys for 20km, past Castello di Velturno on your right and above the river Isarco. Exit for the Val Gardena onto the SS242 for the scenic 15km climb to Ortisei at 1236m.

07 Ortisei

Ortisei is the main hub of the Val Gardena and the Alpe di Siusi mountain region. Like the Alta Badia and Val di Fassa, this is one of only five valleys where Ladin is a majority tongue, while the villages of Ortisei (1236m), **Santa Cristina** (1428m) and **Selva** (1563m) are characterised by folksy architecture and a profusion of woodcarving shops. Ortisei's **Museum de Gherdëina** *(museumgherdeina.it)* has a beautiful collection of wooden toys and sculptures, as does the local church, **St Ulrich**.

From the centre of Ortisei a high-speed cable car ascends the slopes of Alpe di Siusi, Europe's largest high-altitude alpine meadow. To the northeast, another cable car ascends to **Monte Seceda** (2518m) with

Alpe di Siusi

PETR TRAN/SHUTTERSTOCK

unforgettable views of the **Gruppo di Odle**, a cathedral-like series of mountain spires. From Seceda, trail No 2A passes through sloping pastures dotted with wooden *malghe* (shepherds' huts). Afterwards descend for traditional après-ski at the five-star **Hotel Adler** *(adler-dolomiti.com).*

The Drive: The 15km drive to Siusi is staggeringly beautiful. Backtrack 1.2km west on the SS242 towards the autostrada, then veer left onto the SP64, passing through Castelrotto and continuing south on the SP24. The final climb to Alpe di Siusi between the villages of Siusi and Compaccio is off-limits to motorists for much of the year; whenever the Alpe di Siusi Cableway is running, you must park your car at the Siusi base station and take the cable car from there.

08 Alpe di Siusi

There are few more beautiful juxtapositions than the undulating green pastures of the Alpe di Siusi – Europe's largest plateau – ending dramatically at the base of the Sciliar mountains. To the southeast lies the Catinaccio range; its German name 'Rosengarten' is an apt description of the eerie pink hue given off by the dolomite rock at sunset.

Signposted by their onion-domed churches, the villages that dot the valleys – including **Castelrotto** (Kastelruth), **Fié allo Sciliar** (Völs am Schlern) and **Siusi** – are unexpectedly sophisticated.

Part of the Dolomiti Superski network, the gentle slopes of the Alpe di Siusi are even better hiking terrain, and average stamina will get you to the **Rifugio Bolzano** *(schlernhaus.it)*, one of the Alps' oldest mountain huts, which rests at 2457m, just under **Monte Pez** (2564m).

Take the **Panorama chairlift** *(panoramaseiseralm.info)* from Compaccio to the Alpenhotel, from where it's a three-hour walk to the *rifugio* along paths S, No 5 and No 1.

Horses are also a big part of local culture, and there's nothing more picturesque than a chestnut Haflinger pony galloping across the pastures.

Gstatsch-Hof Ponyhof *(gstatschhof.com)* offers accommodation and summer programs.

WESTEND61/GETTY IMAGES

Alta Via No 1

WALK THE HIGH PASSES

The Dolomites' *alte vie* – literally high ways – are high-altitude paths designed for experienced walkers, although most do not require mountaineering skills or equipment. From mid-June to mid-September a network of mountain huts offering food and accommodation lines the route. In high season (July and August) it's advisable to book in advance.

Alta Via No 1 Lago di Braies to Belluno, north to south
Alta Via No 2 Bressanone to Feltre, passing through Odle, the mythical Ladin kingdom
Alta Via No 3 Villabassa to Longarone
Alta Via No 4 San Candido to Pieve di Cadore

STAY AWHILE

VAL BADIA

BY GREGOR CLARK

Summer or winter, Val Badia is a land of enchantment. This stunningly scenic mountain hideaway is one of five Dolomites valleys that retain unique cultural traditions born from centuries of isolation, including the endangered Ladin language, a direct descendent of Vulgar Latin still spoken by 30,000 people. Discover local culture at the **Museum Ladin** *(museumladin.it)*, where displays cover everything from the Dolomites' natural history to Ladin folktales, toy-making and woodworking traditions.

As a Romance language buff, my favourite pastime here is donning headphones to hear native speakers pronouncing everyday words like 'water', 'woman', 'house' and 'field' in five distinct local dialects. A passion for outdoors adventure runs deep in Val Badia. Locals have been scaling the surrounding peaks since the late 1800s, and Alta Badia remains one of Italy's classic ski destinations. For access to more than 100km of spectacular interconnected slopes, grab an **Alta Badia Ski Pass** *(altabadia.org/it/sci/pass-alta-badia)*. Summer is equally splendid, with an endless array of trails climbing to exquisite panoramas of sawtooth peaks, rolling green meadows and rock-strewn uplands. Two of my favorites start within minutes of the valley floor: the **Alta Via 2** from Passo Gardena, and the **Alpe di Fanes-Rifugio Scotoni** loop from Capanna Alpina.

Stay here long enough and you'll inevitably get hooked on the Dolomites' hearty mountain cuisine, combining influences from both Italy and Austria. I'm never happier than when pausing mid-hike on the sunny terrace of **Rifugio Fanes** *(rifugiofanes.com)*, sipping beers and snacking on a *tris de canederli*, a trio of South Tyrolean ricotta and veggie dumplings mimicking the colours of the Italian flag, or dining on *casunziei* (beet ravioli with melted butter and poppy seeds) at **Fana Ladina** *(fanaladina.com)*.

LINK YOUR TRIP

Stop off at Val Badia about halfway along the **16 Grande Strada delle Dolomiti**.

Left: Museum Ladin; Right: Val Badia

FROM LEFT: DAAN KLOEG/SHUTTERSTOCK, MATT MUNRO/LONELY PLANET

PLACES TO STAY

Berghotel Ladinia
The perfect blend of rustic charm and chic comfort, this traditional inn in Corvara has cosy wood-panelled rooms with thick comforters, and a downstairs restaurant serving scrumptious four-course Ladin dinners. *(berghotelladinia.it)*

Camping Sass Dlacia
Backed by a spectacular mountain ridge at 1680m, this San Cassiano campground proudly advertises itself as the Dolomites' highest. Evergreen-shaded sites are nicely complemented by a pizzeria, sauna and store, with easy access to surrounding trailheads. *(campingsassdlacia.it)*

Rifugio Scotoni
Cosy blonde-wood bunk rooms, stunning views and traditional mountain food make this mountain hut a quintessential Val Badia experience for high-country hikers. *(scotoni.it)*

17

THE ITALIAN ALPS

THE VENETIAN DOLOMITES

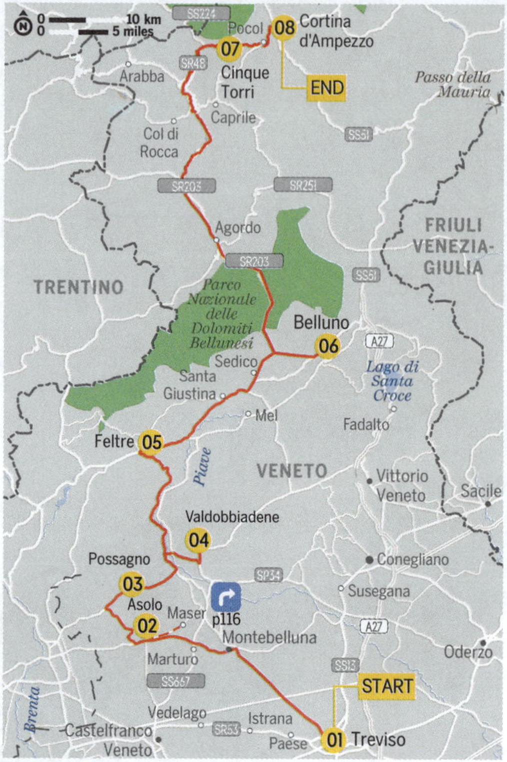

DURATION: 7 DAYS

DISTANCE: 231KM/144 MILES

GREAT FOR: HISTORY, FOOD AND DRINK, FAMILIES

BEST TIME TO GO: DECEMBER TO MARCH FOR SNOW SPORTS; JULY FOR MOUNTAIN HIKES.

A road trip through the Venetian Dolomites takes you through one of Italy's most sophisticated and least visited stretches of countryside. Some of the Veneto's finest country villas and medieval walled towns are to be found here, while a little further north prosecco vines dip and crest across the undulating foothills of the Alps. Crowning it all is the Italian supermodel of ski resorts, Cortina d'Ampezzo – fashionable, pricey and undeniably beautiful.

LINK YOUR TRIP

16 Grande Strada delle Dolomiti
From Cortina head up the SS224 to the Alta Badia. From here you can pick up an epic mountain road trip.

10 A Venetian Sojourn
Continue west from Maser on the SS248 to Bassano del Grappa and then loop around for more countryside culture.

01 Treviso

Treviso has everything you could want from a midsized Veneto city: medieval walls, pretty canals, narrow cobbled streets and frescoed churches. Despite this it receives few visitors, eclipsed by its more impressive neighbour – Venice. However, if you want to experience authentic Veneto life away from the tourist crowds, this is a great place to come.

Like its watery neighbour, Treviso is encircled by water. Its defensive walls are surrounded by a moat fed by the river Sile, which runs to the south of town. Grassy parks, weeping willows and waterwheels lend it a charming air, as does the island-bound **fish market**. Pick up a map from the **tourist office** *(visittreviso.it)* and follow one of the easy walking itineraries, then pop into the **Duomo** (Cattedrale di San Pietro Apostolo) to see the local Titian, and fresco-filled **Chiesa di Santa Lucia** *(santaluciatreviso.it)*, painted by

EMANUS/SHUTTERSTOCK

★ BEST FOR

FOODIES

Refuelling on delicious, deep-fried Schiz cheese after skiing.

Asolo

local talent Tommaso da Modena. For an authentic experience, visit a traditional *osteria* around **Piazza dei Signori**, such as **Osteria Dalla Gigia** or **Hostaria dai Naneti**.

The Drive: Head northwest out of Treviso on the regional road SR348 towards Montebelluna and then Asolo. It's a pleasant 37km drive through flat fields and small provincial towns.

02 Asolo

Asolo with its view of 'a thousand hills' is one of the most beautiful villages in Italy *(borghipiubelliditalia.it)*. It has always been wealthy, starting as a bishopric in the 10th century, then becoming the miniature kingdom of Caterina Cornaro, the Queen of Cyprus in 1489, who gave up her island home to Venice. She filled the town with artists and intellectuals such as Gentile Bellini and humanist Pietro Bembo, who lent it a refined and cosmopolitan air, which has lingered through the centuries.

In their wake came other bohemians such as American author Henry James, English poet Robert Browning, Russian composer Igor Stravinsky, Italian actress and the first woman to grace the cover of *Time* magazine, Eleonora Duse, and English adventurer Freya Stark. There's a small **museum** *(asolo.it)* and a **castle**, but the real pleasure is to wander the romantic alleys and visit the garden of **Villa Freya** *(villafreya.it)* with its dreamy views, then stop for lunch at **Villa Cipriani** *(villacipriani.it)*, once the home of Robert Browning and Lord Guinness, which also has a delightful spa and pool with the most enchanting view.

The Drive: Descend south out of Asolo along Via Forestuzzo until you hit the SP6 where you turn right and then right again at the first roundabout. From here it's a pretty 9km drive up a leafy regional road all the way to Possagno, which perches on a small hill capped by Antonio Canova's Palladian temple.

DETOUR

Maser

Start: 02 Asolo

Andrea Palladio managed to synthesise the classical past without doggedly copying it, creating buildings that were at once inviting, useful and incomparably elegant.

A prime example of this domestic perfection is Palladio's butter-yellow **Villa di Masèr** (*villadimaser.it*) set amid a prosecco vineyard in Maser. Inside, Paolo Veronese nearly upstages his collaborator with wildly imaginative *trompe l'œil* architecture of his own. Vines climb the walls of the Stanza di Bacco; an alert watchdog keeps one eye on the painted door of the Stanza di Canuccio (Little Dog Room); and in a corner of the frescoed grand salon, the painter has apparently forgotten his spattered shoes and broom. In the wine-tasting room by the villa's parking lot, you can raise a toast to Palladio and Veronese with the estate's own prosecco.

03 Possagno

On the slopes of Monte Grappa, the dazzling, white neoclassical **Tempio** peeps above the treetops as if some part of ancient Rome had come to holiday in the Veneto. It's the parish church of Possagno, where Italy's master neoclassical sculptor, Antonio Canova, was born in 1757. Canova laid the first stone in 1819, and came to final rest here in 1822.

More interesting, however, is his home and **Gypsotheca** (*museocanova.it*), a light-filled gallery designed by Carlo Scarpa to showcase Canova's working models and plaster casts; you'll find it at the Museo Canova. The plaster casts reveal the laborious process through which Canova arrived at his glossy, seemingly effortless, marbles. Rough clay models give way to plaster figures cast in gesso, which were then used to map out the final marble in minute detail with small nails. It's the most complete display of an artist's working models in Europe.

The Drive: The short 16km drive east to Valdobbiadene is delightful. Descend from hilltop Possagno on the SP26, through vineyards and green fields. Then take a left onto the SR348 and a right over the Piave river into the vine-draped hills of prosecco country.

04 Valdobbiadene

Prosecco can be traced back to the Romans. It was then known as 'Pucino' and was shipped directly to the court of Empress Livia from Aquileia, where it was produced with grapes from the Carso. During the Venetian Republic the vines were transferred to the Prosecco DOCG (quality-controlled) area, a small triangle of land between the towns of Valdobbiadene, Conegliano and Vittorio Veneto.

Valdobbiadene sits at the heart of prosecco country, vines dipping and cresting across its hillsides. Take the **Strada di Prosecco** (*coneglia novaldobbiadene.it*) to discover some of the area's best wineries, such as **Cantina Bisol** (*bisol.it*), where generations of the Bisol family have been tending Galera vines since 1542. Tastings take place in the atmospheric underground cellars; the signature labels are the award-winning Cartizze Dry and Jeio Brut.

The Drive: Return to the northbound SR348 and take the next 24km alongside the Piave river at a leisurely pace. The views of the river, the vineyards and the approaching foothills of the Alps are timeless and very pretty when set against the blue, blue sky.

TOP TIP

PRIMAVERA DEL PROSECCO

Every May the 30 prosecco-producing villages in the DOC quality-controlled prosecco area participate in the Primavera del Prosecco (Prosecco Spring; *primaveradelprosecco.it*), putting on a weekend party with food stalls and all-day tastings.

05 Feltre

The 'painted city' of Feltre sits in a gorgeous natural setting at the foot of the Dolomites on the banks of the Piave. Since 1404, the city has been inextricably linked to Venice, demonstrating its unflinching loyalty to the Republic when the Holy Roman army ransacked the city and massacred its inhabitants in 1510.

In reward for its faithfulness, Venice refinanced the city's reconstruction, paying for its frescoed and porticoed *palazzi* (mansions) and elegant squares. Wander up **Via Mezzaterra** and **Via Lorenzo Luzzo** to admire the painted facades until you reach Piazza Maggiore,

Valdobbiadene
PAVEL REZAC/SHUTTERSTOCK

PHOTO OPPORTUNITY

The five mythical peaks of the Cinque Torri at sunset.

overlooked by the **Alboino Castle**. In August, a famous historical re-enactment, **Palio di Feltre** *(paliodifeltre.it)*, takes place here with hundreds of citizens dressed in Renaissance garb.

Also worth a look is the **Museo Civico**, which houses an unusually fine art collection, including paintings by major Veneto artists such as Bellini, Cima da Conegliano and Palma il Giovane, while the nearby **Museo d'Arte Carlo Rizzarda** *(comune.feltre.bl.it)* contains modernist pieces by Egon Schiele, Picasso and Adolfo Wildt.

Finally, 5km south of Feltre, on the same road you drove in on, is the unmissable 12th-century, frescoed **Sanctuary of Vittore and Corona** *(santivittoreecorona.it)*, the patron saints of the town.

The Drive: Although a little busier, the 30km drive northeast to Belluno, up the valley, is equally scenic. The SS50 runs between the Piave river to the south and the snowcapped peaks of the Parco Nazionale delle Dolomiti Bellunesi to the north, climbing slowly to Belluno.

06 Belluno

Perched on high bluffs above the Piave river and backed majestically by the snowcapped Dolomites, Belluno makes a scenic and strategic base to explore the 315-sq-km **Parco Nazionale delle Dolomiti Bellunesi** *(dolomitipark.it)*. And you'll be happy to fuel up for ski trails and hikes on the city's hearty cuisine, including some of Italy's most remarkable cheeses: Schiz (semisoft cow's-milk cheese, usually fried in butter) and the flaky, butter-yellow Malga Bellunense. When you're not out on the slopes, the historical old town is its own attraction, mixing stunning views with Renaissance-era buildings. **Piazza dei Martiri**, Belluno's main pedestrian square, is named after four partisans (the 'martyrs') hanged here during WWII. On sunny days and warm nights, its cafes overflow with young and old alike. Nearby, the Piazza del Duomo is framed by the early-16th-century Renaissance **Cattedrale di San Martino**, the 16th-century **Palazzo Rosso** and the **Palazzo dei Vescovi**, with a striking 12th-century tower.

The Drive: The two-hour (81km) drive from Belluno to the Cinque Torri is one of this trip's highlights. Cutting right through Parco Nazionale delle Dolomiti Bellunesi on the SR203, it offers stunning mountain panoramas and a nerve-tingling traverse of the Falzarego pass. Note: in winter, weather conditions may close the high passes. If so, take the A27 and SS51 directly to Cortina d'Ampezzo.

07 Cinque Torri

At the heart of the Dolomites, just 16km west of Cortina at the confluence of the Ampezzo, Badia and Cordevole valleys, is the gorgeous area of **Cinque Torri** *(5torri.it)*. It is accessible from Cortina by buses – ski shuttles in winter (free to ski-pass holders) and a Dolomiti Bus service in summer – which connect with the lifts at Passo Falzarego.

Hard though it is to believe, some of the fiercest fighting of WWI took place in these idyllic mountains between Italian and Austro-Hungarian troops. Now you can wander over 5km of restored trenches in an enormous **open-air museum** *(lagazuoi.it)* between Lagazuoi and the Tre Sassi fort. Guided tours are offered by the Gruppo Guide Alpine, and in winter you can ski the 80km **Great War Ski Tour** *(lagazuoi.it)* with the Dolomiti Superski ski pass. En route, mountain huts provide standout lunches with spectacular views.

The Drive: Another super, swooping drive along mountain roads lined with conifers. At Cinque Torri, pick up the SS48 (Passo Falzarego) and wind your way slowly down the twisting route into Cortina d'Ampezzo, 16km away.

08 Cortina d'Ampezzo

The spiked peaks and emerald-green valleys of the Dolomites are so beautiful, and their ecosystem so unique, they've won UNESCO protection. In winter, Cortina d'Ampezzo is the place to be, with fashion-conscious snow bunnies crowding its excellent slopes. In summer, it doubles as a stunning base for hiking, cycling and rock climbing.

Two cable cars whisk hikers and climbers from Cortina's town centre to a central departure point for chairlifts, cable cars and trails. They usually run from 9am to 5pm daily mid-December to April and resume June to October.

Dolomiti Superski passes provide access to 12 runs in the area, and are sold at Cortina's **ski pass office** *(skipass cortina.com)*. **Guide Alpine Cortina d'Ampezzo** *(guidecortina.com)* runs rock-climbing courses and guided nature hikes.

Cortina's other highlight activity is hunting down its fabulous farm-to-table restaurants, such as **Agriturismo El Brite de Larieto**, in the surrounding larch forests.

Cinque Torri
DIIRT/LONELY PLANET

Mantua
Mincio
Rovigo
Adige
VENETO
LOMBARDY
A13
Po
CROATIA
A22
Ferrara
Parma
Reggio Emilia
Secchia
Modena
Comacchio
E55
26
Bologna
EMILIA-ROMAGNA
Ravenna
Adriatic Sea
A14
A1
Forlì
Rimini
SAN MARINO
Pesaro
21
Pistoia
Serchio
Lucca
A11
Florence
23
22
Urbino
Misa
Ancona
Pisa
Bibbiena
Sansepolcro
Livorno
RA3
Arezzo
24
Gubbio
LE MARCHE
Macerata
Siena
A1
Cortona
TUSCANY
Pienza
Perugia
Assisi
Montalcino
Chiusi
Topino
Ascoli Piceno
E45
25
UMBRIA
Tevere
A14
Lente
Nera
Grosseto
Orvieto
ABRUZZO
E80
Pitigliano
Terni
Pescara
Fonte Cerreto
Porto Ercole
Viterbo
Orte
Rieti
Chieti
L'Aquila
A25
Tarquinia
Guardiagrele
A1
LAZIO
A25
Sulmona
20
Tevere
Avezzano
Cerveteri
Tivoli
Rome
Subiaco
A90
Pescasseroli
Palestrina
Frascati
Ostia Antica
Tyrrhenian Sea
Albano Laziale
A1
Frosinone
Isernia
18
19
MOLISE
Latina
Golfo di Gaeta
CAMPANIA
0 50 km
0 25 miles

REDMASON/SHUTTERSTOCK

Piazza del Popolo (p145)

CENTRAL ITALY

EXPLORE

CENTRAL ITALY

As Florence's Renaissance skyline fades into the background, the open road beckons. Motoring through Tuscany's voluptuous, wine-rich hills is one of Italy's great driving experiences and one of the many on offer in the country's green, rural heartland. To the north of Tuscany, Emilia-Romagna is a paradise for foodies, while to the east and south, Umbria, Le Marche and Abruzzo are made for slow travel with their wooded peaks, hilltop towns and wild landscapes. Artistic treasures, ancient Roman ruins and Etruscan tombs line the way as the road leads inexorably, often tortuously, towards Rome, the Eternal City.

Rome

Many people get their first taste of Italy in Rome, the country's capital and main gateway.

The city sits in the heart of the Lazio region, providing a convenient geographical base for exploring Italy's central territories.

The Roman hinterland, within easy day-tripping distance, is rich in historical interest while to the north you can investigate the lands once ruled by the ancient Etruscans.

To the east, the mountainous region of Abruzzo is about an hour's drive along the A24 *autostrada*.

Rome is, of course, a destination in itself, and it's well set up for visitors with excellent transport links, accommodation for all budgets, and no end of bars, cafes, trattorias and restaurants. It boasts a lifetime's worth of sights, certainly too many for a single trip, but for an introduction to the mysterious Etruscan civilisation, the Museo Nazionale Etrusco di Villa Giulia is well worth searching out.

Perugia

A 2¼-hour drive north of Rome, Perugia is Umbria's historic capital, as well as its largest and most animated city.

Interest is mainly focused on its hilltop centre and rich assortment of medieval treasures, many of which are housed in the superlative Galleria Nazionale dell'Umbria.

The city is also well situated for visiting nearby Assisi, a short hop eastwards, and neighbouring regions: to the east, the lesser-known Le Marche; to the north and west, traveller-favourite Tuscany.

WHEN TO GO

Central Italy looks best in spring when the onset of warm weather causes wildflowers to bloom across the verdant countryside. The blue skies and pleasant temperatures also make city sightseeing a joy. Summer sees plenty of festival action and excellent high-altitude hiking in the Apennines. Early autumn is prime time for lovers of seasonal produce and wine.

Hotels and B&Bs provide accommodation while restaurants, wine bars and trattorias serve up generous helpings of earthy Umbrian fare and local wine.

Florence

As a base for Tuscany, Florence is hard to top. Situated in the north of the region, it's on the main A1 *autostrada* and is served by a constant stream of fast trains and flights to Tuscany's two international airports (one at Florence, the other at Pisa).

Once in town, you'll find plenty of accommodation and dining options, as well as wonderful shopping in markets and artisanal studios.

You'll also come face to face with some of Italy's most celebrated masterpieces and a historic centre that appears to have changed little since Renaissance times.

From the city, roads lead south to the Chianti wine country and on to Siena and the Val d'Orcia.

TRANSPORT

Airports at Rome, Bologna, Florence and Pisa are the main international gateways to the area. Once in Italy, fast trains connect Rome, Florence and Bologna, as does the north–south A1 *autostrada*. Away from the principal towns and cities, rail services are limited and you're better off getting around by bus, or better still, your own car.

To the north, Bologna, gateway to Emilia-Romagna's foodie cities, is about an hour's drive away or 40 minutes by train.

RESOURCES

- **Agriturismi.it**
  Medieval fanfare fuels the atmosphere at Siena's daredevil horse race, held every 2 July and 16 August.
- **Monastery Stays**
  (monasterystays.it) Browse and book bargain accommodation in monasteries and convents.
- **Parco Nazionale d'Abruzzo, Lazio e Molise**
  (parcoabruzzo.it) Website of Abruzzo's largest national park with ideas and practical information, including hiking routes and trail maps.

WHERE TO STAY

Accommodation is plentiful in heavyweight destinations like Rome and Florence. However, places fill quickly, especially at peak periods when prices rise with the heavy demand. Book ahead to avoid disappointment.

Outside the main cities, you'll find rich pickings in the Tuscan and Umbrian countryside where *agriturismi* (farm stays) are a great bet for the period between April and October. At other times, you might find them closed for the season. Another option, particularly popular in religious centres like Assisi, is a convent or monastery, many of which offer basic, inexpensive lodgings.

WHAT'S ON

- **Palio di Siena**
  Medieval fanfare fuels the atmosphere at Siena's daredevil horse race, held every 2 July and 16 August. (p116)
- **Umbria Jazz**
  Perugia's medieval centre swings to the sound of jazz during this renowned music festival, staged over 10 days in July. *umbriajazz.it*
- **Grape Harvest**
  The area's many vineyards are a hive of activity during the annual *vendemmia* (grape harvest) in September and October.

18

★ BEST FOR

WINE

Frascati's traditional cellars.

CENTRAL ITALY

ROAMING AROUND ROME

Vineyards, Frascati

DURATION: 3 DAYS

DISTANCE: 101KM/62 MILES

GREAT FOR: HISTORY, FOOD AND DRINK

BEST TIME TO GO: SPRING'S GOOD FOR THE ANCIENT SITES, EARLY SUMMER FOR ROMANTIC VIEWS.

While Rome (Roma) hogs the limelight, its little-explored hinterland makes for an absorbing drive with its verdant scenery and wealth of historic sights. Headline acts include the remarkably well-preserved ruins of ancient Rome's port at Ostia Antica, and Emperor Hadrian's vast palace complex at Tivoli. Tivoli is one of several hilltop towns featured on this trip, along with the wine town of Frascati and the former papal retreat of Castel Gandolfo.

LINK YOUR TRIP

02 World Heritage Wonders
From Ostia Antica head into Rome along Via Ostiense to join up with this tour of Italy's greatest hits.

27 Shadow of Vesuvius
Take the A1 *autostrada* from near Frascati and head down to Naples (Napoli), the starting point for this exploration of Vesuvius, Pompeii and other classic sites.

01 Ostia Antica

One of Lazio's prize sights, the ruins of ancient Rome's seaport are wonderfully complete, like a smaller version of Pompeii. Ostia was founded in the 4th century BCE at the mouth of the Tiber and developed into a major port with a population of around 50,000. Decline set in after the fall of the Roman Empire and it was gradually abandoned, its citizens driven off by barbarian raids and outbreaks of malaria. Over subsequent centuries, it was slowly buried in river silt, hence its survival.

The **Parco Archeologico di Ostia Antica** *(ostiaantica.cultura.gov.it)* is a vast site and you'll need several hours to do it justice. The main thoroughfare, the **Decumanus Maximus**, leads from the entrance at Porta Romana to highlights such as the **Terme di Nettuno** (Baths of Neptune), whose floor features a famous mosaic of Neptune driving his seahorse chariot. Nearby, the steeply stacked

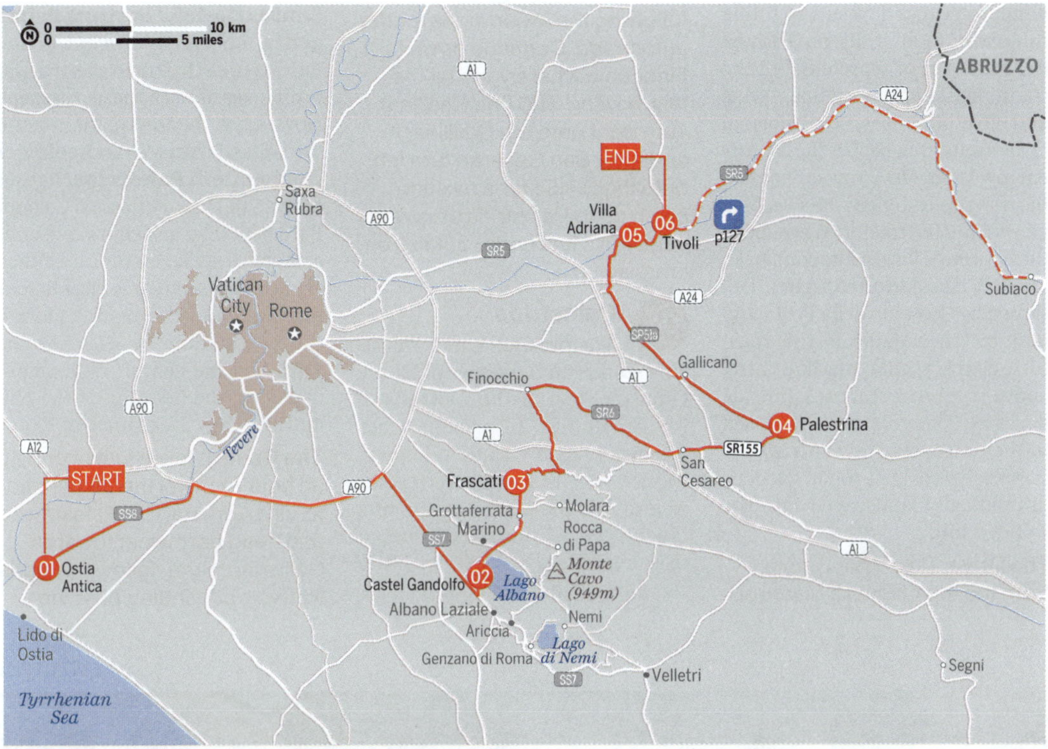

CRISTINA ARBUNESCU/SHUTTERSTOCK

Teatro was built by Agrippa and later enlarged to hold 4000 people. Behind the amphitheatre, the **Piazzale delle Corporazioni** (Forum of the Corporations) housed merchant guilds and is decorated with well-preserved mosaics. Further towards Porta Marina, the **Thermopolium** is an ancient cafe with a bar and fresco advertising the bill of fare.

The Drive: Head back towards Rome and take the Grande Raccordo Anulare (GRA; A90) for Naples. Exit at the Ciampino Airport turnoff and continue up Via Appia (SS7) until you come to traffic lights halfway up a long climb. Make a left turn to Lago Albano and follow this road up under the towering umbrella pines to Castel Gandolfo at the top. All told, it's about 36km.

02 Castel Gandolfo

One of the prettiest towns in the Castelli Romani, an area of wooded, wine-rich hills south of Rome, Castel Gandolfo makes for a memorable stop. It's not a big place but what it lacks in size it makes up for in atmosphere, and on a warm summer's evening there's no better place for a romantic tête-à-tête. Sightseeing action is centred on the **Palazzo Apostolico** *(www.museivaticani.va)*, a 17th-century palace that for centuries served as the pope's summer residence, and the **Giardini di Villa Barberini** *(www.museivaticani.va)*. A stop here is as much about admiring the gorgeous views over Lago Albano and enjoying alfresco meals as it is about sightseeing.

The Drive: To Frascati, it's a pretty straightforward 9km drive. From Castel Gandolfo follow the road for Marino, enjoying glimpses of Lago Albano off to your right, and then Grottaferrata. Here you'll come to a roundabout. Take the third exit and Frascati is 4km further on.

03 Frascati

Best known for its crisp white wine, Frascati is a popular day-trip destination. On hot summer weekends Romans pile into town to hang out in the elegant historic centre and fill up on *porchetta* (herb-roasted pork) and local wine. You can follow suit by filling up at the food stalls on **Piazza del Mercato** or searching out the traditional *cantine* (originally wine and olive-oil cellars, now informal restaurants) that pepper the centre's narrow lanes. Once you've explored the town and admired the sweeping views from the tree-lined avenue at the bottom of Piazza Marconi, head up to **Villa Aldobrandini**. Designed by Giacomo della Porta and built by Carlo Maderno, this regal 16th-century villa sits haughtily above town in a stunning hillside position. The villa itself is closed to the public but you can visit the impressive early-baroque gardens dramatically landscaped into the wooded hill.

The Drive: Take Viale Catone from the top of Piazza Marconi, following the green signs for the *autostrada*. Continue down to Finocchio where you'll hit the fast-flowing SR6 (Via Casilina). Turn right onto the Casilina and after San Cesareo turn left onto the SR155 for a twisting climb up to Palestrina's historic centre. It's just under 30km from Frascati.

04 Palestrina

The pretty town of Palestrina stands on the slopes of Monte Ginestro, one of the foothills of the Apennines. In ancient times Praeneste, as it was then known, was a favourite summer retreat for wealthy Romans and the site of a much-revered temple dedicated to the goddess of fortune. Little remains of the 2nd-century-BCE **Santuario della Fortuna Primigenia**, but much of what is now Palestrina's historic centre was built over its six giant terraces. Nowadays, the town's main act is the fantastic **Museo Archeologico Nazionale di Palestrina**, housed in the 17th-century Palazzo Colonna Barberini. The museum's collection comprises ancient sculpture, funerary artefacts, and some huge Roman mosaics, but its crowning glory is the breathtaking *Mosaico Nilotico,* a detailed 2nd-century-BCE mosaic depicting the flooding of the Nile and everyday life in ancient Egypt.

The Drive: It takes just over half an hour to travel the 21km or so to Villa Adriana. Exit Palestrina and head northwest towards Gallicano. Here, follow the signs to Tivoli, continuing past the

Villa d'Este

MARCO RUBINO/SHUTTERSTOCK

shrubbery and bucolic green fields until you see Villa Adriana signposted a few kilometres short of Tivoli.

05 Villa Adriana

The Emperor Hadrian's sprawling 2nd-century country estate, **Villa Adriana** *(villae.cultura.gov.it)*, was one of ancient Rome's grandest properties, lavish even by the decadent standards of the day. Hadrian personally designed much of the complex, taking inspiration from buildings he'd seen around the world. The *pecile,* the large pool area near the walls, is a reproduction of a building in Athens. Similarly, the *canopo* is a copy of a sanctuary in the Egyptian town of Canopus, with a narrow 120m-long pool flanked by sculptural figures.

To the northeast of the *pecile,* the **Teatro Marittimo** is one of the site's signature buildings. A circular mini-villa set in an artificial pool, this was Hadrian's personal refuge and could only be accessed by swing bridges.

There are also several bath complexes, temples and barracks. Paid parking is available at the site.

The Drive: Pick up Via Tiburtina (SR5), the main Rome–Tivoli road, and head up to Tivoli *centro*. It's a steep, twisting 4km climb up to the town centre.

PHOTO OPPORTUNITY

Fountains at Tivoli's Villa d'Este.

06 Tivoli

Tivoli's elevated historic centre is an attractive, if often busy, spot. Its main attraction is the UNESCO-protected **Villa d'Este** *(villae.cultura.gov.it)*, a one-time Benedictine convent that Lucrezia Borgia's son, Cardinal Ippolito d'Este, transformed into a pleasure palace in the late 16th century. It later provided inspiration for Franz Liszt, who composed *The Fountains of the Villa d'Este* after spending time here between 1865 and 1886.

Before heading out to the gardens, take time to admire the villa's Mannerist frescoes.

Outside, the manicured gardens feature water-spouting gargoyles and shady lanes flanked by lofty cypresses and extravagant fountains, all powered by gravity alone.

Look out for the Bernini-designed **Fountain of the Organ**, which uses water pressure to play music through a concealed organ, and the 130m-long **Avenue of the Hundred Fountains**.

DETOUR

Subiaco

Start: 06 Tivoli

Remote-feeling and dramatic, Subiaco is well worth the trip to see its two breathtaking Benedictine monasteries *(benedettini-subiaco.org)*. The **Monastero di San Benedetto** is carved into the rock over the cave where St Benedict holed up for three years to meditate and pray. As well as a setting described by Petrarch as 'the edge of Paradise', it has an interior covered in 13th- to 15th-century frescoes.

Halfway down the hill from San Benedetto is the **Monastero di Santa Scolastica**, the only one of the 13 monasteries built by St Benedict still standing in the Valley of the Amiene.

If you decide to stay, its Foresteria is a great place to spend a contemplative night. But book ahead, as Benedictine clergy from around the world often make the pilgrimage here to work in the monastery's famous library and archive. There's also a restaurant offering simple meals for €20 to €25.

19

★ BEST FOR

SCENERY

The hills around Pescasseroli.

CENTRAL ITALY

ABRUZZO'S WILD LANDSCAPES

DURATION: 6 DAYS

DISTANCE: 375KM/233 MILES

GREAT FOR: NATURE

BEST TIME TO GO: JUNE, JULY AND SEPTEMBER FOR PERFECT WEATHER AND CLEAR VIEWS.

Parco Nazionale d'Abruzzo (p130)

Although just an hour's drive from Rome, Abruzzo is largely unknown to foreign visitors. Yet with its mountain scenery and rural, back-country charm, it's ideal for a road trip. This route takes in the best of the region's three national parks, winding over green hills and past ancient beech woods populated by wolves and bears, as snow-capped summits shimmer in the distance. Cultural gems also await, such as the charming medieval town of Sulmona.

LINK YOUR TRIP

18 Roaming Around Rome
From Fonte Cerreto take the A24 for about 105km southwest to Tivoli, one of the gems in Rome's fascinating hinterland.

22 Green Heart of Italy
Pick up the A24 near Fonte Cerreto and continue for 140km southwest to Frascati, and a tour of the wine-rich Castelli Romani.

01 Pescara

Before heading into the wild interior spend a day relaxing on the beach in Pescara, Abruzzo's largest city. Action centres on the animated seafront, although there are a couple of small museums worth a look – the **Museo delle Genti d'Abruzzo** *(gentidabruzzo.com)*, which illustrates regional rural culture, and the **Museo Casa Natale Gabriele D'Annunzio**, the birthplace of controversial fascist poet Gabriele D'Annunzio.

Pescara also offers top-notch seafood and a youthful and energetic *aperitivo* (pre-dinner drinks) scene.

The Drive: From central Pescara it's about half an hour to Chieti. Follow the green signs to the *autostrada*, which direct you onto the Raccordo Pescara-Chieti, a fast-moving dual carriageway that runs past factories and warehouses towards the distant mountains. Exit for Chieti and follow signs for Chieti

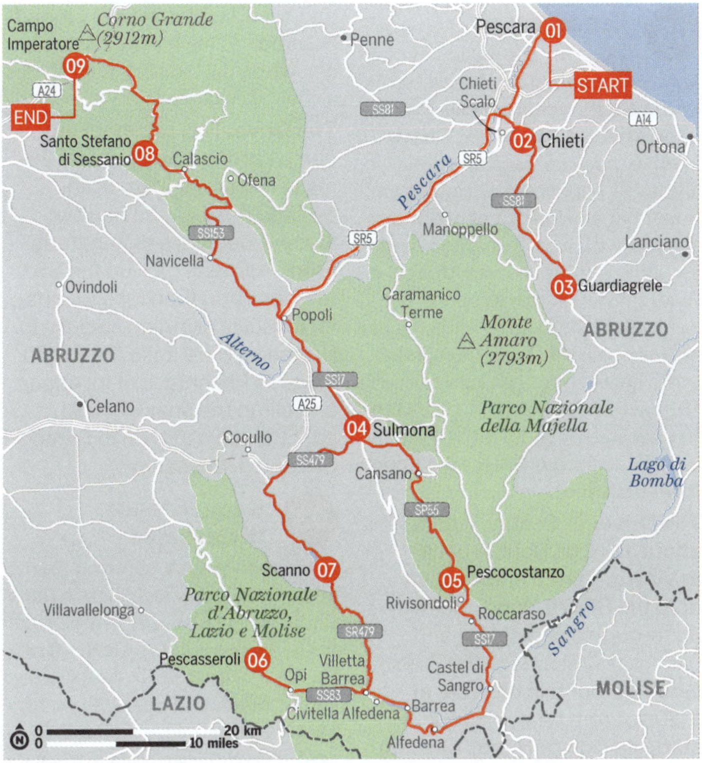

VALERIOMEI/SHUTTERSTOCK

ABRUZZO WILDLIFE

Abruzzo's three national parks – Parco Nazionale del Gran Sasso e Monti della Laga; Parco Nazionale della Majella; and Parco Nazionale d'Abruzzo, Lazio e Molise – are home to thousands of animal species. Most famous of all is the critically endangered Marsican brown bear, of which there are an estimated 50 or so in the Parco Nazionale d'Abruzzo, Lazio e Molise. Apennine wolves also prowl the deep woods, sometimes emerging in winter when thick snow forces them to approach villages in search of food. Other notable animals include the Abruzzi chamois and red deer, and, overhead, golden eagles and peregrine hawks.

centro and then the Civetta and Museo Archeologico Nazionale.

02 Chieti

Overlooking the Aterno valley, hilltop Chieti dates back to pre-Roman times, to the era of feuding Italic tribes. Two museums showcase the town's ancient history. The most important is the **Museo Archeologico Nazionale d'Abruzzo Villa Frigerj**, home to the 6th-century-BCE 'Warrior of Capestrano', the most important pre-Roman find in central Italy and a much-publicised regional icon. Uphill from the Frigerj, the **Museo Archeologico Nazionale d'Abruzzo – La Civitella** is built around a Roman amphitheatre.

The Drive: Descend from Chieti's centre until you see signs for Guardiagrele and the SS81 off to the left. The road twists and turns slowly for the first few kilometres but eventually broadens out and becomes quicker as it runs past woods and vineyards up to Guardiagrele, about 26km (40 minutes) away.

03 Guardiagrele

Described as Abruzzo's terrace by poet Gabriele D'Annunzio, this ancient *borgo* (medieval town) on the eastern flank of the **Parco Nazionale della Majella** *(parcomajella.it)* commands sweeping views. Admire these and the striking **Collegiata di Santa Maria Maggiore** with its elegant Gothic doorway that frames a Romanesque facade topped by a collection of nine bells exposed to the elements.

The Drive: To Sulmona it's about 1½ hours from Guardiagrele. Double back to Chieti on the SS81, then follow signs for the *autostrada* towards L'Aquila then the SR5 to Chieti Scalo and Manoppello. Pass through Popoli and continue on the SS17 until you see Sulmona signposted about 18km on.

04 Sulmona

Overlooked by the grey Morrone massif, Sulmona is a midsized medieval town famous for its *confetti* (sweets traditionally given to guests at Italian weddings). Action is focused on **Corso Ovidio**, named after the local-born poet Ovid, and **Piazza Garibaldi**, a breezy piazza accessed through a 13th-century aqueduct. Here on the square, you can peruse religious and contemporary art at the

Museo Diocesano di Arte Sacra.

At the other end of Corso Ovidio, **Palazzo dell'Annunziata** sits above a 1st-century-BCE Roman *domus* (villa), remains of which can be seen at the **Museo Civico**.

The Drive: The 50-minute run over to Pescocostanzo takes you through some beautiful mountain terrain via the Bosco di Sant'Antonio (ideal for a picnic). From Sulmona head towards Cansano and follow the road as it ascends the increasingly rocky landscape. At Cansano take the SP55 for Pescocostanzo.

05 Pescocostanzo

Surrounded by lush highland meadows, Pescocostanzo (elevation 1400m) is a characteristic hilltop town whose historical core has changed little in over 500 years. Of particular note is the **Collegiata di Santa Maria del Colle**, an atmospheric Romanesque church with a lavish baroque interior. Nearby, **Piazza del Municipio** is flanked by a number of impressive palazzi (mansions), including **Palazzo Comunale** with its distinctive clock tower, and **Palazzo Fanzago**, designed by baroque architect Cosimo Fanzago in 1624. History apart, Pescocostanzo also offers skiing on **Monte Calvario** and summer hiking in the **Bosco di Sant'Antonio**.

The Drive: Reckon on about 75 minutes to Pescasseroli. Continue past Rivisondoli to the SS17, then turn south towards Roccaraso. After Castel di Sangro head right onto the SS83. This beautiful road swoops and dips its way through Alfedena, Barrea, past the artificial Lago di Barrea, and on to Villetta Barrea, Opi and Pescasseroli.

06 Pescasseroli

Deep in the heart of the Marsican mountains, Pescasseroli is the main centre of the **Parco Nazionale d'Abruzzo, Lazio e Molise** *(parcoabruzzo.it)*, the oldest and most popular of Abruzzo's national parks. Hiking opportunities abound with clearly marked paths for all levels. In winter there's a small ski station that's popular with locals. You'll be lucky to see bears or wolves in the wild here (though they exist); however, you can view rescued animals at Pescasseroli's **Centro Visita** and learn about wolves in Civitella Alfedena's **Museo del Lupo Appenninico**.

The Drive: To Scanno it takes about an hour. Double back to Villetta Barrea and turn left onto the SR479. Wind your way up through a pine forest and past grassy slopes to the Passo Godi, a mountain pass set at 1630m. From here, the road starts its slow, tortuous descent to Scanno.

07 Scanno

A tangle of steep alleyways and sturdy, grey-stone houses, prepossessing Scanno is an atmospheric *borgo* known for its finely worked filigree gold jewellery. Explore the pint-sized historic centre and then head down to **Lago di Scanno** – a couple of kilometres out of town on the road to Sulmona – for a cool lakeside drink.

The Drive: This two-hour leg can be broken up by overnighting in Sulmona, 31km from Scanno through the narrow, steep-sided Gole di Sagittario. From Sulmona pick up the SS17 to Popoli and then follow signs for L'Aquila, climbing steadily to Navicella. Here, take the SS153 towards Pescara. Exit for Ofena and climb the snaking road past Calascio and on to Santo Stefano di Sessanio.

> ☑ TOP TIP
>
> ### ARRIVING IN SULMONA
>
> Try to time your arrival in Sulmona between 1.30pm and 5.30pm, when traffic restrictions are lifted and you can drive into the historic centre. It makes getting to your hotel much easier.

08 Santo Stefano di Sessanio

If you really want to slip away from it all, you can't get much more remote than this picturesque village high in the **Parco Nazionale del Gran Sasso e Monti della Laga** *(gransassolagapark.it)*. Once a 16th-century Medici stronghold, it suffered damage in the 2009 earthquake when its emblematic Medici tower collapsed (it's since been rebuilt). Notwithstanding, exploring Santo Stefano's ancient mossy streets with their smattering of local shops and 'diffused' accommodation is a peaceful joy. The helpful **Centro Visite** also contains a small museum about the national park.

The Drive: From Santo Stefano, Campo Imperatore is signposted as 13km away. It's actually more like 20km (20 minutes), but you'll forget about such things as the awesome scenery unfolds ahead of you. Just follow the road and its continuation, the SS17bis, and admire the views.

SERFEO/SHUTTERSTOCK

Scanno

09 Campo Imperatore

The high point – quite literally – of this trip is the highland plain known as Campo Imperatore (average elevation 1800m). Often referred to as Italy's 'Little Tibet', this magnificent grassy plateau provides spectacular views of **Corno Grande** (2912m), the highest mountain in the Apennines. You can climb the mountain on the 11.5km *via normale* (normal route) or just hang around the cable-car station admiring the art deco **Hotel Campo Imperatore** (currently being refurbished) from where German paratroopers famously rescued Mussolini in 1943.

From Campo Imperatore, signs direct you down to **Fonte Cerreto**, a small cluster of hotels set around a *funivia* (cable car) station, and the nearby A24 *autostrada*.

PHOTO OPPORTUNITY

Corno Grande from Campo Imperatore.

20

CENTRAL ITALY

ETRUSCAN TUSCANY & LAZIO

DURATION: 3–4 DAYS

DISTANCE: 231KM/144 MILES

GREAT FOR: HISTORY, NATURE

BEST TIME TO GO: APRIL TO OCTOBER, WHEN THE CASTLES ARE OPEN FOR VIEWING.

Long before Rome came into existence, the Etruscans had forged a great civilisation in the pitted, rugged hills of southern Tuscany, Umbria and northern Lazio. This trip leads through these little-known parts of the country, opening the window onto dramatic natural scenery and spectacular Etruscan treasures. From Tuscany's pock-marked peaks to the haunting tombs that litter Lazio's soft green slopes, it's a beguiling ride.

LINK YOUR TRIP

18 Roaming Around Rome
At Cerveteri, pick up the A12 *autostrada* and continue south 45km, via Fiumicino, to Ostia Antica, Rome's very own Pompeii.

25 Tuscan Landscapes
From Bolsena, head northeast to join the SR71 for the 20km drive to Orvieto, one of the stars of this fabulously scenic trip.

01 Chiusi

Located in Tuscany's Etruscan heartland, in territory where archaeologists still regularly unearth tombs, Chiusi has an outstanding collection of ancient finds. Housed in the **Museo Archeologico Etrusco di Chiusi**, these include a bevy of 9th- to 2nd-century-BCE ceramics, pottery, jewellery and cinerary urns. Don't miss the extraordinary *pietra fetida* (sulphur stone) funerary sphinx and bust of a grieving woman, both dating from the 6th century BCE. The museum ticket also covers entry to two Etruscan tombs in the nearby countryside – free shuttle buses run from the museum to the tombs between April and September.

The Drive: Reckon on 66km for this first leg. From Chiusi, head south through Chiusi Scalo to pick up the southbound SP308. Follow this country road until Piazze where the road bears left and becomes the SP321. Continue onto the SR2 and then the rural SP22 for the last few kilometres to Sovana.

MARTIBSTOCK/SHUTTERSTOCK

Via Cava

02 Sovana

Tuscany's most significant Etruscan tombs are concentrated in the **Necropoli di Sovana** *(cittadeltufo.com)*, an archaeological park encompassing land around the villages of Sovana, Sorano and Vitozza. At Sovana, the best finds are situated just 1.5km west of the village. Here you'll find four major tombs, including the monumental **Tomba Ildebranda**, with traces of carved columns and stairs, as well as two stretches of original Etruscan road – **Via del Cavone** and **Via Cava di Poggio Prisca**.

The village itself has a pretty main street and two beautiful Romanesque churches – the **Cattedrale di San Pietro**, with its austere vaulted interior, and the **Chiesa di Santa Maria Maggiore**, notable for its 16th-century apse frescoes.

The Drive: Head east out of Sovana and after a couple of kilometres turn right onto the SP46. This winding road twists through scorched open peaks and occasional pockets of woodland as it wends its way to Pitigliano, about 7km away.

03 Pitigliano

Sprouting from a towering tufa outcrop and surrounded by dramatic gorges on three sides, Pitigliano is a lovely knot of twisting stairways, cobbled alleys and quaint stone houses. In the middle of it all, the **Museo Civico Archeologico di Pitigliano** has a small but rich collection of local Etruscan finds, including some huge *bucchero* (black earthenware pottery) dating from the 6th century BCE.

The town also has an interesting Jewish history – at one point it was dubbed 'Little Jerusalem' – which you can find out about at **La Piccola Gerusalemme** *(lapiccolagerusalemme.it)*.

The Drive: Head east on the SR74 until the road forks. Bear right onto the SP489 for Gradoli and follow through the increasingly lush countryside until you hit the fast-flowing SR2 (Via Cassia). Go right and skirt the northern banks of Lago di Bolsena into Bolsena town. It's about 30km in total.

04 Bolsena

The main town on **Lago di Bolsena**, Italy's largest volcanic lake, Bolsena was a major medieval pilgrimage destination after a miracle supposedly took place here in 1263, leading Pope Urban IV to establish the festival of Corpus Domini. Other than the lake, the main reason to stop by is to visit the **Rocca Monaldeschi**, a 13th-century fortress that dominates the skyline and houses a small collection of locally unearthed artefacts in the **Museo Territoriale del Lago di Bolsena** *(simulabo.it)*.

The Drive: It's a straightforward 31km drive to Viterbo along the SR2. This takes you down Lago di Bolsena's eastern side, past orchards, vineyards and olive groves through the medieval town of Montefiascone and on to Viterbo.

PHOTO OPPORTUNITY

Pitigliano rising out of the rock.

05 Viterbo

Founded by the Etruscans and later taken over by the Romans, Viterbo became an important medieval centre, and in the 13th century was briefly the seat of the papacy.

Its Etruscan past is chronicled at the **Museo Nazionale Etrusco**, one of several interesting sights in the town's well-preserved *centro storico* (historic centre). To the south, the Renaissance Piazza del Plebiscito is overlooked by **Palazzo dei Priori**, Viterbo's city hall, which has some fine 16th-century frescoes. Southwest of here, **Piazza San Lorenzo** was the medieval city's religious heart, where cardinals came to vote for their popes and pray in the 12th-century **Cattedrale di San Lorenzo**. Next door, the **Museo del Colle del Duomo** *(archeoares.it/musei/viterbo)* displays a small collection of archaeological artefacts and religious art. Also on the piazza is the **Palazzo dei Papi**, a handsome Gothic palace that was built for the popes who lived in Viterbo from 1257 to 1281. Its main feature is the **Sala del Conclave**, scene of the first and longest ever papal conclave.

The Drive: Exit Viterbo and pick up the SS675 heading towards Rome. Continue on this fast dual carriageway until the turnoff for SR2 (Via Cassia).

Pitigliano (p133)

DAVIDE MARZOTTO/SHUTTERSTOCK

Take this and continue to Vetralla, where you should go right onto the SS1bis (Via Aurelia bis) and continue to Tarquinia. It's about 44km in total.

06 Tarquinia

The pick of Lazio's Etruscan towns, Tarquinia is a gem. Its highlight is the 7th-century-BCE **Necropoli di Tarquinia**, one of Italy's most important Etruscan sites. Some 6000 tombs have been excavated here since 1489, of which 22 are currently open to the public, including the Tomba della Caccia e della Pesca, the richly decorated Tomba dei Leopardi, and the Tomba della Fustigazione with its erotic depiction of ancient S&M.

In the *centro storico,* the **Museo Archeologico Nazionale Tarquiniense** is a delightful museum, showcasing some wonderful Etruscan artefacts, including a breathtaking terracotta frieze of winged horses (the *Cavalli Alati*).

The Drive: The easiest way to Cerveteri, about 53km away, is via the A12 *autostrada*. Take this towards Rome/Civitavecchia and exit at the Cerveteri/Ladispoli turnoff. After the toll booth, head left into town.

THE ETRUSCANS

Of the many Italic tribes that emerged from the Stone Age, the Etruscans left the most enduring mark. By the 7th century BCE their city-states – places such as Caere (modern-day Cerveteri), Tarquinii (Tarquinia), Veii (Veio), Perusia (Perugia), Volaterrae (Volterra) and Arretium (Arezzo) – were the dominant forces in central Italy. Debate rages about their origins – Roman historian Herodotus claimed they came to Italy from Asia Minor to escape famine – but what is not disputed is that they gave rise to a sophisticated society based on agriculture, trade and mineral mining. They were skilled architects, and although little remains of their buildings, archaeologists have found evidence of aqueducts, bridges and sewers, as well as temples. In artistic terms, they were known for their jewellery and tomb decoration, producing elaborate stone sarcophagi and bright, vivid frescoes.

For much of their existence, the Etruscans were rivals of the Greeks, who had colonised much of southern Italy from the 8th century BCE, but in the end it was the Romans who finally conquered them. In 396 BCE they lost the key town of Veii, and by the 2nd century BCE they and their land had largely been incorporated into the rapidly expanding Roman Republic.

07 Cerveteri

Cerveteri, or Kysry to the Etruscans and Caere to Latin-speakers, was one of the most important commercial centres in the Mediterranean from the 7th to the 5th centuries BCE. Its main sight is the UNESCO-listed **Necropoli di Banditaccia** just outside town. This 12-hectare site is a veritable city of the dead, with streets, squares and terraces of *tumuli* (circular tombs cut into the earth and capped by turf). Look out for the 6th-century-BCE **Tomba dei Rilievi**, which retains traces of painted reliefs.

In Cerveteri itself, the **Museo Nazionale Cerite** displays finds from the tombs, including the Euphronios Krater, a celebrated 1st-century-BCE vase.

21

CENTRAL ITALY

MONASTERIES OF TUSCANY & UMBRIA

★ BEST FOR

HIKING

The forests around the Santuario della Verna.

DURATION: 5 DAYS

DISTANCE: 262KM/163 MILES

GREAT FOR: HISTORY, NATURE

BEST TIME TO GO: SUMMER AND EARLY AUTUMN ARE BEST FOR MONASTIC VISITS.

Santuario della Verna (p139)

Away from the crowds and bright lights, an austere 11th-century monastery sits in silence surrounded by forest and rocky mountainsides. Welcome to the Monastero e Sacro Eremo di Camaldoli, one of the starkly beautiful monasteries that you'll discover on this tour of central Umbria and Tuscany. Most people don't venture into the remote and densely forested locations where these monasteries are set, but they set the scene for a gripping drive.

LINK YOUR TRIP

02 World Heritage Wonders
From Florence, head 73km south to Siena, one of the stars of this classic trip.

23 Piero della Francesca Trail
Push north from Cortona to Arezzo and join up with this art-based trail that runs from Urbino to Florence.

01 Assisi

Both the birthplace and the final resting place of St Francis, this medieval hilltop town is a major destination for millions of pilgrims. Its biggest drawcard is the **Basilica di San Francesco** *(sanfrancescoassisi.org)*, which comprises two gloriously frescoed churches – the Gothic **Basilica Superiore** (upper church), which was built between 1230 and 1253 and features a celebrated fresco cycle by Giotto, and the dimly lit **Basilica Inferiore** (lower church), with frescoes by Simone Martini, Cimabue and Pietro Lorenzetti.

At the other end of the *centro storico,* the 13th-century **Basilica di Santa Chiara** *(assisisantachiara.it)* is the last resting place of St Clare, a contemporary of St Francis and founder of the Order of the Poor Ladies, aka the Poor Clares.

The Drive: From Assisi you can get to Perugia in about 40 minutes, but if you've got time it's worth stopping off to admire

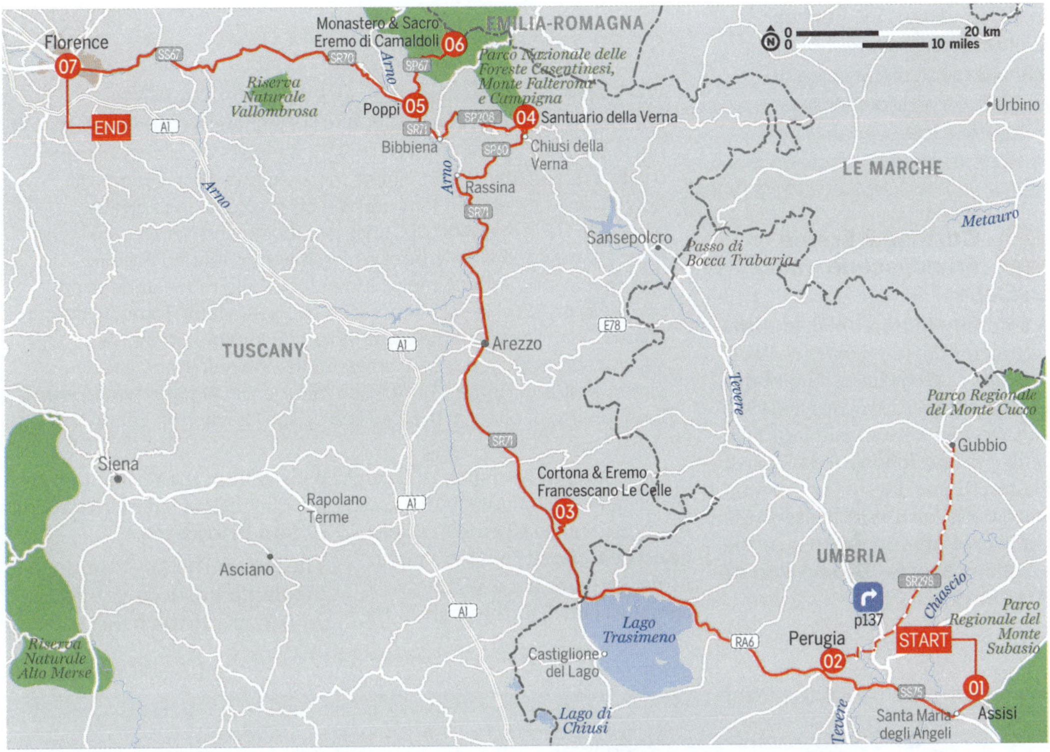

MNSTUDIO/SHUTTERSTOCK

the basilica at Santa Maria degli Angeli. From Assisi head down the snaking road to Santa Maria degli Angeli and pick up the fast-running SS75 to Perugia.

02 Perugia

With its hilltop medieval centre and international student population, Perugia is as close as Umbria gets to a heaving metropolis – which isn't all that close. Action is focused on the main strip, **Corso Vannucci**, and **Piazza IV Novembre**, home to the austere 14th-century **Cattedrale di San Lorenzo** with its unfinished two-tone facade.

Over the square, the 13th-century **Palazzo dei Priori** houses Perugia's best museums, including the **Galleria Nazionale dell'Umbria** (*gallerianazionaledellumbria.it*), with a collection containing works by local heroes Perugino and Pinturicchio. Close to the palazzo (mansion), the impressive **Nobile Collegio del Cambio** (*Exchange Hall*; *collegiodelcambio.it*) also has some wonderful frescoes by Perugino.

The Drive: From Perugia it's just under an hour's drive to Cortona. Pick up the RA6 Raccordo Autostradale Bettolle-Perugia and head west, skirting Lago Trasimeno before joining the northbound SR71 at the lake's northwestern corner. From there the pace slackens as the road cuts through vineyards and sunflower fields up to Cortona.

DETOUR
Gubbio
Start: 02 Perugia

Stacked on the steep slopes of an Umbrian mountainside, the medieval town of Gubbio is well worth a visit. Highlights include **Piazza Grande**, with grandstand views over the surrounding countryside, and the **Museo Civico Palazzo dei Consoli** (*palazzodeiconsoli.it*), where you'll find Gubbio's most famous treasures – the Iguvine Tablets. Dating to between 300 BCE and 100 BCE, these bronze tablets are inscribed with ancient text, the finest existing samples of the ancient Umbrian language. For a change of scene, and yet more views, take the **Funivia Colle Eletto** *(funiviagubbio.it)* up to the Basilica di Sant'Ubaldo high above on Monte Ingino.

Gubbio is just over an hour's drive northeast of Perugia on the SR298.

03 Cortona & Eremo Francescano Le Celle

A stunning hilltop town, and the setting for the film *Under the Tuscan Sun,* Cortona has a remarkable artistic pedigree. Fra' Angelico lived and worked here in the late 14th century, and fellow artists Luca Signorelli and Pietro da Cortona were both born within its walls – all three are represented in the excellent **Museo Diocesano di Arte Sacra**.

ST FRANCIS OF ASSISI

The son of a wealthy merchant and a French noblewoman, Francesco was born in Assisi in 1181. He enjoyed a carefree youth, but in his early 20s he went off to fight against Perugia and spent a year in an enemy prison. Illness followed and after a series of holy visions he decided to renounce his possessions and live a humble life in imitation of Christ, preaching and helping the poor. He travelled widely, performing miracles (curing the sick, communicating with animals) and establishing monasteries until his death in 1226. He was canonised two years later. Today, various places claim links with the saint, including Gubbio where he supposedly brokered a deal between the townsfolk and a man-eating wolf, and Rome where Pope Innocent III allowed him to found the Franciscan order at the Basilica di San Giovanni in Laterano.

Three kilometres north of town in dense woodland, the Franciscan hermitage called **Eremo Francescano Le Celle** sits next to a picturesque stream. It's a wonderfully tranquil spot, disturbed only by the bells calling the resident friars to mass in the cave-like **Chiesa Cella di San Francesco**.

The Drive: The 1¾-hour drive to the Santuario della Verna takes you deep into the heart of the

Castello dei Conti Guidi

MARCO TALIANI DE MARCHIO/SHUTTERSTOCK

Casentino hills. From Cortona head north on the SR71. About 25km beyond Arezzo, in Rassina, follow signs right and continue up the densely wooded slopes to Chiusi della Verna. The sanctuary is about 3km above Chiusi.

04 Santuario della Verna

St Francis of Assisi is said to have received the stigmata at the **Santuario della Verna** *(laverna.it)* on the southeastern edge of the **Parco Nazionale delle Foreste Casentinesi Monte Falterona e Campigna** *(parcoforestecasentinesi.it)*. The sanctuary, which is dramatically positioned on a windswept mountainside, holds some fine glazed ceramics by Andrea Della Robbia and his studio, including a magnificent *Crucifixion* in the **Cappella delle Stimmate**, the 13th-century chapel built on the spot where the saint supposedly received the stigmata.

The Drive: Allow about 45 minutes to Poppi from the sanctuary. The first leg, along the SP208, winds through the lush tree-covered mountains to Bibbiena, from where it's an easy 5km north on the SR71. You'll know you're near when you see Poppi's castle up on your left.

PHOTO OPPORTUNITY

The towered castle at Poppi.

05 Poppi

Perched high above the Arno plain, Poppi is crowned by the **Castello dei Conti Guidi**. Inside the 13th-century structure, you'll find a fairy-tale courtyard, a library full of medieval manuscripts, and a chapel with frescoes by Taddeo Gaddi, including a gruesome depiction of *Herod's Feast* with a dancing Salome and headless John the Baptist.

The Drive: Camaldoli is about 13km from Poppi. Take SP67 (Via Camaldoli) and follow it up through the forest until you come to a fork in the road – the hermitage is uphill to the right; the monastery is downhill to the left.

06 Monastero & Sacro Eremo di Camaldoli

The 11th-century **Sacro Eremo e Monastero di Camaldoli** *(camaldoli.it)* sits immersed in thick forest on the southern fringes of the Parco Nazionale delle Foreste Casentinesi Monte Falterona e Campigna. Home to a small group of Benedictine monks, it has some wonderful art; in the monastery's church you'll find three paintings by Vasari: *Deposition from the Cross; Virgin with Child, St John the Baptist & St Girolamo;* and a Nativity. At the hermitage, the small church harbours an exquisite altarpiece by Andrea Della Robbia.

For a souvenir, pop into the 16th-century **pharmacy** and pick up soap, perfumes and other items made by the resident monks.

The Drive: From the Monastero di Camaldoli, it's a 1½-hour drive to the Florentine monastery now housing the Museo di San Marco. From Camaldoli, double back along the SP67 and then head west along the SR70 through Poppi and then over the Passo della Consuma, a scenic mountain pass in the Tuscan section of the Apennine mountains, before following the river Arno through Pontassieve and into Florence's historic centre.

07 Museo di San Marco, Florence

This 15th-century Dominican monastery located next to the Chiesa di San Marco in the Florentine neighbourhood of the same name is one of the city's most spiritually uplifting museums, showcasing frescoes by Fra' Angelico ('Il Beato Angelico', or 'The Blessed Angelic One'), an artist and monk who was made a saint by Pope John Paul II in 1984. Major works here include Fra' Angelico's haunting *Annunciation* (c 1440) on the staircase leading to the monks' cells, one of the best-loved of all Renaissance artworks.

22

CENTRAL ITALY

GREEN HEART OF ITALY

DURATION: 4-5 DAYS

DISTANCE: 309KM/192 MILES

GREAT FOR: HISTORY, FOOD AND DRINK, NATURE

BEST TIME TO GO: JUNE TO SEPTEMBER FOR WILDFLOWERS, ARTS FESTIVALS AND HIKING.

★ BEST FOR

FOODIES

Veal-stuffed *olive all'ascolana* in its hometown, Ascoli Piceno.

Olive all'ascolana

From otherworldly caves to the wild green peaks of the Monti Sibillini, this trip weaves through the rural heartland of Umbria and Le Marche. Few places are as off the beaten track as this swath of central Italy. Here small rural roads run past sun-ripened wheat fields while dark mountains brood in the distance and medieval hill towns cling onto wooded slopes. But it's not all nature and stunning scenery – there's also culture aplenty with several fine art galleries, striking basilicas and opera in the summer sun.

LINK YOUR TRIP

23 Piero della Francesca Trail
Some 62km north of Gubbio, Urbino is the starting point for this art-lovers's pilgrimage through Tuscany.

21 Monasteries of Tuscany & Umbria
Head west from Perugia to join this tour of monasteries in the forests and forgotten mountains of Tuscany and Umbria.

01 Perugia

With a pristine medieval centre and an international student population, Perugia is Umbria's largest and most cosmopolitan city. Its *centro storico*, seemingly little changed in more than 400 years, rises in a helter-skelter of cobbled alleys, arched stairways and piazzas framed by solemn churches and magnificent Gothic palazzi.

Flanking the main strip, **Corso Vannucci**, the 14th-century Gothic **Palazzo dei Priori** was the headquarters of the local magistracy, but now houses Umbria's foremost art gallery, the **Galleria Nazionale dell'Umbria** *(gallerianazionaledellumbria.it)* and its impressive collection of Italian masterpieces. Of particular note are the Renaissance works of hometown heroes Pinturicchio and Perugino. Also in the Palazzo is the **Nobile Collegio del Cambio** (*Exchange Hall; collegiodelcambio.it*),

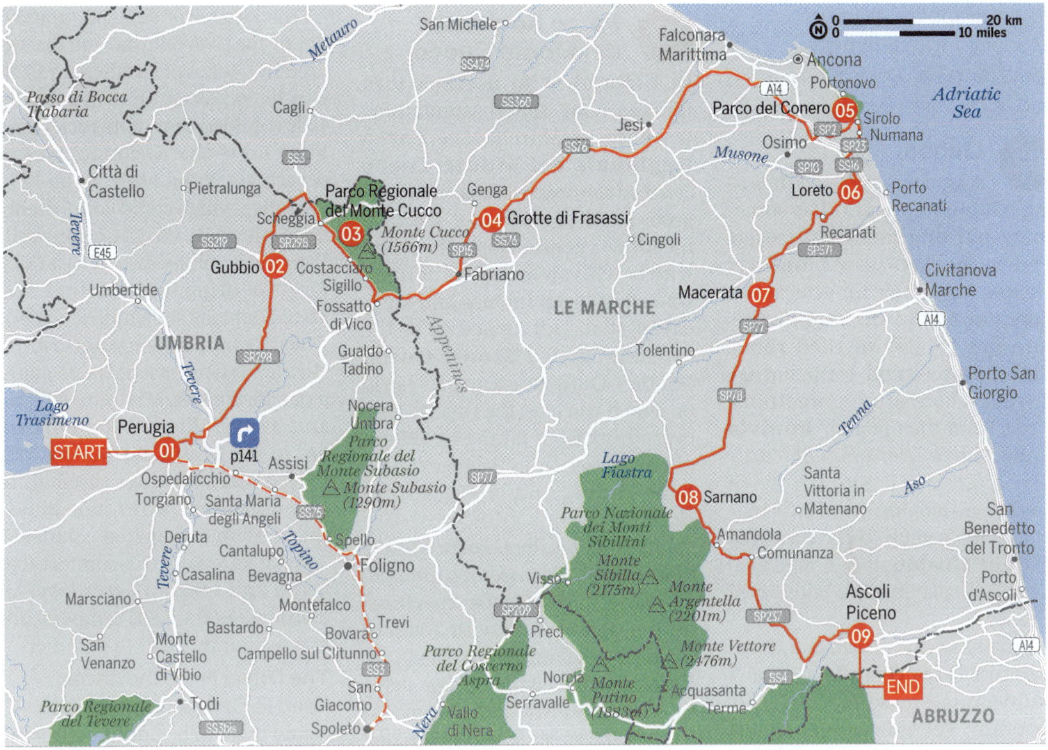

home to yet more Perugino paintings. At the end of Corso Vannucci, **Piazza IV Novembre** is a local hang-out where people gather to chat, soak up the sun and watch street entertainers in the shadow of the city's cathedral, the **Cattedrale di San Lorenzo**.

The Drive: From east of town pick up the northbound SS3bis and after less than a kilometre bear right onto the SR298. This easy-going country road climbs and twists and turns through verdant hills and past cultivated fields up to Gubbio. Although it's only 42km you should allow about an hour for the drive.

DETOUR

Spoleto

Start: 01 Perugia

Presided over by a formidable medieval fortress and backed by the broad-shouldered Apennines, their summits iced with snow in winter, the hill town of Spoleto is visually stunning.

At its heart is the pretty, pale-stone **Duomo** (Cattedrale di Santa Maria Assunta; *duomo spoleto.it*), originally built in the 11th century and subsequently enriched by the addition of a Renaissance portico in the 15th century. Inside, marvel at a rainbow swirl of mosaic frescoes by Filippo Lippi and assistants.

For a different view of things, head up to the **Rocca Albornoziana**, a glowering 14th-century former papal fortress that now houses the **Museo Nazionale del Ducato**, a small museum dedicated to the Duchy of Spoleto.

Before leaving town, make sure to photograph the medieval **Ponte delle Torri**, a 10-arch bridge that leaps spectacularly across a steeply wooded gorge – a scene beautifully captured by Turner in his 1840 oil painting.

Spoleto is worth visiting any time, but come in summer and you'll find it a hive of cultural activity as it hosts the mammoth, 17-day **Festival dei Due Mondi** *(festivaldispoleto.it)*. To get to Spoleto, it's a 65km drive south from Perugia via the SS75 and SS3.

02 Gubbio

Angular, sober and imposing, Gubbio appears like something out of a medieval fresco. Tightly packed grey buildings cluster together on the steep slopes of Monte Ingino in a picturesque jumble of tiled roofs, Gothic towers and 14th-century turrets. There are unforgettable views from the open-air **Funivia Colle Eletto** *(funiviagubbio.it)* – like a glorified ski lift with precarious-looking metal baskets – as it hauls you up to the **Basilica di Sant'Ubaldo**, a fine medieval church displaying the body of St Ubaldo.

Once back on terra firma, head over to **Piazza Grande**, Gubbio's panoramic showpiece square, to enjoy yet more panoramas and visit the **Museo Civico** *(palazzodeiconsoli.it)*. Occupying the 14th-century Palazzo dei Consoli, this museum has a picture gallery, archaeological artefacts and, most notably, seven bronze tablets known as the Iguvine Tablets (also called the Eugubian Tablets). These are considered the best existing samples of ancient Umbrian script.

The Drive: The 19km drive to Costacciaro takes you east to the Parco Regionale del Monte Cucco, via the SR298 and spectacular SS3. This scenic road winds down the western fringes of the park, with mood-lifting views on almost every corner, passing quaint mountain hamlets and woods where wolves, lynx and wild boar roam.

03 Parco Regionale del Monte Cucco

In Umbria's wild northeastern fringes near the regional border with Le Marche, the **Parco Regionale del Monte Cucco** *(parcodelmontecucco.it)* is a gorgeous swath of wildflower-speckled meadows, gentle slopes brushed with beech, yew and silver fir trees, waterfalls, deep ravines and karst cave systems, all topped off by the oft-snowcapped **Monte Cucco** (1566m). Outdoor escapades beckon, and if you have the time, there's everything from hiking on 120km of waymarked trails to horse riding, hang-gliding and cross-country skiing.

A highlight is the **Grotta Monte Cucco** *(grottamontecucco.umbria.it)*, one of Europe's most spectacular limestone caves, with 30km of galleries reaching depths of 900m. Those up for a challenge can delve into its underground forest of stalactites and stalagmites on a guided two- to three-hour 'discovery' tour. For more details on the caves and park, stop by the info point in the village of **Costacciaro**.

The Drive: Push on down the park's western flank on the SS3 to pick up the eastbound SS76 near Fossato di Vico. Continue on this fast road to Fabriano where you'll need to join the SP15. Head on to Frazione Pianello near Genga where a right will lead on to the Grotte. All in, it's about 40km.

04 Grotte di Frasassi

Further subterranean displays await at the **Grotte di Frasassi** *(frasassi.com)*, one of Europe's largest cave systems, near the village of Genga.

This karst wonderland, gouged out by the river Sentino and discovered by a team of climbers in 1971, can be explored on a 75-minute, 1.5km guided tour of its rock stars. First up is the Ancona Abyss, a cavernous 200m-high, 180m-long chamber, which could comfortably accommodate Milan cathedral. Your gaze will be drawn to a fairy forest of dripping stalactites and giant 20m-long stalagmites, some of which took 1.4 million years to form. Highlights here include the Niagara, a petrified cascade of pure calcite, and a crystallised lake. Further on, in the Gran Canyon, look out for parallel stalactites resembling pipe organs and waxy stalagmites that rise up like melted candles.

Make sure to wear comfortable shoes and take an extra layer of clothing, as the 14°C temperature can feel nippy, even in summer.

The Drive: From the caves, head to Camponocecchio to rejoin the SS76. Continue northeast on this dual carriageway as it traverses farmland to pick up the southbound A14 *autostrada* near Chiaravalle. Push on towards Pescara until the Ancona-Sud Osimo exit. From there take the SP2 to Sirolo in the Parco del Conero, some 75km from the Grotte.

05 Parco Del Conero

Just south of Ancona, Le Marche's main city and port, the Parco del Conero *(parcodelconero.org)* has a stunning stretch of coastline. Limestone cliffs soar above the cobalt-blue Adriatic as crescent-shaped, white pebble bays hide behind fragrant woods of pine, oak, beech, broom and oleander trees. Walking trails thread through the

Parco Nazionale dei Monti Sibillini (p145)
MNSTUDIO/SHUTTERSTOCK

60-sq-km regional park, which is remarkably still off the radar for many travellers and retains a peaceful, unspoilt air found nowhere else along Le Marche's coast. Its highest peak is the 572m-high **Monte Conero**, which takes a spectacular nosedive into the sea and provides fertile soil for the vineyards that taper down its slopes, giving rise to the excellent, full-bodied Rosso Conero red wine. In the south of the park, the cliff-backed resort of **Sirolo** is one of several that makes a fine base for exploring the area. A boat trip is the best way to cove hop.

The Drive: It's just short of 15km to Loreto. South of Sirolo pick up the SP23 and head inland. It's a slow, country drive, past hedgerows and sunflower fields, to near Crocette where you should turn left onto the SS16 and follow signs to Loreto.

PHOTO OPPORTUNITY

The plunging coastline around Sirolo in the Parco del Conero.

06 Loreto

Straddling a hilltop and visible from miles around, Loreto is dominated by the domed **Basilica della Santa Casa** *(www.santuarioloreto.va)*. This magnificent sanctuary, built between 1469 and 1587, is a stunning hybrid of Gothic and Renaissance architectural styles. Inside, the chief focus is the Santa Casa di Loreto, a tiny brick house that's said to be where the Virgin Mary grew up. Each year, thousands of pilgrims flock to the Casa, now enclosed in an ornately sculpted marble screen by Bramante, to glimpse a bejewelled black statue of the Virgin and pray in the candlelit twilight. According to legend, a host of angels brought the house from Nazareth in 1294 after the Crusaders were expelled from Palestine.

The Drive: More back-country roads await on the 28km stretch to Macerata. From Loreto head south to pick up the SP571. Continue on to Fontenoce where you should bear left onto the SP77, which will take you to the village of Sambucheto. Go left here and continue on the bucolic green scenery to Macerata.

07 Macerata

Straddling low-rise hills, Macerata combines charming hill-town scenery with the verve of student life – its university is one of Europe's oldest, dating

View from Monte Conero

TRABANTOS/SHUTTERSTOCK

to 1290. Its old town, a jumbled maze of cobblestone streets and honey-coloured palazzi, springs to life in summer for the month-long **Macerata Opera Festival** *(sferisterio.it)*, one of Italy's foremost musical events during which big-name opera stars take to the stage at the stunning outdoor **Arena Sferisterio** *(musei.macerata.it)*.

Of the numerous Renaissance palazzi in the *centro storico*, the **Loggia dei Mercanti** stands out. An arcaded building commissioned for Cardinal Alessandro Farnese and built in 1505, it originally housed travelling merchants selling their wares. A short walk away, the fabulous **Musei Civici di Palazzo Buonaccorsi** *(macerata musei.it)* harbour an eclectic collection of horse-drawn carriages and artworks. A real highlight are the dynamic paintings of Ivo Pannaggi, one of the driving forces behind Italian futurism in the 1920s and '30s.

The Drive: Exit Macerata and head south on the SP77 to Sforzacosta where you'll need to hook up with the SP78. Continue southwards, past the ancient Roman ruins of Urbs Salvia, and on to Sarnano, 40km away.

08 Sarnano

Spilling photogenically down a hillside, its medieval heart a maze of narrow cobbled lanes, Sarnano looks every inch the prototype Italian hill town, particularly when its red-brick facades glow warmly in the late-afternoon sun. There are no must-see sights but it makes a charming, hospitable base for exploring the Monti Sibillini range, much of which is encompassed in the **Parco Nazionale dei Monti Sibillini** *(sibillini.net)*. Sarnano is also the main gateway to the **Sassotetto-Santa Maria Maddalena ski resort**, about 15km to the west. In winter, alpine and cross-country skiing, snowboarding and snowshoeing are all available on its 11km of pistes. In warmer weather you can take to the hills on 100km of waymarked hiking and cycling trails. For more dramatic thrills, Sarnano is also a popular paragliding site.

The Drive: Driving this 50km leg you'll understand why this part of Italy is referred to as the country's green heart. The SP237 runs past overhanging trees and overgrown hedgerows before opening up to reveal wooded peaks as far as the eye can see. Continue for about 46km and then join the eastbound SS4 for the last few kilometres into Ascoli.

PARCO NAZIONALE DEI MONTI SIBILLINI

Straddling the Le Marche–Umbria border in rugged splendour, the wild and wonderfully unspoiled Parco Nazionale dei Monti Sibillini *(sibillini.net)* never looks less than extraordinary, whether visited in winter, when its peaks are dusted with snow, or in summer, when its highland meadows are carpeted with poppies and cornflowers.

The 700-sq-km park has some of central Italy's most dramatic landscapes, with great glacier-carved valleys, beautifully preserved hilltop hamlets, beech forests where deer roam, and mountains, 10 of which tower above 2000m.

The park is a magnet for hikers and outdoor enthusiasts, with an expansive network of walking trails, mountain-biking circuits and a series of summer *rifugi* (mountain huts) offering basic accommodation. Most trails are now open after the 2016 earthquakes but a number of *rifugi* remain closed – check the park website for updates.

09 Ascoli Piceno

The charming town of Ascoli Piceno marks the end of the road. With a continuous history dating from the 9th century BCE, it's like the long-lost cousin of ancient Rome and a small Marchigiani village, heavy on history and food – it's famous as the birthplace of Italy's much-loved *olive all'ascolana* (veal-stuffed fried olives).

In the centre of town, the harmonious and lovely **Piazza del Popolo** has been Ascoli's *salotto* (drawing room) since Roman times. An elegant rectangular square, it's flanked by the 13th-century **Palazzo dei Capitani del Popolo** and the beautiful **Chiesa di San Francesco**. Virtually annexed to the church is the **Loggia dei Mercanti**, built in the 16th century by the powerful guild of wool merchants to hide their rough-and-tumble artisan shops. To finish on a high note, Ascoli's fine **Pinacoteca** *(ascolimusei.it)* holds an outstanding display of art, sculpture, and religious artefacts including paintings by Titian, Carlo Crivelli and Guido Reni.

23

CENTRAL ITALY

PIERO DELLA FRANCESCA TRAIL

★ BEST FOR

FILM BUFFS

Arezzo's Piazza Grande, a location for scenes in *La vita è bella* (Life Is Beautiful).

Arezzo (p148)

DURATION: 7 DAYS

DISTANCE: 185KM/115 MILES

GREAT FOR: HISTORY

BEST TIME TO GO: JUNE TO SEPTEMBER FOR SUMMER PAGEANTRY.

Follow in the footsteps of the Renaissance painter Piero della Francesca as you wind your way from medieval Urbino to Florence, admiring his greatest works en route. The trail was first advocated by British author Aldous Huxley in *The Best Picture*, a 1925 essay he wrote in praise of Della Francesca's *Resurrezione* (Resurrection). The roads have improved since Huxley's day but the trail remains a labour of love for art fans.

LINK YOUR TRIP

24 Tuscan Wine Tour
From Florence head south on the SR222 to the Castello di Verrazzano, one of the historic Chianti vineyards on this classic wine tour.

26 Foodie Emilia-Romagna
Head 125km north from Urbino via the A14 *autostrada* to connect with Ravenna and this tasty trip through Emilia-Romagna.

01 Urbino

Hidden away in hilly Le Marche, the charming town of Urbino was a key player in the Renaissance art world. Its ruler, the Duca Federico da Montefeltro, was a major patron and many of the top artists and intellectuals of the day spent time here at his behest. Piero della Francesca arrived in 1469 and, along with a crack team of artists and architects, worked on the duke's palatial residence, the Palazzo Ducale. This magnificent palace now houses the **Galleria Nazionale delle Marche** *(gndm.it)* and its rich collection of Renaissance paintings, including Piero della Francesca's great *Flagellazione di Cristo* (Flagellation of Christ).

A short walk away, you can pay homage to Urbino's greatest son at the **Casa Natale di Raffaello** *(casaraffaello.com)*, the house where superstar painter Raphael was born in 1483.

The Drive: The 50km (one-hour) drive up to the Passo di Bocca

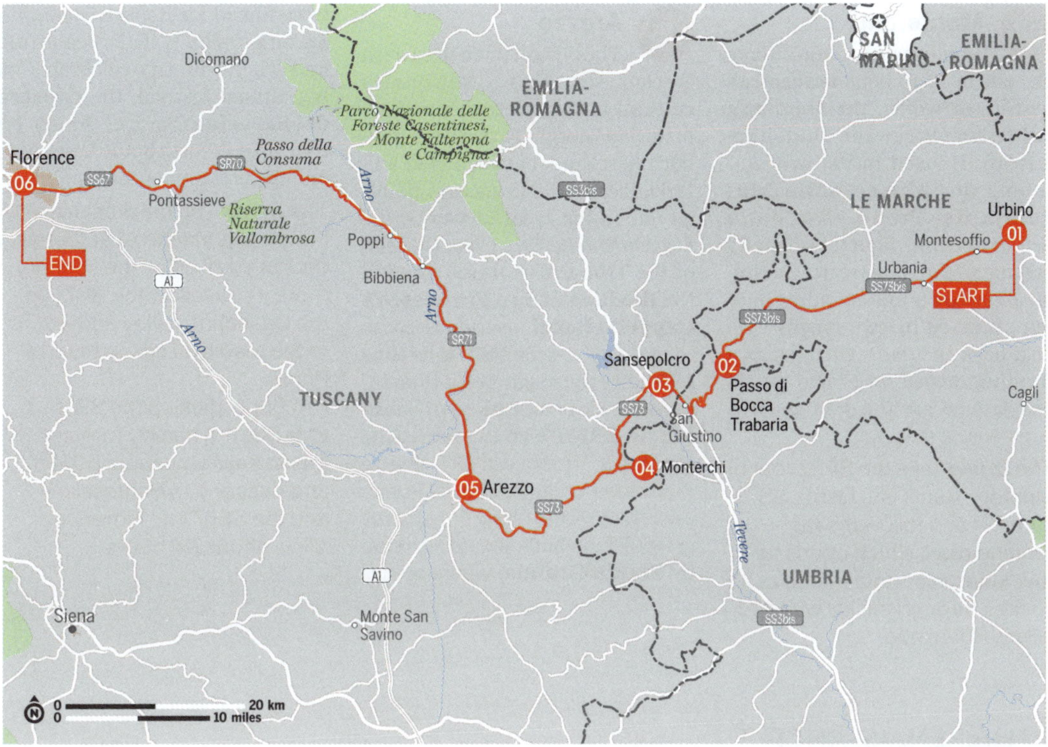

MASSIMO SANTI/SHUTTERSTOCK

Trabaria involves multiple of hairpin bends and tortuous climbing as it traverses a magnificent stretch of Apennine mountains. From Urbino pick up the SS73bis and head through Montesoffio and Urbania before climbing up to the pass.

02 Passo di Bocca Trabaria

The Bocca Trabaria mountain pass (1049m) divides the Valtiberina (Tiber valley), on the Urbino side, from the upper Valle del Metauro (Metauro valley).

It's a spectacular spot, well worth a quick pause, with sweeping views over the Apennines and several hiking trails heading into the surrounding mountains.

The Drive: Allow about half an hour for the 20km descent from Bocca Trabaria to Sansepolcro. For the first 15km or so the meandering road plunges down the valley slopes to San Giustino, from where it's an easy hop northwest to Sansepolcro.

03 Sansepolcro

Sansepolcro the birthplace of Piero della Francesca and home to two of his greatest works. Its unspoiled historic centre is also littered with palazzi and churches harbouring great works of art, including the 14th-century **Cattedrale di San Giovanni Evangelista**, which contains an *Ascension* by Perugino. The highlight, though, is the **Museo Civico** *(www.museocivicosansepolcro.it)*, whose small but top-notch collection includes Della Francesca's *Resurrection* (1458–74) and *Madonna della Misericordia* (Madonna of Mercy) polyptych (1445–56) as well as two fresco fragments portraying *San Ludovico* (St Ludovic, 1460) and *San Giuliano* (St Julian, 1460).

The Drive: Head southwest from Sansepolcro along the SS73 following signs for Arezzo. After roughly 12km of easy driving through pleasant green countryside, turn left onto the SP42 and continue for 3km to Monterchi. It takes about 25 minutes.

04 Monterchi

This unassuming village has one of Piero della Francesca's best-loved works, the *Madonna del Parto* (Pregnant Madonna, c 1460). Housed in its own museum, the **Museo della Madonna del Parto** *(madonnadelparto.it)*, it depicts a heavily pregnant Madonna wearing a simple blue gown and standing in a tent, flanked by two angels who hold back the tent's curtains as a framing device. In a nice touch, people who are pregnantget free entry to the museum.

The Drive: Take the SP221 out of Monterchi until you hit the SS73. Turn left and follow the fast-running road, which opens to four lanes in certain tracts, as it snakes through thickly wooded hills up to Arezzo.

05 Arezzo

The biggest town in eastern Tuscany, Arezzo has a distinguished cultural history. Petrarch and art historian Giorgio Vasari were both born here, and, between 1452 and 1466, Piero della Francesca painted one of his greatest works, the *Leggenda della Vera Croce* (Legend of the True Cross) fresco cycle in the **Basilica di San Francesco's Cappella Bacci** *(museiarezzo.it)*.

Once you've seen that, take time to admire the magnificent Romanesque facade of the **Chiesa di Santa Maria della Pieve** en route to the **Duomo** (Cattedrale di SS Donato e Pietro) and yet another della Francesca fresco – his *Mary Magdalene* (c 1460). Film buffs should also stop by **Piazza Grande**, where scenes were filmed for Roberto Benigni's *La vita è bella* (Life Is Beautiful), and where the city celebrates its big annual festival, the **Giostra del Saracino** (Saracen Joust), on the third or fourth Saturday of June and the first Sunday of September.

The Drive: The quickest route to Florence is via the A1 *autostrada*, but you'll enjoy the scenery more if you follow the SR71 up the Casentino valley and on to the medieval castle town of Poppi.

At Poppi pick up the SR70 to tackle the heavily forested Passo della Consuma (1050m) and descend to Pontassieve and the SS67 into Florence. Allow about 2¾ hours.

THE RENAISSANCE

Bridging the gap between the Middle Ages and the modern world, the Renaissance *(il Rinascimento)* emerged in 14th-century Florence and quickly spread throughout Italy.

The Early Days

Giotto di Bondone (1267–1337) is generally considered the first great Renaissance artist, and with his exploration of perspective and a new interest in realistic portraiture, he inspired artists such as Lorenzo Ghiberti (1378–1455) and Donatello (c 1382–1466).

In architectural terms, the key man was Filippo Brunelleschi (1377–1446), whose dome on Florence's Duomo was one of the era's blockbuster achievements.

Of the following generation, Sandro Botticelli (c 1444–1510) was a major player and his *Birth of Venus* (c 1485) was one of the most successful attempts to resolve the great conundrum of the age – how to give a painting both a realistic perspective and a harmonious composition.

The High Renaissance

By the early 16th century, the focus had shifted to Rome and Venice.

Leading the way in Rome was Donato Bramante (1444–1514), whose classical architectural style greatly influenced the Veneto-born Andrea Palladio (1508–80).

One of Bramante's great rivals was Michelangelo Buonarrotti (1475–1564), whose legendary genius was behind the Sistine Chapel frescoes, the dome over St Peter's Basilica, and the *David* sculpture.

Other headline acts included Leonardo da Vinci (1452–1519), who developed a painting technique *(sfumato)* enabling him to modulate his contours using colour, and Raphael (1483–1520), who more than any other painter mastered the art of depicting large groups of people in a realistic and harmonious way.

CLAUDIO GIOVANNI COLOMBO/SHUTTERSTOCK

PHOTO OPPORTUNITY

Views from the Passo della Consuma.

Passo della Consuma

06 Florence

The last port of call is Florence, the city where the Renaissance kicked off in the 14th century. Paying the way was the Medici family, who sponsored the great artists of the day and whose collection today graces the **Galleria degli Uffizi** *(uffizi.it)*.

Here you can admire Piero della Francesca's famous portrait of the red-robed *Duke and Duchess of Urbino* (1465–72) alongside works by Renaissance giants, from Giotto and Cimabue to Botticelli, Leonardo da Vinci, Raphael and Titian. Elsewhere in town, you'll find spiritually uplifting works by Fra' Angelico in the wonderful **Museo di San Marco,** and superb frescoes by Masaccio, Masolino da Panicale and Filippino Lippi at the **Cappella Brancacci** *(cultura.comune.fi.it/musei)*, over the river in the **Basilica di Santa Maria del Carmine**. The historic centre is a great place to explore on foot.

PIERO DELLA FRANCESCA

Though many details are hazy, it's believed that Piero della Francesca was born around 1415 in Sansepolcro and died in 1492. Trained as a painter from the age of 15, his use of perspective, mastery of light and synthesis of form and colour set him apart from his contemporaries. His most famous works are the *Leggenda della Vera Croce* (Legend of the True Cross) in Arezzo, and *Resurrezione* (Resurrection) in Sansepolcro, but he is most fondly remembered for his luminous *Madonna del Parto* (Pregnant Madonna) in Monterchi.

24

CENTRAL ITALY

TUSCAN WINE TOUR

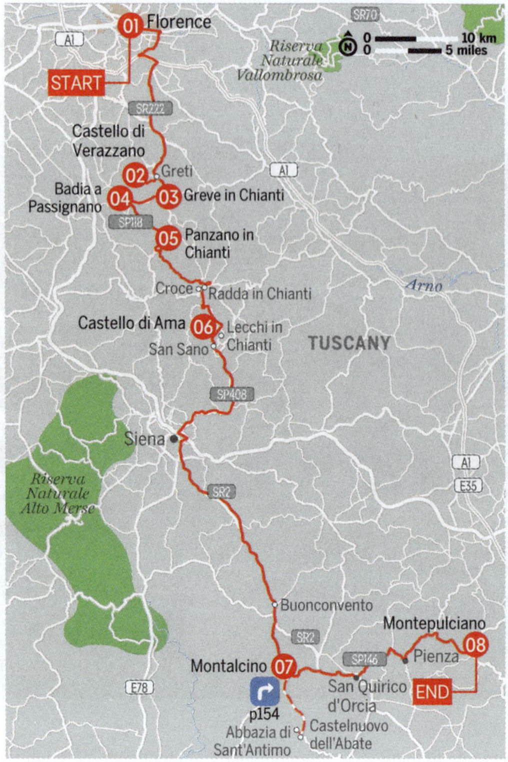

DURATION: 4 DAYS

DISTANCE: 185KM/115 MILES

GREAT FOR: WINE

BEST TIME TO GO: AUTUMN FOR EARTHY HUES AND THE GRAPE HARVEST.

Tuscany has its fair share of highlights, but few can match a drive through its wine country. This classic Chianti tour offers a taste of life in the slow lane. Once out of Florence, you'll find yourself on quiet back roads driving through wooded hills and immaculate vineyards, stopping off at estates and hilltop towns to try the local vintages. En route, you'll enjoy soul-stirring scenery, farmhouse food and some captivating towns.

LINK YOUR TRIP

23 Piero della Francesca Trail
Starting in Florence, you can join this trail of revered Renaissance frescoes.

26 Foodie Emilia-Romagna
Also from Florence, continue 120km north on the A1 to Bologna and a tour of Emilia-Romagna's great food towns.

01 Florence

Whet your appetite for the road ahead with a one-day cooking course at the **Cucina Lorenzo de' Medici** *(cucinaldm.com)*, one of Florence's many cookery schools. Once you're done at the stove, sneak out to visit the **Chiesa e Museo di Orsanmichele**, an inspirational 14th-century church and one of Florence's lesser-known gems. Over the river, you can stock up on Tuscan wines and gourmet foods at **Obsequium** *(obsequium.it)*, a well-stocked wine shop on the ground floor of a medieval tower. Or, explore the old town on foot before you hit the road.

The Drive: From Florence it's about an hour to Verrazzano. Head south along the scenic SR222 (Via Chiantigiana) towards Greve. When you get to Greti, you'll see a shop selling wine from the Castello di Verrazzano and, just before it, a right turn up to the castle.

HLPHOTO/SHUTTERSTOCK

★ BEST FOR

FOODIES

Tuscan *bistecca* (steak) in Panzano in Chianti.

Tuscan bistecca (steak)

02 Castello di Verrazzano

Some 26km south of Florence, the **Castello di Verrazzano** *(verrazzano.com)* lords it over a 230-hectare estate where Chianti Classico, Vin Santo, grappa, honey, olive oil and balsamic vinegar are produced. In a previous life, the castle was home to Giovanni di Verrazzano (1485–1528), an adventurer who explored the North American coast and is commemorated in New York by the Verrazzano-Narrows bridge linking Staten Island to Brooklyn.

At the *castello* (castle), you can choose from a range of guided tours, which include a tasting and can also include lunch with the estate wines. Book ahead.

The Drive: From the *castello* it's a simple 10-minute drive to Greve in Chianti. Double back to the SR222 in Greti, turn right and follow for about 3km.

03 Greve in Chianti

The main town in the Chianti Fiorentino, the northernmost of the two Chianti districts, Greve in Chianti has been an important wine centre for centuries. It has an amiable market-town air, and several eateries and *enoteche* (wine bars) that showcase the best Chianti food and drink. To stock up on picnic supplies, head to **Antica Macelleria Falorni** *(falorni.it)*, an atmospheric butcher's shop-bistro that the Bencistà Falorni family has been running since the early 19th century and which specialises in delicious *finocchiona briciolona* (pork salami made with fennel seeds and Chianti wine). The family also runs the **Enoteca Falorni**, the town's top cellar, where you can sample all sorts of local wine.

The Drive: From Greve turn off the main through road, Viale Giovanni di Verrazzano, near the Esso petrol station, and head up towards Montefioralle. Continue on as the road climbs past olive groves and through woods to Badia a Passignano, about 15 minutes away.

04 Badia a Passignano

Encircled by cypress trees and surrounded by swaths of olive groves and vineyards, the 11th-century

Chiesa di San Michele Arcangelo at Passignano sits at the heart of a historic wine estate run by the Antinoris, one of Tuscany's oldest and most prestigious winemaking families. The estate offers a range of guided tours, tastings and cookery courses. Most require prior booking, but you can just turn up at the estate's wine shop, **La Bottega** *(osteriadipassignano.com)*, to taste and buy Antinori wines and olive oil.

The Drive: From Badia a Passignano, double back towards Greve and pick up the signposted SP118 for a pleasant 15-minute drive along the narrow tree-shaded road to Panzano.

05 Panzano in Chianti

The quiet medieval town of Panzano is an essential stop on any gourmet's tour of Tuscany. Here you can stock up on meaty picnic fare at **L'Antica Macelleria Cecchini** *(dariocecchini.com)*, a celebrated butcher's shop run by the poetry-spouting guru of Tuscan meat, Dario Cecchini. Alternatively, you can dine at one of his three eateries: the **Officina della Bistecca**, which serves a simple set menu based on *bistecca* (steak); **Solociccia**, where guests share a communal table to sample meat dishes other than *bistecca*; and **Cecchini Panini Truck**, a casual daytime option. Book ahead for the Officina and Solociccia.

The Drive: From Panzano, it's about 20km to the Castello di Ama. Strike south on the SR222

WINE TASTING GOES HIGH TECH

One of Tuscany's biggest cellars, the **Enoteca Falorni** *(enotecafalorni.it)* in Greve in Chianti stocks more than 1000 labels, of which around 100 are available for tasting. It's a lovely, brick-arched place, but wine tasting here is a very modern experience, thanks to a sophisticated wine-dispensing system that preserves wine in an open bottle for up to three weeks and allows tasters to serve themselves by the glass. Leave your credit card as a guarantee or buy a nonrefundable prepaid wine card (€5 to €100) to test your tipples of choice at the various 'tasting islands' dotted around the cellar. Curated tastings are also available.

Enoteca Falorni (p151)

KATUKA/SHUTTERSTOCK

towards Radda in Chianti, enjoying views off to the right as you wend your way through the green countryside. At Croce, just beyond Radda, turn left and head towards Lecchi and San Sano. The Castello di Ama is signposted after a further 7km.

06 Castello di Ama

To indulge in some contemporary-art appreciation between wine tastings, make for **Castello di Ama** *(castellodiama.com)* near Lecchi. This highly regarded wine estate produces a fine Chianti Classico and has an original sculpture park showcasing 14 site-specific works by artists including Louise Bourgeois, Chen Zhen, Anish Kapoor, Kendell Geers and Daniel Buren. Book ahead.

The Drive: Reckon on about 1½ hours to Montalcino from the **Castello di Ama**. Double back to the SP408 and head south to Lecchi and then on towards Siena. Skirt around the east of Siena and pick up the SR2 (Via Cassia) to Buonconvento and hilltop Montalcino, off to the right of the main road.

07 Montalcino

Montalcino, a pretty medieval town perched above the Val d'Orcia, is home to one of Italy's great wines, Brunello di Montalcino (and the more modest, but still very palatable, Rosso di Montalcino). There are plenty of *enoteche* where you can taste and buy, including one in the **Fortezza**, the 14th-century fortress that dominates the town's skyline.

For a historical insight into the town's winemaking past, head to the **Museo della Comunità di Montalcino e del Brunello** *(fattoriadeibarbi.it/museo-del-brunello)*, a small museum at

FRANCESCO LORENZETTI/SHUTTERSTOCK

Brunello di Montalcino

TUSCAN REDS

Something of a viticultural powerhouse, Tuscany excites wine buffs with its myriad full-bodied, highly respected reds. Like all Italian wines, these are classified according to strict guidelines, with the best denominated Denominazione di Origine Controllata e Garantita (DOCG), followed by Denominazione di Origine Controllata (DOC) and Indicazione di Geografica Tipica (IGT).

Chianti Cheery, full and dry, contemporary Chianti gets the thumbs up from wine critics. Produced in eight subzones from Sangiovese and a mix of other grape varieties, Chianti Classico is the best known, with its Gallo Nero (Black Cockerel) emblem, which once symbolised the medieval Chianti League.

Brunello di Montalcino Brunello is among Italy's most prized wines. The product of Sangiovese grapes, it must be aged for a minimum of 24 months in oak barrels and four months in bottles, and cannot be released until five years after the vintage. Intense and complex with an ethereal fragrance, it is best paired with game, wild boar and roasts. Brunello grape rejects go into Rosso di Montalcino, Brunello's substantially cheaper but wholly drinkable kid sister.

Vino Nobile di Montepulciano Prugnolo Gentile grapes (a clone of Sangiovese) form the backbone of the distinguished Vino Nobile di Montepulciano. Its intense but delicate nose and dry, vaguely tannic taste make it the perfect companion to red meat and mature cheese.

Super Tuscans Developed in the 1970s, the Super Tuscans are wines that fall outside the traditional classification categories. They are often made with a combination of local and imported grape varieties, such as merlot and cabernet. Sassacaia, Solaia, Bolgheri, Tignanello and Luce are all super-hot Super Tuscans.

WHY I LOVE THIS TRIP

DUNCAN GARWOOD, WRITER

The best Italian wine I've ever tasted was a Brunello di Montalcino. I bought it directly from a producer after a tasting in the Val d'Orcia and it was a revelation. It was just so thrilling to be drinking wine in the place it had been made. And it's this, combined with the inspiring scenery and magnificent food, that makes this tour of Tuscan wineries so uplifting.

the Fattoria dei Barbi wine estate, one of the oldest in the region.

The Drive: From Montalcino, head downhill and then, after about 8km, turn onto the SR2. At San Quirico d'Orcia pick up the SP146, a fabulously scenic road that weaves along the Val d'Orcia through rolling green hills, past the pretty town of Pienza, to Montepulciano. Allow about an hour.

DETOUR

Abbazia di Sant'Antimo

Start: 07 Montalcino

The striking Romanesque **Abbazia di Sant'Antimo** *(antimo.it)* lies in an isolated valley just below the village of Castelnuovo dell'Abate, 10.5km from Montalcino.

According to tradition, Charlemagne founded the original monastery in 781.

The exterior, built in pale travertine stone, is simple but for the stone carvings, which include various fantastical animals.

Inside, look for the polychrome 13th-century *Madonna and Child* and 12th-century *Crucifixion* above the main altar. The abbey's church, crypt, upper loggia, chapel, pharmacy and garden can be visited with a rented video guide.

PHOTO OPPORTUNITY

Val di Chiana and Val d'Orcia panoramas from Montepulciano's upper town.

08 Montepulciano

Set atop a narrow ridge of volcanic rock, the Renaissance centre of Montepulciano produces the celebrated red wine Vino Nobile.

To sample it, head up the main street, called in stages Via di Gracciano nel Corso, Via di Voltaia del Corso and Via dell'Opio nel Corso, to the **Enoliteca Consortile** *(enolitecavinonobile.it)*, a modern tasting room operated by local wine producers.

Housed on the ground floor of the town's **Medicean fortress**, it offers over 70 wines for tasting and purchase.

Vineyard, Chianti
PETER ZELEI IMAGES/GETTY IMAGES

✔ TOP TIP

DRIVING IN CHIANTI

To cut down on driving stress, purchase a copy of *Le strade del Gallo Nero*, a useful map that shows major and secondary roads and has a comprehensive list of wine estates. It's available at the tourist office in Greve and at **Casa Chianti Classico** *(chianticlassico.com)*, the headquarters of the Consorzio di Chianti Classico in Radda.

STAY AWHILE

SIENA

BY GREGOR CLARK

Smack in the heart of Tuscany, Siena is one of Italy's most exquisitely preserved medieval towns. My perfect day here begins at **Panificio Il Magnifico** *(ilmagnifico.siena.it)* for a breakfast of cappuccino and *ricciarelli* – Siena's delightfully chewy, orange-zesty almond cookies. From here it's an easy stroll to Siena's star attraction, the gracefully sloping, seashell-shaped **Piazza del Campo**, paved in a herringbone pattern of red brick and travertine. Even after decades exploring Italy, I always feel a visceral thrill emerging from one of Siena's narrow alleyways into this vast and elegant public square.

For aerial perspectives, climb the **Torre del Mangia**, a pencil-thin 14th-century bell tower that commands bird's-eye views across the medieval centre to Siena's **Duomo** (cathedral), resplendent in candy-striped white and greenish-black marble. Next door, the crenellated, Gothic-arched **Palazzo Pubblico** abounds in frescoes offering insights into the Sienese worldview at the dawn of the Renaissance. I love Ambrogio Lorenzetti's allegorical cycle of Good and Bad Government, where Justice, Wisdom and Concord preside over thriving scenes of fertile farmland and industrious tradespeople, while on the adjacent wall, a horned tyrant sits surrounded by figures portraying Avarice, Vanity, Cruelty and Division. Equally engaging is Simone Martini's wall-sized equestrian portrait of Guidoriccio da Fogliano, celebrating his victory at the Siege of Montemassi against a backdrop of Tuscan towers and a deep cobalt sky – a reminder of the days when battles between Italian city-states were commonplace.

Surrounding Siena are some of Tuscany's most evocative landscapes, including the Chianti vineyards and the wheat fields and cypresses of the Crete Senesi. My favourite way to experience them is on foot along the **Via Francigena** *(viefrancigene.org)*, the ancient pilgrimage route to Rome that passes through the heart of town; with a car, you can reach either place in less than an hour.

LINK YOUR TRIP

Siena is the starting point of the grand **25 Tuscan Landscapes** road trip.

Left: Piazza del Campo; Right: Basilica di San Clemente

FROM LEFT: JON DAVISON/LONELY PLANET, TOMMASO LIZZUL/SHUTTERSTOCK

PLACES TO STAY

Albergo Bernini
With only 10 rooms, this family-run hotel in the northern end of the city centre makes for a cosy stay with beautiful terrace views. *(albergobernini.com)*

Hotel Santa Caterina
Located outside the historic centre, steps away from the Porta Romana, this small, welcoming hotel is great for those seeking peace and quiet. *(hotelsantacaterinasiena.com)*

Hotel Chiusarelli
Elegantly furnished, well positioned and a scrumptious breakfast to prepare you for long art-filled days. *(chiusarelli.com)*

Antica Residenza Cicogna
As the name suggests, this charming old hotel has its roots in the Middle Ages – don't worry, though, amenities have been elegantly updated since then. *(anticaresidenzacicogna.it)*

25

CENTRAL ITALY

TUSCAN LANDSCAPES

★ BEST FOR

RENAISSANCE ARCHITECTURE

Montepulciano's historic centre

Montepulciano (p160)

DURATION: 3–4 DAYS

DISTANCE: 160KM/99 MILES

GREAT FOR: FOOD AND DRINK, HISTORY

BEST TIME TO GO: MAY TO SEPTEMBER FOR BLUE SKIES AND FAB PHOTOS.

Ever since medieval pilgrims discovered Tuscany en route from Canterbury to Rome, the region has been captivating travellers. This trip strikes south from Siena, running through the Crete Senesi, an area of clay hills scored by deep ravines, to the UNESCO-listed Val d'Orcia, whose soothing hills and billowing plains are punctuated by delightful Renaissance towns. The end of the road is Orvieto, home to one of Italy's most feted Gothic cathedrals.

LINK YOUR TRIP

20 Etruscan Tuscany & Lazio
From Orvieto continue 20km southwest to Bolsena and join up with this Etruscan treasure hunt.

21 Monasteries of Tuscany & Umbria
Head east from Montepulciano along the SP438 to visit a string of ancient, isolated monasteries.

01 Siena

With its medieval palazzi and humbling Gothic architecture, Siena's historic centre is a sight to compare with any in Tuscany. To admire it from above, climb to the top of the **Torre del Mangia** *(museo civico.comune.siena.it)*, the slender 14th-century tower that rises above **Piazza del Campo**, and look down on a sea of red-tiled roofs and, beyond, to the green, undulating countryside that awaits you on this trip. At the foot of the tower, **Palazzo Pubblico** is a magnificent example of Sienese Gothic architecture and home to the city's best art museum, the **Museo Civico**.

To the southwest of Palazzo Pubblico, another inspiring spectacle awaits. Siena's 13th-century **Duomo** *(Cattedrale di Santa Maria Assunta; operaduomo.siena.it)* is one of Italy's greatest Gothic churches, and its magnificent facade of white, green and red polychrome marble is one you'll remember long after you've left town.

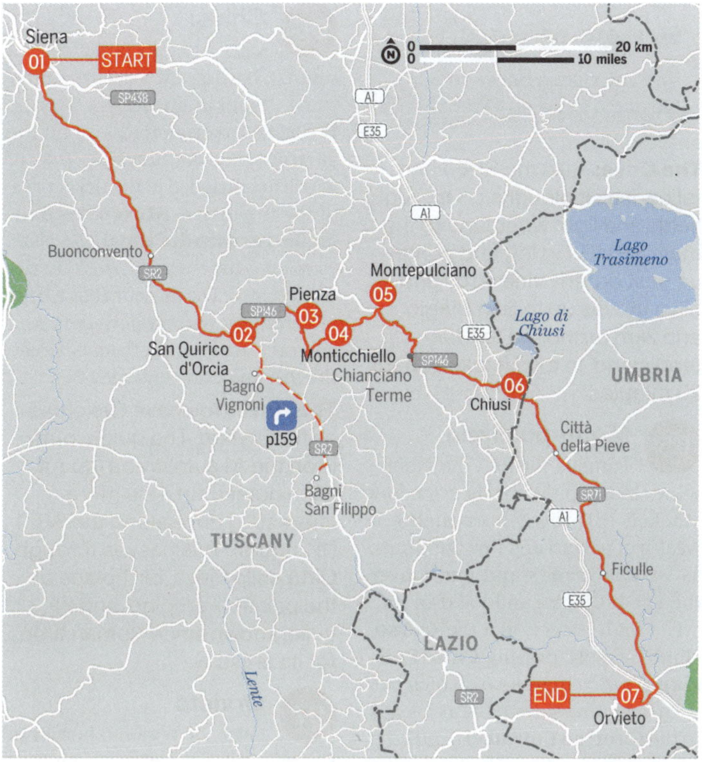

VUNAV/SHUTTERSTOCK

THE PALIO

Siena's Palio is one of Italy's most spectacular annual events. Dating from the Middle Ages, it comprises a series of colourful pageants and a wild horse race on 2 July and 16 August. Ten of Siena's 17 *contrade* (town districts) compete for the coveted *palio* (silk banner). From about 5pm, representatives from each *contrada* parade around the Campo in historical costume, all bearing their individual banners. Then, at 7.30pm in July and 7pm in August, the race gets the green light. For scarcely one exhilarating minute, the 10 horses and their bareback riders tear three times around the temporarily constructed dirt racetrack with a speed and violence that makes spectators' hair stand on end.

The Drive: The first leg to San Quirico d'Orcia, about an hour's drive, takes you down the scenic SR2 via the market town of Buonconvento. En route you'll pass cultivated fields and swaths of curvaceous green plains.

02 San Quirico d'Orcia

First stop in the UNESCO-protected Val d'Orcia is San Quirico d'Orcia. A fortified medieval town and one-time stopover on the Via Francigena pilgrim route between Canterbury and Rome, it's now a lovely, low-key village. There are no great must-see sights, but it's a pleasant place for a stroll, with a graceful Romanesque **Collegiata** (church) and formal Renaissance gardens known as the **Horti Leononi**.

The Drive: From San Quirico d'Orcia it's a quick 15-minute drive to Pienza along the SP146. This is one of the trip's most beautiful stretches, offering unfettered views over undulating grasslands peppered by stone farmhouses and lines of elegant cypress trees.

DETOUR

Bagno Vignoni & Bagni San Filippo

Start: 02 San Quirico d'Orcia

Some 9km south of San Quirico d'Orcia along the SR2 hot sulphurous water (around 49°C) bubbles up into a picturesque pool in the centre of Bagno Vignoni. You can't actually enter the pool, but there are various spa complexes offering a full range of treatments. For free hot-water frolics continue 18km further along the SR2 to the tiny village of Bagni San Filippo, where there are thermal cascades in an open-air reserve. You'll find these just uphill from Hotel le Terme – follow a sign marked 'Fosso Bianco' down a lane for about 150m and you'll come to a series of mini pools, fed by hot, tumbling cascades of water. Not unlike a free, alfresco spa, it's a pleasant if slightly whiffy spot for a picnic.

03 Pienza

One of the most popular tourist destinations in the Val d'Orcia, pint-sized Pienza has a Renaissance centre that has changed little since local boy Pope Pius II had it built between 1459 and 1462. Action is centred on Piazza Pio II, where the solemn **Duomo** (Concattedrale di Santa Maria Assunta) is flanked by two Renaissance palazzi – on the right, **Palazzo Piccolomini** (*palazzopiccolominipienza.it*), the former papal residence; on the left, **Palazzo Vescovile**, home to the **Museo Diocesano** (*palazzoborgia.it*) and an intriguing miscellany of artworks, manuscripts, tapestries and miniatures.

Before leaving town make sure you pick up some of the local *pecorino* (sheep's milk) for which the area is justly famous.

The Drive: From Pienza strike south on the SP18 and head into the heart of the countryside, enjoying more bucolic scenery as you go. After 6km or so you'll see a sign to Monticchiello off to the left. Take this road and continue for another 4km.

04 Monticchiello

A 15-minute drive southeast from Pienza brings you to Monticchiello, a sleepy medieval hilltop village with two good eateries. Choose between **Osteria La Porta** (*osterialaporta.it*), just inside the main gate, which has a small terrace with panoramic views of the Val d'Orcia; and stylish **Ristorante Daria** (*ristorantedaria.it*), a short walk away, which offers a menu of dishes that successfully marry rustic inspiration and refined execution.

> **PHOTO OPPORTUNITY**
>
> The Val d'Orcia between San Quirico d'Orcia and Pienza.

The Drive: Take the SP88 and follow it as it ploughs on through fields and light woodland to the main SP146. Go left and continue past orderly vineyards and olive groves up to San Biagio and 2km further on to Montepulciano. In total it takes about 20 minutes.

05 Montepulciano

Famous for its Vino Nobile wine, Montepulciano is a steeply stacked hill town harbouring a wealth of palazzi and fine buildings, as well as grandstand views over the Val di Chiana and Val d'Orcia.

The main street, aka the **Corso**, climbs steeply, passing **Caffè Poliziano** (*caffepoliziano.it*), which has been operating since 1868, as it leads to the **Cantine Contucci** (*contucci.it*), one of a number of historic wine cellars in town.

Nearby Piazza Grande is flanked by the 14th-century **Palazzo Comunale** and the late-16th-century **Duomo** (Cattedrale di Santa Maria Assunta; *montepulcianochiusipienza.it*).

The Drive: Reckon on about 40 minutes to cover the 25km to Chiusi. From Montepulciano head southeast along the SP146 to Chianciano Terme, a popular spa town. Continue on towards the A1 *autostrada*, and Chiusi is just on the other side of the highway.

06 Chiusi

Once an important Etruscan centre, Chiusi is now a sleepy country town. Its main attractions are the Etruscan tombs dotted around the surrounding countryside, two of which are included in the ticket price of the impressive **Museo Archeologico Etrusco di Chiusi** (*facebook.com/museoetrusco.dichiusi*) in the town centre. The museum has a bevy of ceramics, pottery, jewellery and cinerary urns dating from between the 9th and 2nd centuries BCE.

The Drive: You have two choices for Orvieto. The quick route is on the A1 *autostrada* (about 45 minutes), but it's a more interesting drive along the SR71 (1½ hours). This passes through Città della Pieve, birthplace of the painter Perugino, and Ficulle, known since Roman times for its artisans.

07 Orvieto

Over the regional border in Umbria, the precariously perched town of Orvieto has one of Italy's finest Gothic cathedrals. The **Duomo di Orvieto** (*opsm.it*) took 30 years to plan and three centuries to complete. Work began in 1290, originally to a Romanesque design, but as construction proceeded, Gothic features were incorporated into the structure. Highlights include the richly coloured facade, and, in the Cappella di San Brizio, Luca Signorelli's fresco cycle *The Last Judgement*.

Across the piazza from the cathedral, the **Museo Claudio Faina e Civico** (*museofaina.it*) houses an important collection of Etruscan archaeological artefacts.

San Quirico d'Orcia (p159)
RWEISSWALD/SHUTTERSTOCK

26

★ BEST FOR

ART LOVERS

Ravenna's sparkling mosaics.

CENTRAL ITALY

FOODIE EMILIA-ROMAGNA

Mosaic, Basilica di Sant'Apollinare Nuovo (p165)

DURATION: 7 DAYS

DISTANCE: 255KM/158 MILES

GREAT FOR: FOOD AND DRINK, HISTORY

BEST TIME TO GO: AUTUMN IS IDEAL FOR FRESH SEASONAL PRODUCE.

Sandwiched between Tuscany and the Veneto, Emilia-Romagna is a foodie's dream destination. Many of Italy's signature dishes originated here, and its regional specialities are revered across the country. This tasty trip takes in the region's main culinary centres of Parma, Modena and Bologna, as well as the charming Renaissance town of Ferrara and art-rich Ravenna, which is celebrated for its glorious Byzantine mosaics.

LINK YOUR TRIP

06 Cinematic Cinque Terre
From Parma head 120km along the A15 *autostrada* to La Spezia, gateway to the spectacular Cinque Terre coastline.

07 Northern Cities
From Ferrara take the A13 *autostrada* for 75km to Padua, home of one of Italy's great Renaissance masterpieces.

01 Parma

Handsome and prosperous, Parma is one of Italy's culinary hot spots, producing the country's finest ham *(prosciutto di Parma)* and its most revered cheese *(parmigiano reggiano)*. To stock up on these, as well as local Lambrusco wines and other regional delicacies, head to the **Salumeria Garibaldi** *(salumeriagaribaldi.com)*, a divine deli in the historic centre. Once you've sated your appetite, sate your soul at the city's 12th-century **Duomo** (*Cattedrale di Santa Maria Assunta; piazza duomoparma.com*), with its classic Lombard-Romanesque facade and ornate baroque interior. Nearby, the octagonal **Battistero** displays a hybrid Romanesque-Gothic look in pink and white marble. Parma's main art collection, which includes works by locals Parmigianino and Correggio alongside paintings by Fra' Angelico, El Greco and a piece attributed to Leonardo da Vinci, is in the **Galleria Nazionale**, one of

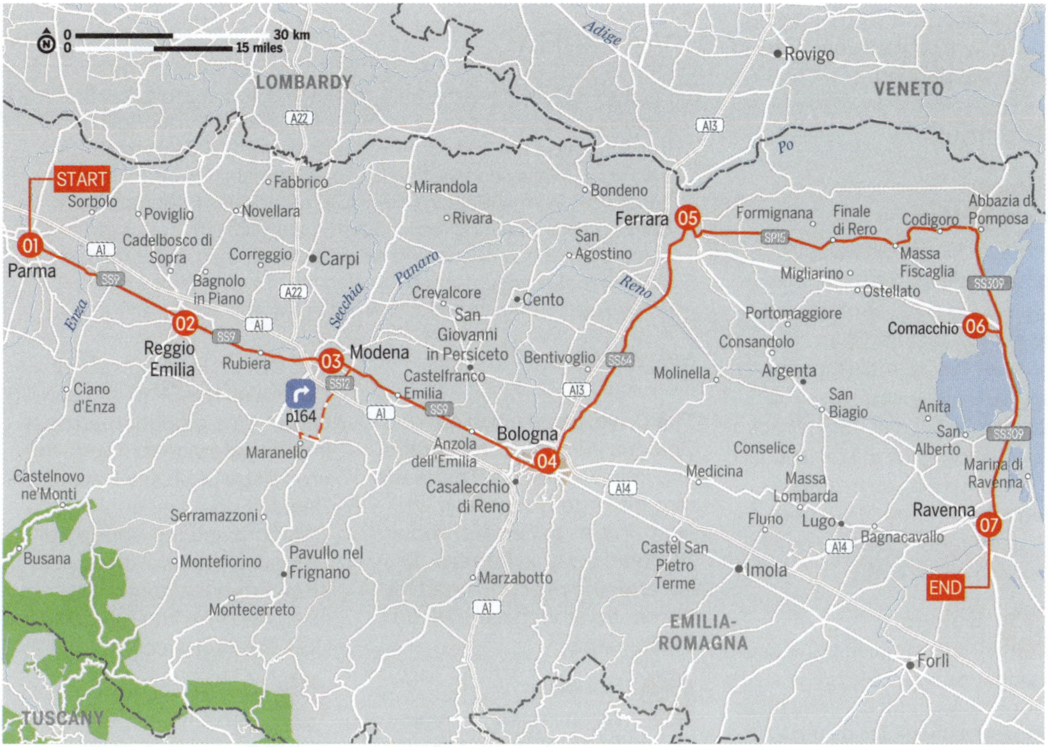

VVOE/SHUTTERSTOCK

several museums in the monumental **Palazzo della Pilotta** *(complesso pilotta.it)*.

The Drive: From Parma, it's a straightforward 50-minute drive southeast on the SS9 (Via Emilia) through fairly uninspiring flat farmland to Reggio Emilia. If you're in a hurry, the quicker A1 *autostrada* covers the same route.

02 Reggio Emilia

Genteel Reggio Emilia puts the *reggiano* in *parmigiano reggiano* (Parmesan). Apart from its cheese, the city is best known as the birthplace of the Italian flag – the famous red, white and green tricolour – whose history is chronicled at the **Museo del Tricolore** *(musei.re.it/sedi/museo-del-tricolore)*. There are several other museums and galleries in town, including the **Galleria Parmeggiani** *(musei.re.it/sedi/galleria-parmeggiani)*, which has some interesting Italian, Flemish and Spanish paintings.

The Drive: The run down to Modena takes about an hour on the SS9. The scenery is much like the first leg from Parma – flat fields, petrol stations, agricultural buildings and the occasional stone farmhouse. At Modena head for the *centro*.

03 Modena

Modena is one of Italy's great gastro centres, the creative force behind *aceto balsamico* (balsamic vinegar), *zamponi* (pig's trotters), *cotechino* (stuffed pork sausage) and sparkling Lambrusco wines. You'll find shops all over town selling local delicacies, including **La Consorteria 1966** *(laconsorteria1966.it)*.

Modena also has a wonderfully suggestive medieval core, centred on **Piazza Grande** and the **Duomo** (*Cattedrale Metropolitana di Santa Maria Assunta e San Geminiano*; *duomodimodena.it*), considered by many to be the finest Romanesque church in Italy. Inseparable from the cathedral is the early-13th-century tower, the **Torre Ghirlandina** *(visitmodena.it)*.

The Drive: From Modena take the SS9 southeast to Bologna. It's only about 45km away, but traffic is often heavy and it can take up to 1½ hours to get there. Bologna's centre is closed to most traffic, so if you're staying downtown, contact your hotel to ask about parking.

DETOUR

Maranello

Start: 03 Modena

A mecca for petrolheads, Maranello is the hometown of Ferrari. The world's sportiest cars have been manufactured here since the early 1940s, and although the factory is off-limits (unless you happen to own a Ferrari), you can get your fix ogling the flaming red autos on display at the **Museo Ferrari** *(museomaranello.ferrari.com)*. Maranello is 17km south of Modena on the SS12.

04 Bologna

Emilia-Romagna's vibrant regional capital, Bologna is a city with serious culinary credentials. It's most famous for inspiring the eponymous bolognese sauce with its own (and tastier) dish known as *ragù,* but it also gifted the world lasagne, *mortadella* (pork cold cut) and *tortellini* (pockets of meat-stuffed pasta). These and other local goodies appear on menus across the city, but for a real gastro treat, sniff out the fabulous old-style delis in the bustling **Quadrilatero** district.

Overshadowing the Quadrilatero's medieval streets are **Le Due Torri**, Bologna's two leaning towers. If vertigo is not a problem, you can climb the taller of the two, the 97.6m-high **Torre degli Asinelli** *(duetorribologna.com)*, and survey the historic centre from on high. The big barn-like structure you'll see to the northwest is the **Basilica di San Petronio** *(basilicadisanpetronio.org)*, the world's fifth-largest basilica, which lords it over **Piazza Maggiore**, Bologna's striking showpiece square.

The Drive: Head north out of Bologna along Via Stalingrado and follow the SS64. This leads through orderly farmland and neat villages to Ferrara, about 1½ hours away. In Ferrara, turn left after the river and head for the *centro storico* car park on Via Darsena.

VIA EMILIA

For the first half of the trip from Parma to Bologna you follow the region's most famous road, the ruler-straight Via Emilia. Built by the Romans in the 2nd century BCE, it ran for 206km through the Po river valley connecting the region's main cities – Placentia (Piacenza), Parma, Regium (Reggio Emilia), Mutina (Modena), Bononia (Bologna) and Ariminum (Rimini). Within decades of completion, it had opened up Italy's fertile northern hinterland to economic expansion, and converted the rich river plain into the empire's proverbial breadbasket – a position it still enjoys today.

05 Ferrara

Ferrara was once the seat of the powerful Este family (1260–1598), and although it is often bypassed by travellers, it's an attractive place with an austere UNESCO-listed cityscape and compact historic centre. In food terms, specialities include the town's uniquely shaped bread, known as *coppia ferrarese,* and *cappellacci di zucca* (hat-shaped pasta stuffed with pumpkin, herbs and nutmeg).

The town centre, which is easily explored on foot, is focused on **Castello Estense** *(castelloestense.it)*, a martial 14th-century castle complete with moat and drawbridge. Linked to the castle by an elevated passageway is the 13th-century crenellated **Palazzo Municipale**, now largely occupied by administrative offices. Opposite, Ferrara's pink-and-white, 12th-century **Duomo** (Cattedrale di San Giorgio) sports a graphic three-tier facade, combining Romanesque and Gothic styles.

The Drive: Head east out of Ferrara on the SP15 and continue on the straight road past immaculate vineyards into the tiny village of Massa Fiscaglia. Bear left here and continue to Codigoro and the Abbazia di Pomposa (well worth a quick stop). From the abbey it's a straight 20-minute run down the SS309 to Comacchio.

06 Comacchio

Resembling a mini Venice with its canals and brick bridges, Comacchio is the main centre in the Po delta (Foci del Po). This area of dense pine forests and extensive wetlands, much of it protected in the **Parco del Delta del Po** *(parcodeltapo.it)*, offers superlative birdwatching and excellent cycling. Foodies can try the prized local speciality, eel, which is served at the many restaurants on Comacchio's canals. Don't miss the excellent **Museo Delta Antico** *(museodeltaantico.com)*.

The Drive: From Comacchio, Ravenna is only an hour's drive away, 40km south on the SS309. The road spears down a narrow strip of land between a lagoon and the Adriatic coast, but you won't see much water thanks to lengthy curtains of verdant trees and heavy foliage.

SIMONA BOTTONE/SHUTTERSTOCK

Market, Bologna

07 Ravenna

No tour of Emilia-Romagna would be complete without a stop at Ravenna to see its remarkable UNESCO-protected mosaics. Relics of the city's golden age as capital of the Western Roman and Byzantine Empires, they are described by Dante in his *Divine Comedy*, much of which he wrote here. The **mosaics** (*ravenna mosaici.it*) are spread over several sites, five of which are covered by a single ticket – **Basilica di San Vitale** and **Mausoleo di Galla Placidia** on Via San Vitale, **Basilica di Sant'Apollinare Nuovo** on Via di Roma, **Museo Arcivescovile** on Piazza Arcivescovado, and **Battistero Neoniano** on Piazza del Duomo 1. Outside town you'll find more mosaics at the **Basilica di Sant'Apollinare in Classe**.

PHOTO OPPORTUNITY

Food stalls and delis in Bologna's Quadrilatero district.

0
100 km
0
50 miles
ABRUZZO
Termoli
A14
Vieste
Monte
Sant'Angelo
MOLISE
Fortore
San
Severo
Golfo di
Manfredonia
Adriatic Sea
Campobasso
PUGLIA
Foggia
Cervaro
Carapelle
Volturno
31
Trani
Bari
A16
Conversano
27
CAMPANIA
PUGLIA
32
A14
Valle
d'Itria
34
Martina
Franca
Brindisi
Naples
Mt Vesuvius
BASILICATA
Matera
Golfo di
Napoli
Pompeii
Salerno
28
Sele
Potenza
Sorrento
Capri
Amalfi
Castelmezzano
Taranto
Lecce
Golfo di
Salerno
Paestum
Padula
29
CAMPANIA
Gallipoli
Sapri
Golfo di
Taranto
Palinuro
Maratea
Santa
Maria di
Leuca
Golfo di
Policastro
Morano
Calabro
30
Crati
33
A3
Crati
Cosenza
Camigliatello
Silano
Tyrrhenian
Sea
Crotone
35
CALABRIA
Catanzaro
Golfo di
Sant'Eufemia
Golfo di
Squillace
Tropea
Pizzo
Golfo di
Gioia
A3
Aeolian
Islands
Ionian
Sea
Gerace
Messina
Milazzo
Reggio
Calabria
Cefalù
A20
SICILY
Taormina

ALEXIS DOYLE/LONELY PLANET

Amalfi (p183)

SOUTHERN ITALY

EXPLORE

SOUTHERN ITALY

Nature itself seems a little wilder in southern Italy, a fiery land of moody volcanoes, spectacular coastlines, rocky landscapes and ravishing food. Italy's greatest hits may lie further north, but the south tugs hard at the heartstrings offering charm, culinary good times and ancient treasures at every turn. Away from Naples' traffic-clogged streets, it's also adventurous driving country. Naples, Vesuvius and the Amalfi Coast are are must-sees, but lesser-known routes reveal some wonderful surprises, from the Cilento's pristine beaches to Calabria's remote mountains and Puglia's unique *trulli* (conical-capped houses).

Naples

First port of call for many travellers to southern Italy is Naples. Italy's third-largest city makes an immediate impression with its in-your-face energy and Dickensian backstreets.

And once you've found your feet, you'll discover there's a lot to love here with priceless art packed into regal palaces and sweeping bay views over to Vesuvius on the horizon.

Accommodation is plentiful and the food is magnificent – a *pizza margherita* in Naples' historic centre is one of Italy's quintessential eating experiences.

Transport-wise, Naples is well connected to the rest of the country. To the south of the city, urban development skirts the Gulf of Naples as it curves around to the Sorrentine Peninsula and the sunny resort of Sorrento.

This animated seaside town heaves in summer and serves as a local transport hub with buses and seasonal ferries to the Amalfi Coast, hydrofoils to Capri and a direct rail service to Pompeii.

Bari

On the Adriatic coast, Bari makes a good initial base for Puglia, the heel of the Italian boot. As regional capital and a major transport hub, it's well served by road, rail, sea and air, and its central location makes it convenient for heading either north or south.

It's not a big touristy place and interest is largely focused on the old town (Bari Vecchia) and nearby

WHEN TO GO

Southern Italy's coast bursts into life in summer, particularly in August when Italian holidaymakers swarm to its many beach resorts. That means crowds, sky-high prices and traffic jams. If you can, spring and early autumn are a better bet, offering reliable sunshine without the holiday mayhem. Winter, when many resorts close for the season, is quiet.

seafront, both of which are worth investigating.

Accommodation is largely in B&Bs and business hotels, and there's a ready supply of trattorias and pizzerias serving fantastic regional fare.

For an authentic local bite try a slice of fluffy focaccia or a bread roll stuffed with freshly caught octopus.

North of the city, the road leads to a string of attractive towns and on to the Gargano National Park, an area of stunning coastal beauty. To the south, country roads wind through the Valle d'Itria, renowned for its Hobbit-like *trulli,* and down to Lecce and the beaches of the Salento.

Matera

Set around a rocky gorge in the heart of Basilicata, is a fascinating city, reckoned to be one of the world's oldest continuously inhabited settlements. It's renowned for its frescoed *chiese rupestri* (cave churches) and *sassi* (cave dwellings), a number of which have been resurrected as boutique hotels, ideal for some R&R after a week on the road.

TRANSPORT

Domestic and international flights serve airports at Naples (for Campania and the Amalfi Coast), Bari and Brindisi (both for Puglia). Fast Alta Velocità trains also run to the main cities on both coasts while regional buses are best for smaller towns and villages, particularly inland. Realistically, you'll want your own wheels for getting to the remote internal areas.

WHERE TO STAY

Accommodation, which is concentrated in the main cities and coastal resorts, runs the gamut from B&Bs and family-run *pensioni* (small hotels) to self-catering apartments, resort hotels and luxury five-stars. Popular holiday destinations such as Sorrento, the Amalfi Coast and Puglia's Salento area are particularly well supplied, even if places fill quickly in summer and many close over winter.

The south also boasts some wonderful alternative accommodation: you can bed down in a *sasso* (cave) hotel in Matera or a *trullo* (stone house) in Puglia. Puglia is also renowned for its *masserie* (working farms), many of which house stunning rural retreats.

RESOURCES

- **Alilauro**
  For info on ferries to/from Naples, the Amalfi Coast and Bay islands. *alilauro.it*
- **Pompeii Sites**
  Get the lowdown on Pompeii: ticket prices, hours, what's open and the Great Pompeii Project. *pompeiisites.org*
- **Viaggiare in Puglia**
  Puglia's multilingual tourist website is packed with ideas, inspiration and practical info. *viaggiareinpuglia.it*

WHAT'S ON

- **Ravello Festival**
  (ravellofestival.info) Music and art fill Ravello high above the Amalfi Coast in July and August.
- **La Notte della Taranta**
  (lanottedellataranta.it) Puglia rocks to the rhythms of the *pizzica* dance in August. Events, held across the Salento, culminate in a mega concert at Melpignano.
- **Christmas Presepi**
  Shoppers flock to Via San Gregorio Armeno in Naples' historic centre to check out traditional *presepi* (Nativity scenes).

27

★ BEST FOR

HISTORY

Relive history amid Herculaneum's ruins.

SOUTHERN ITALY

SHADOW OF VESUVIUS

DURATION: 2–3 DAYS

DISTANCE: 90KM/56 MILES

GREAT FOR: FOOD AND DRINK, HISTORY, NATURE

BEST TIME TO GO: SPRING AND AUTUMN FOR THE BEST WEATHER; DECEMBER FOR CHRISTMAS DISPLAYS.

Mosaic, Herculaneum (p172)

This trip begins in Naples (Napoli), a city that rumbles with contradictions – grimy streets hit palm-fringed boulevards, crumbling facades mask golden baroque ballrooms. Rounding the Bay of Naples and the dense urban sprawl, you quickly reach some of the world's most spectacular Roman ruins including Pompeii and Herculaneum, as well as lesser-known jewels, from Portici's royal getaway to sprawling ancient villas. Above it all looms Vesuvius' dark beauty.

LINK YOUR TRIP

28 Southern Larder
From Sorrento, you can embark on this culinary adventure along the Amalfi Coast and the Golfo di Salerno, where mozzarella rules the roost.

29 Amalfi Coast
Vico Equense kicks off this week-long adventure of hairpin turns and vertical landscapes amid the world's most glamorous stretch of coastline.

01 Naples

Italy's most misunderstood city is also one of its finest – an exhilarating mess of frescoed cupolas, mysterious shrines and catacombs, and boisterous, hyperactive street markets. Contradiction is the catchphrase here. It's a place where anarchy, pollution and poverty share the stage with lavish theatres, glorious museums and cafe-lounging artists and intellectuals.

The UNESCO-listed *centro storico* (historic centre) is an intoxicating warren of streets packed with ancient churches, citrus-filled cloisters and first-rate pizzerias. It's here, under the washing lines, that you'll find classic Neapolitan street life – overloaded Vespas hurtling through cobbled alleyways and clued-up *casalinghe* (housewives) bullying market vendors. Move towards the sea and the cityscape opens up. Imperious palaces flank show-off squares, and seafront panoramas take in fabled Capri and mighty Vesuvius. This is Royal Naples,

ALYSTA/SHUTTERSTOCK

the Naples of the Bourbons that so impressed the 18th-century Grand Tourists.

To prepare for Pompeii and Herculaneum, head to the **Museo Archeologico Nazionale** *(museoarcheologiconapoli.it)*. With one of the world's finest collections of Graeco-Roman artefacts, it stars a series of stunning sculptures, mosaics from Pompeii and a room full of ancient erotica.

The Drive: A straight 8km drive along the SS18 provides a relatively easy journey from central Naples straight to Portici – if the other drivers behave, of course.

DETOUR

Campi Flegrei

Start: 01 Naples

Stretching west of Posillipo Hill to the Tyrrhenian Sea, the oft-overlooked **Campi Flegrei** (Phlegrean Fields) counterbalances its ugly urban sprawl with lush volcanic hillsides and priceless ancient ruins without the crowds. While its Greek settlements are Italy's oldest, its Monte Nuovo is Europe's youngest mountain. It's not every week that a mountain just appears on the scene. At 8pm on 29 September 1538, a crack appeared in the earth near the ancient Roman settlement of Tripergole, spewing out a violent concoction of pumice, fire and smoke over six days. By the end of the week, Pozzuoli had a new 134m-tall neighbour.

Today, Europe's newest mountain is a lush and peaceful nature reserve. Before exploring the Campi Flegrei, stop at the **tourist office** *(infocampiflegrei.it)* in Pozzuoli to get local information and purchase a cumulative ticket (valid for two days) to four of the area's key sites: the **Anfiteatro Flavio**, the **Parco Archeologico di Baia**, the **Museo Archeologico dei Campi Flegrei** and the **Parco Archeologico di Cuma**.

02 Portici

The town of Portici lies at the foot of Mt Vesuvius and had to be rebuilt in the wake of its ruin by the 1631 eruption. Charles III of Spain, king of Naples and Sicily, erected a stately royal palace here between 1738 and 1748. Known as the **Reggia di Portici** *(centromusa.it)*, the palace today houses a couple of worthwhile museums, most notably the **Herculanense Museum** with artefacts from Pompeii and Herculaneum. Even if the museum is closed, the palace is worth a stop for its string of colourfully frescoed rooms. Outside, the exquisite **botanic gardens** are operated by the University of Naples Federico II.

The Drive: The entrance to the ruins of Herculaneum lies just a couple of kilometres along the SS18.

03 Herculaneum

The ruins of ancient **Herculaneum** *(ercolano.beniculturali.it)* are smaller, less daunting and easier to navigate than Pompeii. They also include some of the area's richest archaeological finds, offering a rare, intimate glimpse of daily life as it was when the Romans ruled the region.

Heavily damaged by an earthquake in 63 CE, Herculaneum was completely submerged by the 79 CE eruption of Mt Vesuvius. However, because it was much closer to the volcano than Pompeii, it drowned in a sea of mud, essentially fossilising the town and ensuring that even delicate items were discovered remarkably well preserved.

Seek out the **Casa d'Argo** (Argus House), a well-preserved example of a Roman noble family's house, complete with porticoed garden and *triclinium* (dining area). The **Casa dei Cervi** (House of the Stags) is an imposing example of a Roman noble's villa, with two storeys arranged around a central courtyard and animated with murals and still-life paintings. And don't miss the **Terme del Foro** (Forum Baths), with deep pools, stucco friezes and, in the female *apodyterium* (changing room), a striking mosaic of a naked Triton.

The Drive: The Mt Vesuvius museum is only 10km from Herculaneum. Keep heading down the SS18 until you reach the centre of Torre del Greco, where you will turns left on Via Vittorio Veneto, which will quickly turn into Via Guglielmo Marconi. Follow the signs as you wind your way up the lower elevations of Mt Vesuvius, and the Bay of Naples comes into view. The museum is only 10km from Herculaneum.

04 Museo dell'Osservatorio Vesuviano

Halfway up Mt Vesuvius, this **museum** *(www.ov.ingv.it)* contains an interesting array of artefacts telling the history of 2000 years of Vesuvius-watching. Founded in 1841 to monitor Vesuvius' moods, it is the oldest volcanic observatory in the world. To this day, scientists are still constantly monitoring the active volcanoes at Vesuvius, Campi Flegrei and Ischia

The Drive: It's many more hairpin turns as you make your way along the same road almost to Vesuvius' crater, about 7km away. Views across the Bay of Naples and Campania are magnificent.

> ☑ TOP TIP
>
> ### PASS TO THE PAST
>
> If you plan on blitzing the archaeological sites around Pompeii, consider purchasing a multi-attraction ticket. Valid for three days, the pass includes entry to Pompeii, Boscoreale and Oplontis. The ticket is available at the ticket offices of all three sites.

05 Mt Vesuvius

Since exploding into history in 79 CE, **Mt Vesuvius** *(parconazionaledelvesuvio.it)* has blown its top more than 30 times. The most devastating of these was in 1631, and the most recent was in 1944. It is the only volcano on the European mainland to have erupted within the last 100 years. What redeems this lofty menace is the spectacular view from its crater – a breathtaking panorama that takes in Naples, its world-famous bay and part of the Apennine mountains.

The end of the road is the summit car park, from where a shuttle bus reaches the ticket office and entry point further up the volcano. From here, a relatively easy 860m path leads up to the actual summit (allow 25 minutes), best tackled in comfy sneakers and with a jacket in tow (it can be chilly up top, even in summer). When the weather is bad the summit path is closed.

The Drive: The first part of this 21km stretch heads back down Vesuvius the same way you came up. Head all the way down to the A3 motorway, turn left onto it and head southeast.

Pompeii (p175)
A-BABE/SHUTTERSTOCK

VESUVIAN WINES

Vesuvian wine has been relished since ancient times. The rare combination of rich volcanic soil and a favourable microclimate created by its slopes makes the territory one of Italy's most interesting viticultural areas. Lacryma Christi (literally 'tears of Christ') is the name of perhaps the most celebrated wine produced on the slopes of Mt Vesuvius.

Further afield, other top regional wines include Taurasi, Fiano di Avellino, Aglianico del Taburno and Greco di Tufo.

06 Oplontis

Buried beneath the unappealing streets of modern-day Torre Annunziata, **Oplontis** *(pompeiisites.org)* was once a seafront suburb under the administrative control of Pompeii. First discovered in the 18th century, only two of its houses have been unearthed, and only one, **Villa Poppaea**, is open to the public. This villa is a magnificent example of an *otium* villa (a residential building used for rest and recreation), and may once have belonged to Emperor Nero's second wife.

The Drive: This brief 5km jaunt has you once again heading southeast, this time on the SS18, to SS268 (Via Settetermini), which leads through scruffy Neapolitan suburbs to Boscoreale.

07 Boscoreale

Some 3km north of Pompeii, the archaeological site of **Boscoreale** *(pompeiisites.org)* consists of a rustic country villa dating back to the 1st century BCE, and a fascinating antiquarium showcasing artefacts from Pompeii, Herculaneum and the surrounding region. Especially evocative is the reconstructed ceremonial chariot, ornately decorated in bronze and silver.

The Drive: Head straight back down the SS268 all the way to the SS18, which will take you through about 2km of suburbs right up next to the ruins of Pompeii.

Sorrento

ALEXIS DOYLE/LONELY PLANET

08 Pompeii

Nothing piques human curiosity like a mass catastrophe, and few beat the ruins of **Pompeii** *(pompeiisites.org)*, a stark reminder of Vesuvius' malign forces.

Of Pompeii's original 66 hectares, 44 have now been excavated, with new discoveries unearthed regularly. Audio guides are a sensible investment, and a good guidebook will help – try *Pompeii*, published by Electa Napoli. To do justice to the site, allow at least three hours.

Highlights include the 1st-century-BCE **Terme Suburbane**, famous for their risqué frescoes, and the **foro**, ancient Pompeii's main piazza. To the northeast of the *foro*, the **Lupanare** (brothel) harbours a series of erotic frescoes that originally served as a menu for clients. At the far east of the site, the **Anfiteatro** is the oldest known Roman amphitheatre in existence. Over on the opposite side of town, the **Villa dei Misteri**, one of the site's most complete structures, contains the remarkable fresco *Dionysiac Frieze*. One of the world's largest ancient paintings, it depicts the initiation of a bride-to-be into the cult of Dionysus, the Greek god of wine.

> PHOTO OPPORTUNITY
>
> Capture Vesuvius' brooding majesty from Naples' waterfront.

The Drive: The 9km trip from Pompeii begins heading south along the SS145 (Corso Italia). It will take you through a mixture of suburbs and small farms. Ahead, you will see the mountains of the Amalfi Coast rear up. The ancient villas of Stabiae are just east of Corso Italia, off Via Giuseppe Cosenza.

09 Castellammare di Stabia

South of Oplontis in modern-day Castellammare di Stabia, **Stabiae** *(pompeiisites.org)* was once a popular resort for wealthy Romans. It stood on the slopes of the Varano hill overlooking the entire Bay of Naples, and according to ancient historian Pliny it was lined for miles with extravagant villas. You can visit two of these frescoed villas: the 1st-century-BCE **Villa Arianna** and the larger **Villa San Marco**, said to measure more than 11,000 sq metres.

The Drive: This trip is a bit longer, at 21km, than the last few. Head back to the SS145, which will soon head over to the coast. Enjoy beautiful views over the Bay of Naples as you wind your way past Vico Equense, Meta and Piano di Sorrento to Sorrento.

10 Sorrento

For an unabashed tourist town, Sorrento still manages to preserve the feeling of a civilised coastal retreat. Even the souvenirs are a cut above the norm, with plenty of fine old shops selling ceramics, lacework and marquetry items. It is also the spiritual home of *limoncello*, a delicious lemon liqueur traditionally made from the zest of Femminello St Teresa lemons, also known as Sorrento lemons. Its tart sweetness makes the perfect nightcap, as well as a brilliant flavouring for both sweet and savoury dishes.

28

★ BEST FOR

FOODIES

Going to mozzarella's source in Paestum.

SOUTHERN ITALY

SOUTHERN LARDER

DURATION: 3–4 DAYS

DISTANCE: 119KM/73 MILES

GREAT FOR: FOOD AND DRINK, NATURE

BEST TIME TO GO: SPRING FOR SUNNY, CLEAR WEATHER; EARLY AUTUMN FOR ABUNDANT PRODUCE.

Making mozzarella cheese, Paestum (p178)

Breathtaking natural beauty aside, this trip is a gourmand's Elysium. Food lovers flock to the Amalfi and Cilento coasts from across the globe for local specialities such as *limoncello* (lemon liqueur), ricotta-stuffed sfogliatella pastries, and wildly creamy mozzarella made from water-buffalo milk. Burn off the extra calories hiking the Amalfi's jaw-dropping coastal trails or clambering over Paestum's robust Greek ruins.

LINK YOUR TRIP

27 Shadow of Vesuvius
From Sorrento, follow this itinerary in reverse, heading around the Bay of Naples to wander the ruins of Pompeii and Herculaneum, brave the slopes of Vesuvius, and conquer high-energy Naples.

29 Amalfi Coast
Vico Equense kicks off this week-long adventure of hairpin turns and vertical landscapes along the world's most glamorous stretch of coastline.

01 Sorrento

Most people come to seaside Sorrento as a pleasant stopover between Capri, Naples and the Amalfi Coast. And while it does offer dramatic views of the Bay of Naples and an upbeat holiday vibe, gluttons converge here for a very specific treat: *limoncello,* a simple lemon liqueur made from the zest of lemons (preferably the local Femminello St Teresa lemons), plus sugar and grain alcohol. It's traditionally served after dinner in chilled ceramic cups, and its combination of sweetness and biting tartness makes for a satisfying culinary epilogue.

The Drive: Head north on the SS145, including a beautiful stretch along the Bay of Naples, for 12km to Vico Equense.

DETOUR

Capri

Start: 01 Sorrento

A mass of limestone rock that rises sheer through impossibly

HIGH FLIERS/SHUTTERSTOCK

blue water, Capri is the perfect microcosm of Mediterranean appeal – a smooth cocktail of chi-chi piazzas and cool cafes, Roman ruins and rugged seascapes.

Need any more reason to go? OK, here's one more: the *torta caprese*. Back in the 1920s, when an absent-minded baker forgot to add flour to the mix of a cake order, a great dessert was born. Now an Italian chocolate-and-almond (or chocolate-and-walnut) cake that is traditionally gluten-free, it is named for the island of Capri from which it originated. The cake has a hard shell covering a moist interior. It is usually covered with a light dusting of fine powdered sugar, and sometimes made with a small amount of Strega or other liqueur.

02 Vico Equense

Known to the Romans as Aequa, Vico Equense is a small clifftop town east of Sorrento. Largely bypassed by international tourists, it's a laid-back, authentic place worth a quick stopover, if only to experience some of the famous pizza served by the metre at the justly celebrated **Ristorante & Pizzeria da Gigino** *(pizzametro.it)*. Save room for some superb, made-from-scratch gelato at **Gabriele** *(gabrieleitalia.com)*, another local institution.

The Drive: From Vico Equense to Pimonte is 18km. You'll again hug the beautiful Bay of Naples for a while, reaching the turnoff for the SR ex SS366 in Castellammare di Stabia. From here, head inland and uphill as you wind your way to Pimonte.

03 Pimonte

Tucked into the mountains in the easternmost end of the Amalfi peninsula, this small town is a far cry from the high-rolling coast, with tractors trundling through the narrow streets. Make a point of stopping at **Bar Pasticceria Palummo** for its cult-status *torta palummo*, a delicious concoction of *pan di spagna* (sponge cake) and almond cream. For a savoury snack, seek out the *taralli noci e provolone del monaco*, crunchy, savoury biscuits made with walnuts and a semi-hard local cheese.

The Drive: The 8km drive from Pimonte to Agerola takes you along a winding road through forested countryside along the SR ex SS366.

04 Agerola

Agerola is located amid a wide green valley approximately 600m above sea level. It is surrounded by natural forests and offers amazing views of the nearby mountains and Mediterranean Sea. Be sure to make a stop here for the legendary *fior di latte* (cow's-milk mozzarella) and *caciocavallo* (gourd-shaped traditional curd cheese) produced on the fertile slopes around town.

The Drive: From Agerola, hop back on the SR ex SS366 for a quick 2km jaunt to Bomerano, enjoying a forest of beech trees and a backdrop of mountains thickly quilted with pines. You are now in the depths of the verdant Parco Regionale dei Monti Lattari.

05 Bomerano

Just a stone's throw from Agerola, you can easily follow your nose to tiny Bomerano for delicious buffalo-milk yogurt, an ultra-rich, mildly tangy and creamy treat. While in town, feast your eyes on the ornate ceiling frieze in the 16th-century **Chiesa San Matteo Apostolo**.

The Drive: From Bomerano to Conca dei Marini, continue on the same road, SS366, for 9km as it twists dramatically down to the sea, with strategically placed lookouts along the way. From the SR ex SS366, you will do more switchbacking down to the town of Conca dei Marini itself.

06 Conca dei Marini

This charmingly picturesque fishing village has been beloved by everyone from Princess Margaret to Gianni Agnelli, Jacqueline Onassis and Carlo Ponti. Work up an appetite with an excursion to the **Grotta dello Smeraldo**, a seaside cavern where the waters glow an eerie emerald green. Then head back to the town for a *sfogliatella,* a scrumptious shell-shaped, ricotta-stuffed pastry that was probably invented here in the 18th century in the monastery of Santa Rosa. The local pastry is even honoured with its own holiday: the first Sunday in August.

The Drive: Head northeast on the SS163 to the town of Amalfi.

07 Amalfi

A picturesque ensemble of whitewashed buildings and narrow alleyways set around a sun-kissed central piazza, Amalfi is the main centre on the Amalfi Coast. To glean a sense of its medieval history, explore the hidden lanes that run parallel to the main street, with their steep stairways, covered porticos and historic shrine niches. And, of course, gourmets shouldn't miss *scialatielli.* A fresh pasta resembling short, slightly widened strips of *tagliatelle,* it is a local speciality, most commonly accompanied by courgette and mussels or clams, or a simple sauce of fresh cherry tomatoes and garlic.

The Drive: It's about 15km on the SS163 from Amalfi to Cetara. Silver birches and buildings draped in bougainvillea add to the beauty of the drive.

08 Cetara

A picturesque tumble-down fishing village, Cetara is also a gastronomic highlight. Tuna and anchovies are the local specialities, especially the sauce from the latter. Known as *colatura di alici,* it flavours home-made pasta dishes like *scialatielli* with local yellow tomatoes and ravioli stuffed with buffalo mozzarella at **Cetara Punto e Pasta** *(facebook.com/cetarapuntoepasta),* a humble, affordable eatery a short walk up from the beach.

The Drive: Head northeast on SS163 for Salerno. En route, colourful wildflowers spill over white stone walls as you travel the sometimes hair-raising 11km along the coast.

09 Salerno

Salerno may seem like a bland big city after the Amalfi Coast's glut of pretty towns, but the place has a charming, if gritty, individuality, especially around its vibrant *centro storico.* Don't miss the **Duomo** *(cattedraledisalerno.it),* built in the 11th century and graced by a magnificent main entrance, the 12th-century Porta dei Leoni. And for *torta di ricotta e pera* (ricotta-and-pear tart), Salerno is the place. This dessert is an Amalfi Coast speciality, deriving its unique tang from the local sheep's-milk ricotta.

The Drive: Head south on the SP175 and hug the coast. Lush palm and lemon trees and the sparkling sea are your escorts for this 38km drive to Paestum.

10 Paestum

Work up an appetite amid Paestum's UNESCO-listed **Greek temples** *(parchipaestumvelia.cultura.gov.it),* some of the best-preserved in the world. Then head to **Tenuta Vannulo** *(vannulo.it),* a 10-minute drive from Paestum, for a superbly soft and creamy mozzarella made from the organic milk of water buffalo. Group tours are available (reservations are essential), but you can also stop just to buy the cheese. Be warned, though, it usually sells out by early afternoon.

Agerola
IVANGAR_FOTOGRAFIA/SHUTTERSTOCK

PHOTO OPPORTUNITY

Capture the hypnotically terraced cliffs of Agerola at sunset.

29

★ BEST FOR

OUTDOORS

Hiking Ravello and its environs.

SOUTHERN ITALY

AMALFI COAST

DURATION: 7 DAYS

DISTANCE: 100KM/62 MILES

GREAT FOR: FOOD AND DRINK, NATURE

BEST TIME TO GO: JUNE OR SEPTEMBER FOR BEACH WEATHER WITHOUT THE PEAK SUMMER CROWDS.

Ravello (p184)

Not for the faint-hearted, this trip along the Amalfi Coast tests your driving skill on a 100km stretch, featuring dizzying hairpin turns and pastel-coloured towns draped over sea-cliff scenery. Stops include the celebrated coastal resorts of Positano and Amalfi, as well as serene, mountain-top Ravello, famed for its gardens and views. Walking trails that provide a wonderful escape from the built-up coastal clamour

LINK YOUR TRIP

27 Shadow of Vesuvius
Follow the curve of the Bay of Naples, from simmering Vesuvius to loud, gregarious Naples.

28 Southern Larder
From Sorrento to Paestum, this trip savours the flavours of Campania's bountiful coast.

01 Vico Equense

The Bay of Naples is justifiably famous for its pizza, invented here as a savoury way to highlight two local specialities: mozzarella and sun-kissed tomatoes. Besides its pretty *centro storico,* this little clifftop town overlooking the Bay of Naples claims some of the region's top pizza, including a by-the-metre version at cult-status **Ristorante & Pizzeria da Gigino** *(pizzametro.it).*

The Drive: From Vico Equense to Sorrento, your main route will be the SS145 roadway for 12km. Expect to hug the sparkling coastline after Marina di Equa before venturing inland towards Meta and Piano do Sorrento.

02 Sorrento

On paper, cliff-straddling Sorrento is a place to avoid – a package-holiday centre with few sights, no beach to speak of and a glut of brassy English-style pubs. In reality, it's strangely appealing, its laid-back southern Italian charm resisting all attempts to swamp

ALEXIS DOYLE/LONELY PLANET

it in souvenir tat and graceless development.

According to Greek legend, it was in Sorrento's waters that the mythical sirens once lived. Sailors of antiquity were powerless to resist the beautiful song of these charming maiden-monsters, who would lure them to their doom.

The Drive: Take the SS145 for 8km to Sant'Agata sui Due Golfi. Sun-dappled village streets give way to forest as you head further inland.

03 Sant'Agata sui Due Golfi

Perched high in the hills above Sorrento, sleepy Sant'Agata sui Due Golfi commands spectacular views of the Bay of Naples on one side and the Bay of Salerno on the other (hence its name, Saint Agatha on the Two Gulfs). The best viewpoint is the **Convento del Deserto**, a Carmelite convent 1.5km uphill from the village centre. It's a knee-wearing hike, but make it to the top and you're rewarded with fabulous 360-degree vistas.

The Drive: From Sant'Agata sui Due Golfi to Marina del Cantone it's a 9km drive, the last part involving some serious hairpin turns. Don't let the gorgeous sea views distract you.

04 Marina del Cantone

From **Nerano**, where you'll park, a beautiful hiking trail leads down to the stunning Bay of Ieranto and one of the coast's top swimming spots, Marina del Cantone. This unassuming village with its small pebble beach is a lovely, tranquil place to stay as well as a popular diving destination. The village also has a reputation as a gastronomic hot spot and VIPs regularly catch a boat over from Capri to dine on superlative seafood at **Lo Scoglio** *(hotelloscoglio.com)*.

The Drive: First, head back up that switchbacks to Sant'Agata sui Due Golfi. Catch the SS145 and then the SS163 as they weave their way along bluffs and cliff sides to Positano. Most of the 24km offers stunning sea views.

♥ WHY I LOVE THIS TRIP

CRISTIAN BONETTI, WRITER

From Richard Wagner to Gore Vidal, the Amalfi Coast has bewitched some of the world's most illustrious figures. This is Italy's most arresting coastline, with a natural beauty that borders on the ethereal. While this trip takes in the fabled, sun-drenched towns the Amalfi Coast is famous for, it also sees you hitting the sleepy, hiking-friendly hills above, where the views demand a symphony.

05 Positano

The pearl in the pack, Positano is the coast's most photogenic and expensive town. Its steeply stacked houses are a medley of peaches, pinks and terracottas, and its near-vertical streets (many of which are, in fact, staircases) are lined with voguish shop displays, elegant hotels and smart restaurants. Look closely, though, and you'll find reassuring signs of everyday reality – crumbling stucco, streaked paintwork and occasionally a faint whiff of problematic drainage.

John Steinbeck visited in 1953 and was so bowled over that he wrote of its dream-like qualities in an article for *Harper's Bazaar*.

The Drive: From Positano to Praiano it's a quick 6km spin on the SS163, passing Il San Pietro di Positano at the halfway point, then heading southeast along the peninsula's edge.

DETOUR

Nocelle

Start: 05 Positano

A tiny, still relatively isolated mountain village above Positano, Nocelle (450m) commands some of the most memorable views on the entire coast. A world apart from touristy Positano, it's a sleepy, silent place where not much ever happens, nor would its few residents ever want it to. If you want to stay, consider delightful **Villa della Quercia** *(villalaquercia.com)*, a former monastery with spectacular vistas. Nocelle lies eight very winding kilometres northeast of Positano.

Positano

KATERINA KODYAKOVA/SHUTTERSTOCK

PHOTO OPPORTUNITY

Positano's vertiginous stack of pastel-coloured houses cascading down to the sea.

06 Praiano

An ancient fishing village, a low-key summer resort and, increasingly, a popular centre for the arts, Praiano is a delight. With no centre as such, its whitewashed houses pepper the verdant ridge of Monte Sant'Angelo as it slopes towards Capo Sottile. Exploring involves lots of steps and there are several trails that start from town, including the legendary **Sentiero degli Dei**.

For those who'd rather venture below sea level, **La Boa** *(laboa.com)* runs dives that explore the area's coral, marine life and grottoes.

The Drive: From Praiano, Marina di Furore is just 3km further on, past beautiful coves that cut into the shoreline.

07 Marina di Furore

Marina di Furore sits at the bottom of what's known as the fjord of Furore, a giant cleft that cuts through the Lattari mountains. The main village, however, stands 300m above, in the upper Vallone del Furore. A one-horse place that sees few tourists, it breathes a distinctly rural air despite the presence of colourful murals and unlikely modern sculpture.

The Drive: From Marina di Furore to Amalfi, the sparkling Mediterranean Sea will accompany you as you drive eastward along the SS163 coastal road for 6km. Look for Vettica Minore and Conca dei Marini along the way, along with fluffy bunches of fragrant cypress trees.

08 Amalfi

It is hard to grasp that pretty little Amalfi, with its sun-filled piazzas and small beach, was once a maritime superpower with a population of more than 70,000. For one thing, it's not a big place – you can easily walk from one end to the other in about 20 minutes. For another, there are very few historical buildings of note. The explanation is chilling – most of the old city, along with its populace, simply slid into the sea during an earthquake in 1343.

One happy exception is the striking **Cattedrale di Sant'Andrea**,

WALK OF THE GODS

Probably the best-known walk on the Amalfi Coast is the three-hour, 12km **Sentiero degli Dei**, which follows the high ridge linking Praiano to Positano. The walk commences in the heart of Praiano, where a thigh-challenging 1000-step start takes you up to the path itself. The route proper is not advised for vertigo sufferers: it's a spectacular, meandering trail along the top of the mountains, with caves and terraces set dramatically in the cliffs and deep valleys framed by the brilliant blue of the sea. You'll eventually emerge at Nocelle, from where a series of steps will take you through the olive groves and deposit you on the road just east of Positano.

parts of which date from the early 10th century. Between 10am and 5pm entrance to the cathedral is through the adjacent **Chiostro del Paradiso**, a 13th-century Moorish-style cloister.

Be sure to take the short walk around the headland to neighbouring **Atrani**, a picturesque tangle of whitewashed alleys and arches centred on a lively, lived-in piazza and popular beach.

The Drive: Start the 7km trip to Ravello by heading along the coast to Atrani. Here turn inland and follow the SR373 as it climbs the steep hillside in a series of second-gear hairpin turns up to Ravello.

09 Ravello

Sitting high in the hills above Amalfi, polished Ravello is a town almost entirely dedicated to tourism. With impeccable artistic credentials – Richard Wagner, DH Lawrence and Virginia Woolf all lounged here – it's known today for its ravishing gardens and stupendous views, the best in the world according to former resident, the late Gore Vidal.

To enjoy these views, head south of Ravello's cathedral to the 14th-century tower that marks the entrance to **Villa Rufolo** *(villarufolo.it)*. Created by Scotsman Scott Neville Reid in 1853, these gardens combine celestial panoramic views, exotic colours, artistically crumbling towers and luxurious blooms.

Also worth seeking out is the wonderful **Camo** *(museodelcorallo.com)*. Squeezed between tourist-driven shops, this very special place is, on the face of it, a cameo shop. And exquisite they are too, crafted primarily out of coral and shell. But don't stop here; ask to see the treasure trove of a museum beyond the showroom.

The Drive: Head back down to the SS163 for a 19km journey that twists and turns challengingly along the coast to Cetara. Pine trees and a variety of flowering shrubs line the way.

Ravello

ALEXIS DOYLE/LONELY PLANET

DETOUR

Ravello Walks

Start: 09 Ravello

Ravello is the starting point for numerous walks that follow ancient paths through the surrounding Lattari mountains. If you've got the legs for it, you can walk down to **Minori** via an attractive route of steps, hidden alleys and olive groves, passing the picturesque hamlet of **Torello** en route. Alternatively, you can head the other way, to Amalfi, via the ancient village of **Scala**. Once a flourishing religious centre with more than 100 churches and the oldest settlement on the Amalfi Coast, Scala is now a pocket-sized, sleepy place where the wind whistles through empty streets, and gnarled locals go patiently about their daily chores.

10 Cetara

Cetara is a picturesque, tumbledown fishing village with a reputation as a gastronomic delight. Since medieval times it has been an important fishing centre, and today its deep-sea tuna fleet is considered one of the Mediterranean's most important. At night, fishers set out in small boats armed with powerful lamps to fish for anchovies. No surprise then that tuna and anchovies dominate local menus, including at **Cetara Punto e Pasta**, a sterling seafood restaurant near the small harbour.

The Drive: From Cetara to Vietri sul Mare, head northeast for 6km on the SS163 for more twisting, turning and stupendous views across the Golfo di Salerno.

ALEXANDREE/SHUTTERSTOCK

Amalfi Coast

THE BLUE RIBBON DRIVE

Stretching from Vietri sul Mare to Sant'Agata sui Due Golfi near Sorrento, the SS163 – nicknamed the Nastro Azzurro (Blue Ribbon) – remains one of Italy's most breathtaking roadways. Commissioned by Bourbon king Ferdinand II and completed in 1853, it wends its way along the Amalfi Coast's entire length, snaking round impossibly tight curves, over deep ravines and through tunnels gouged out of sheer rock. It's a magnificent feat of civil engineering – although it can be challenging to drive – and in certain places it's not wide enough for two cars to pass, a fact John Steinbeck alluded to his 1953 essay for *Harper's Bazaar*.

11 Vietri sul mare

Marking the end of the coastal road, Vietri sul Mare is the ceramics capital of Campania. Although production dates back to Roman times, it didn't take off as an industry until the 16th and 17th centuries. Today, ceramics shopaholics can get their fix at the **Ceramica Artistica Solimene** *(ceramicasolimene.it)*, a vast factory outlet with an extraordinary glass and ceramic facade.

For a primer on the history of the area's ceramics, seek out the **Museo della Ceramica** in the nearby village of Raito.

30

★ BEST FOR

HISTORY

Paestum's magnificent ancient Greek temples.

SOUTHERN ITALY

CILENTO COASTAL TRAIL

DURATION: 4–5 DAYS

DISTANCE: 143KM/89 MILES

GREAT FOR: FOOD AND DRINK, NATURE

BEST TIME TO GO: SPRING AND AUTUMN FOR HIKING; HIGH SUMMER FOR BEACH DAYS.

Paestum

Barely accessible by road until the 20th century, the jagged cliff-bound Cilento peninsula is one of Italy's least-explored stretches of coastline. After flourishing under the Greeks and Romans, the Cilento was abandoned for centuries to the vagaries of Mediterranean pirates. Today, its fishing villages and pretty hill towns remain largely free of mass development, despite long, sandy beaches, pristine blue waters and superb seafood.

LINK YOUR TRIP

28 Southern Larder
Join this culinary adventure through Campania where this trip begins – amid the ancient ruins of Paestum.

34 Across the Lucanian Apennines
A stunning 20km from Sapri along Basilicata's coastline, Maratea kicks off this journey over the gorgeous Lucanian Apennines to otherworldly Matera.

01 Paestum

The three stately, honey-coloured temples at **Paestum** *(parchi paestumvelia.cultura.gov.it)* are among the best preserved in Magna Graecia – the Greek colonies that once held sway over much of southern Italy. The Greeks capitulated to the Romans in 273 BCE, and Poseidonia, as it was known, remained a thriving trading port until the fall of the Roman Empire.

Buy tickets to the temples at the **museum**, itself a fascinating repository of frescoes, statues and archaeological artefacts, before entering the site's main entrance. The first structure you encounter is the 6th-century-BCE **Tempio di Cerere** (Temple of Ceres), the smallest of the three temples, which later served as a Christian church. As you head south, you can pick out the remnants of the Roman city, including an amphitheatre, housing complexes and the **foro** (forum). Beyond lies the **Tempio di Nettuno** (Temple of Neptune), the largest and best preserved of the three temples.

Almost next door, the equally beautiful **basilica** (in reality, a temple to the goddess Hera) is Paestum's oldest surviving monument, dating from the middle of the 6th century BCE.

The Drive: Heading 10km south down the SP430 from Paestum, you quickly start winding into the foothills of the Cilento. Agropoli's historic centre will loom up on the right. Follow signs to the *centro storico*.

DETOUR

Parco Nazionale del Cilento e Valle di Diano

Start: 01 Paestum

Italy's second-largest national park, the **Parco Nazionale del Cilento e Vallo di Diano** *(cilentoediano.it)* occupies the lion's share of the Cilento peninsula. Some of the most interesting and accessible parts lie within an hour's drive northeast of Paestum, in the park's northwest corner. Near the town of **Castelcivita**, you can explore the **Grotte di Castelcivita** *(grottedi castelcivita.com)*, a complex of otherworldly prehistoric caves. For hikers, the town of **Sicignano degli Alburni**, capped by a medieval castle, makes a good base for the tough trek up 1742m-high **Monte Panormo**. Finally, the medieval centre of **Postiglione**, crowned by an 11th-century Norman castle, makes for a lovely stroll.

02 Agropoli

Guarding the northern flank of the Cilento peninsula, the ancient town of Agropoli proffers stunning views across the Gulf of Salerno to the Amalfi Coast. The outskirts are made up of a rather faceless grid of shop-lined streets, but the historic kernel, occupying a rocky promontory, is a charming tangle of cobbled streets with ancient churches, the remains of a castle and superlative views up and down the coast.

The Drive: South of Agropoli, the 13km stretch of the SR ex SP267 turns inland, giving a taste of the rugged interior, but you'll quickly head west to the sea.

03 Santa Maria di Castellabate

Because of the danger of sudden pirate attacks, all the coastal towns on the Cilento once consisted of a low-lying coastal fishing community and a nearby highly defended hilltop town where the peasants and fishing families could find quick refuge.

These days, the fishing district of Castellabate – known as Santa Maria di Castellabate – has outgrown its hilltop protector, thanks to the town's 4km beach of golden sand. Despite the development, the town's historic centre preserves a palpable southern Italian feel, with dusky-pink and ochre houses blinkered by traditional green shutters. The little harbour is especially charming, with its 19th-century palazzi (mansions) and the remnants of a much older castle. Note that these charms can diminish quickly when summer crowds overwhelm the scant parking.

The Drive: Just past Santa Maria di Castellabate along the SR ex SS267 is the turnoff to Castellabate. The road then winds through orchards and olive groves for 8km.

04 Castellabate

One of the most endearing towns on the Cilento coast, medieval Castellabate clings to the side of a steep hill 280m above sea level. Its summit is marked by the broad **Belvedere di San Costabile**, from where there are sweeping coastal views, and the shell of a 12th-century castle. The surrounding labyrinth of narrow streets is punctuated by ancient archways, small piazzas and the occasional palazzo.

The Drive: Head back down to the SR ex SS267 and follow it for 21km. The road leads inland, but you'll see the sea soon enough as you twist down to Acciaroli.

05 Acciaroli

Despite a growing number of concrete resorts on its outskirts, the tastefully restored historic centre of this fishing village makes it worth a stop, especially for lovers of Ernest Hemingway. The author spent time here in the early 1950s, and some say he based *The Old Man and the Sea* on a local fisherman.

The Drive: After Acciaroli, the coastal highway climbs quickly for 8km to Pioppi, proffering stunning views down the Cilento coast to Capo Palinuro.

06 Pioppi

A tiny, seaside hamlet, Pioppi enjoys culinary fame as the spiritual home of the Mediterranean diet. For more than 30 years, the American medical researcher Dr Ancel Keys lived here, observing the vigorous residents and studying the health benefits of their diet. Join the latest generation of locals on lovely **Piazza del Millenario**, before heading to the pristine, pale pebble beach a few steps away for a picnic.

The Drive: By Cilento standards, it's practically a straight shot for 8km along the coast to the archaeological site of Velia.

07 Velia

Founded by the Greeks in the mid-6th century BCE, and subsequently a popular resort for wealthy Romans, Velia (formerly Elea) was once home to philosophers Parmenides and Zeno. Today, you can wander around the town's evocative ruins at the **Parco Archeologico di Elea Velia** *(parchipaestumvelia.cultura.gov.it)*, and explore intact portions of the original city walls, plus remnants of thermal baths, an Ionic temple, a Roman theatre and even a medieval castle.

The Drive: You are now headed into the most hair-raising stretch of the Cilento's coastal highway, but spectacular views are your reward. At Ascea, 6km from Velia, coastal mountains make way for the small but rich plains that once fed ancient Velia. Olive trees start multiplying as you near Pisciotta. The total distance is about 10km.

08 Pisciotta

The liveliest town in the Cilento and also its most dramatic, hilltop Pisciotta consists of a steep maze of medieval streets. Life centres on the main square, **Piazza Raffaele Pinto**, where the town's elderly residents rule the roost. The surrounding hills are terraced into rich olive groves and produce particularly prized oil, while local fishers specialise in anchovies. When their catch is marinated in the local oil, the result is mouthwateringly good.

The Drive: The 11km trip begins with a steep descent from Pisciotta, and a straight road to Palinuro. Before reaching town, you'll see its beautiful, miles-long beach.

09 Palinuro

The Cilento's main resort, Palinuro remains remarkably low-key, with a fishing-village feel, though its beaches become crowded in August. Extending past its postcard-pretty harbour, the 2km-long promontory known as **Capo Palinuro** affords wonderful walking trails and views up and down the coast. Better yet, you can visit its sea cliffs and hidden caves, including Palinuro's own version of Capri's famous Grotta Azzurra, with a spectacular display of water, colour and light. To arrange an excursion, **Da Alessandro** *(costieradelcilento.it)* runs two-hour trips to the grotto and other local caves.

The Drive: Begin the 27km drive with a jaunt along the water before heading inland at Marina di Camerota. Get ready for plenty of sharp turns as you wind up the stunning SR ex SP562.

10 San Giovanni a Piro

With its historic centre and jaw-dropping views across the Gulf of Policastro to the mountains of Basilicata and Calabria, this little agricultural town makes a worthy stop as you wind your way around the wild, southern tip of the peninsula.

The Drive: The final 21km of this trip begins with a winding descent from San Giovanni a Piro to the pretty port town of Scario; the road flattens out as you make your way around the picturesque Golfo di Policastro.

11 Sapri

Set on an almost perfectly round natural harbour, Sapri is the ideal place to wave goodbye to the Cilento. The peninsula's dramatic interior mountains rear up across the beautiful Golfo di Policastro. Admire the views from the town's promenade or one of its nearby beaches.

Pisciotta

MAY004/SHUTTERSTOCK

PHOTO OPPORTUNITY

Capture rugged coast and royal-blue sea from hilltop Pisciotta.

31

★ BEST FOR

HISTORY

Conversano's restrained medieval splendour.

SOUTHERN ITALY

PUGLIA'S PILGRIM TRAIL

DURATION: 4 DAYS

DISTANCE: 312KM/194 MILES

GREAT FOR: FOOD AND DRINK, HISTORY, NATURE

BEST TIME TO GO: APRIL TO JUNE FOR HIKING AMID WILDFLOWERS; AUTUMN FOR MUSHROOMS AND MILD WEATHER.

Conversano

Both pilgrims and princes have long been partial to this stretch of the Adriatic coast. Weave your way from the sun-kissed seaside to fertile inland plains, which together form the basis for Puglia's extraordinary cuisine. All the way to the dramatic Promontorio del Gargano, you'll see evidence of Puglia's medieval golden age, when Norman and Swabian overlords built bristling castles and distinctive Romanesque churches.

LINK YOUR TRIP

33 Salento Surprises
From Bari, head 153km along coastal highways SS16, SS379 and SS613 until you reach jewel-like Lecce, then along the fascinating, beach-lined high heel of the Italian boot.

34 Across the Lucanian Apennines
About 67km south of Bari via the SS96 and SS99 lies Matera, the culmination of this trip over the gorgeous and little-explored Lucanian Apennines.

01 Conversano

Conversano's historic centre is a medieval jewel that generates its own austerely intriguing atmosphere. The main attraction is the Norman-Swabian **Castello di Conversano**, which commands views over the coastal plains all the way to Bari. And don't miss the beautiful Romanesque **cathedral** (Largo Cattedrale). Built between the 9th and the 14th centuries, it has a typical graven portal, large rose window and pointy gabled roof.

The Drive: Head northwest through Puglia's rich agricultural flatlands along the SP240 for the 31km to Bari.

DETOUR

Valle d'Itria

Start: 01 Conversano

Just south of Conversano rises the great limestone plateau of the **Murgia** (473m), a strange landscape riddled with holes and ravines through which small

streams and rivers gurgle. At the heart of the Murgia lies the idyllic **Valle d'Itria**, famous for its *trulli*. Unique to Puglia, these UNESCO-protected circular stone-built houses have curious conical roofs. The Murgia is also famous for its *masserie* – modelled on the classical Roman villa, these fortified farmhouses – equipped with oil mills, storehouses, chapels and accommodation for workers and livestock – functioned as self-sufficient communities. These days, many offer stylish country accommodation, including lovely **Biomasseria Lama di Luna** *(lamadiluna.com)*, a working farm redesigned according to principles of green architecture.

02 Bari

A lively university town and regional transport hub, Bari is often overlooked by time-poor travellers. But Puglia's capital, and southern Italy's second-largest city, deserves more than a cursory glance. The most interesting area is **Bari Vecchia** (Old Bari), an atmospheric warren of tight alleyways, unfussy trattorias and graceful piazzas.

In the heart of the district, the 12th-century **Basilica di San Nicola** *(basilicasannicola.it)* was one of the first Norman churches built in southern Italy. A splendid example of Puglian-Romanesque architecture, it's best known for housing the bones of St Nicholas (aka Santa Claus).

The Drive: A not-very-interesting 19km drive leads to Bitonto. From Bari, follow the SS96 through the city's flat, industrial suburbs to the town of Modugno, where you should connect with the SP231 to Bitonto.

03 Bitonto

Surrounded as it is by olive groves, it's no surprise Bitonto produces a celebrated extra-virgin oil. However, it is the town's medieval core that makes it worth seeking out.

Its magnificent 12th-century **cathedral** is romantically dedicated to St Valentine. There's also an impressive 14th-century tower, and smaller medieval churches.

The Drive: Heading along the SP231, the flat landscape becomes increasingly rural, until you reach the outskirts of Ruvo di Puglia, 19km to the west.

04 Ruvo di Puglia

Situated on the eastern slopes of the Murgia plateau and surrounded by olive and almond orchards, Ruvo is an attractive country town. Its historic core is dominated by a famous 13th-century **cathedral**, a gorgeous example of Puglia's distinctive version of Romanesque architecture. A short walk away, the **Museo Nazionale Jatta** *(museipuglia.cultura.gov.it)* showcases an interesting collection of ancient Greek ceramics. Don't leave town without trying the exquisite cakes and pastries made with Ruvo's prized local almonds.

The Drive: Head through fields and olive orchards along the SP2 for 8km to Corato, where you'll catch the SP238 – a straight shot north for 14km through dozens of olive groves to seaside Trani.

05 Trani

Known as the 'Pearl of Puglia', Trani has a sophisticated feel, particularly in summer when well-heeled visitors pack the bars on the marina. The marina is the place to promenade and watch the boats, while the historic centre, with its medieval churches, glossy limestone streets and faded yet charming palazzi, is enchanting. The most arresting sight is the austere, 12th-century **Cattedrale di Trani** *(cattedraletrani.it)*, white against the deep-blue sea.

The Drive: Following the coastline, the SS16 heads quickly into agricultural land until you reach Barletta's suburbs after 15km.

06 Barletta

Barletta's crusading history is a lot more exotic than the modern-day town, although the historic centre is pretty enough with its cathedral, colossus and fine castle. However, the history of the town is closely linked with the nearby archaeological site of **Canne della Battaglia**, where Carthaginian Hannibal whipped the Romans. Barletta also has some of the nicest beaches along this stretch of coast.

The Drive: From Barletta it's a 31km drive south to Andria along the SS170dir. Continue on the same road and follow as the land begins to rise near Castel del Monte.

Monte Sant'Angelo

ALEXANDRE.ROSA/SHUTTERSTOCK

07 Castel del Monte

With its unearthly geometry and hilltop location, the 13th-century, UNESCO-protected **Castel del Monte** *(casteldelmonte.cultura.gov.it)* is visible for miles around. No one knows why Frederick II built this mysterious structure – there's no nearby town or strategic crossroads, and it lacks typical defensive features like a moat or arrow slits. Some theories claim that, in accordance with mid-13th-century beliefs, the octagon represented the union between the circle (representing the sky and the infinite) and square (the Earth and the temporal).

The Drive: From Castel del Monte this leg is 34km, heading south along the SS170dir, then picking up the SP234 and SP149 at Montegrosso. The road meanders through a hilly and rather barren stretch until you reach the SP231 and the flatter lands around Canosa di Puglia.

08 Canosa di Puglia

Predating the arrival of the Romans by many centuries, this rather drab provincial town was once rich and powerful Canusium, Roman capital of the region. Today you can see remnants of this prosperity in the massive **Arco Traiano**, the **Roman Bridge** and the **Basilica di San Leucio**. Once a huge Roman temple, it was converted into a massive Christian basilica in the 4th and 5th centuries. Today only tantalising fragments remain at the **Parco Archeologico di San Leucio**.

The Drive: From Canosa head towards Cerignola on the A14 *autostrada*. Exit at Cerignola Est and follow the SP77 past olive groves to Manfredonia at the southern end of the Promontorio del Gargano. Join the SS89 and then the SP55 for the climb to hilltop Monte Sant'Angelo. Allow two hours for the 85km drive.

> PHOTO OPPORTUNITY
>
> Capture the isolated mountaintop splendour of Monte Sant'Angelo.

DETOUR

Lucera

Start: 08 Canosa di Puglia

About 85km northwest of Canosa di Puglia, Lucera has one of Puglia's most impressive castles and a handsome old town centre of mellow sand-coloured brick and stone, with chic shops lining wide, shiny stone streets. Frederick II's enormous castle, built in 1233, lies 14km northwest of the town on a rocky hillock surrounded by a perfect 1km-long pentagonal wall, guarded by 24 towers.

09 Monte Sant'Angelo

One of Europe's most important pilgrimage sites: it was here in 490 CE that St Michael the Archangel is said to have appeared in a grotto. During the Middle Ages, the **Santuario di San Michele** *(santuariosanmichele.it)* marked the end of the Route of the Angel, which began in Mont St-Michel in Normandy and passed through Rome. Today the sanctuary is a remarkable conglomeration of Romanesque, Gothic and baroque elements. Etched bronze and silver doors, cast in Constantinople in 1076, open into the grotto itself. Inside, a 16th-century statue of the archangel covers a sacred spot: the site of St Michael's footprint.

The Drive: From Monte Sant'Angelo, head back towards the sea, rejoining the SS89 and then the fiercely winding SP53 as you head to the tip of the peninsula. This 56km drive is the most scenic of the trip.

10 Vieste

Jutting off the Gargano's easternmost promontory into the Adriatic, Vieste is an attractive whitewashed town overlooking a lovely sandy beach – a gleaming wide strip flanked by sheer white cliffs and overshadowed by the towering rock monolith, **Scoglio di Pizzomunno**. It's packed in summer and ghostly quiet in winter.

DETOUR

Isole Tremiti

Start: 10 Vieste

This three-island archipelago is a picturesque vision of rugged cliffs, medieval structures, lonesome caves, sandy coves and thick pine woods – all surrounded by a glittering, dark-blue sea. It's packed to the gills in July and August, but makes a wonderful off-season getaway. Ferries depart in summer from Vieste and Peschici, and year-round from Termoli, about a three-hour drive up the Adriatic coast.

32

SOUTHERN ITALY

VALLE D'ITRIA

DURATION: 2–3 DAYS

DISTANCE: 176KM/109 MILES

GREAT FOR: ARCHITECTURE, HISTORY, NATURE

BEST TIME TO GO: MAY AND JUNE WHEN THE WEATHER'S WARM AND SPRING FLOWERS ARE OUT.

★ BEST FOR

FOODIES

A grilled *bombetta* (a ball of local *capocollo* meat) in Cisternino.

Apulian food

It might only be an hour's drive from big-city Bari but the Valle d'Itria is another world. This is farming country, where quiet back roads run past orderly fruit orchards and gnarled, centuries-old olive trees writhe out of the rusty red soil. Attractive hilltop towns harbour whitewashed historic centres, and strange *trulli* (circular stone-built houses) litter the rock-strewn landscape. Marking the end of the road is Lecce, Puglia's great baroque city.

LINK YOUR TRIP

31 Puglia's Pilgrim Trail
Instead of turning south at Bari, head north to join this tour of Puglia's architectural splendours and medieval castles.

33 Salento Surprises
Lecce is the starting point for this trip through the fashionable summer hot spots of Puglia's deep south.

01 Bari

Start your trip with a blast of urban grit in Bari. Pugila's regional capital and main transport hub is a city of busy, shop-lined boulevards and grand municipal buildings, its large student population ensuring there's always plenty of life in its piazzas, bars and cafes.

Much of the city's grid-patterned centre dates to the 19th century, but it's in the tightly packed **Bari Vecchi** (Old Bari), that you'll find the city's greatest treasures. Chief among these is the mighty **Basilica di San Nicola** *(basilicasannicola.it)*, a towering Puglian-Romanesque cathedral that houses the miraculous bones of St Nicholas (aka Santa Claus). Nearby, the hulking **Castello Svevo** (Swabian Castle) harks back to Puglia's golden age under the Swabian king Frederick II.

The Drive: From Bari pick up the SS100, following signs for Taranto. Exit at Casamassima and push on to Turi on the SS172. The road traverses typical Pugliese countryside,

ANGELO DAMICO/SHUTTERSTOCK

drystone walls and orchards of fruit and olive trees. After Turi, head left on the SP32 for the Grotte, some 43km from Bari.

02 Grotte di Castellana

On the northwestern edge of the Valle d'Itria, the **Grotte di Castellana** *(grottedicastellana.it)* are a series of spectacular limestone caves that link to form Italy's longest natural subterranean network. The galleries, first discovered in 1938, contain an incredible range of underground landscapes, with extraordinary stalactite and stalagmite formations – look out for the jellyfish, the bacon and the stocking. The highlight is the **Grotta Bianca** (White Grotto), visitable on a full tour only, an eerie white alabaster cavern hung with stiletto-thin stalactites.

The Drive: On this short 17km drive up to Alberobello via the SP237 to Putignano and then the SS172, you'll catch sight of the Valle d'Itria's unique *trulli* houses dotted amid the roadside fields and olive groves.

03 Alberobello

The UNESCO-listed town of Alberobello is Puglia's *trulli* capital. There are more than 1000 of these gnomic conical-capped houses spread across town, many huddled together on the hillside in the **Rione Monti** district southwest of the central strip, Via Indipendenza. Alberobello, which was named after a primitive oak forest, Arboris Belli (beautiful trees), that once covered the area, is an amazing sight, but it does get very touristy – from May to October busloads of tourists pile into *trullo* homes, drink in *trullo* bars and shop in *trullo* shops.

To get the best views of the whole higgledy-piggledy scene, park in Largo Martellotta and follow the steps up to Piazza del Popolo and the **Belvedere Trulli** lookout.

The Drive: It's a straightforward 9km drive up along the SS172 to Locorotondo. Once you arrive, don't attempt to take your car into the *centro storico*; instead, but park on the road downhill from the centre.

TRULLI

Unique to this part of Puglia, the white-grey, conical-capped *trulli* are a characteristic part of the Valle d'Itria's landscape. They first appeared in the late 15th century when they were built without mortar, making them easy to dismantle and allowing their wily owners to avoid local taxes. But while their design looks simple, it is well suited to the local climate – they are made out of whitewashed limestone and have thick walls that keep them cool in the baking summers.

04 Locorotondo

Perched on a ridge overlooking the valley, Locorotondo has one of Puglia's most beautiful historic centres. There are few 'sights' as such; rather, the town is a sight in itself with its circular *centro storico* – the name Locorotondo is a derivation of the Italian for 'round place' – where everything is a shimmering white, and blood-red geraniums tumble down from pretty window boxes. The streets are paved with smooth ivory-coloured stones, with the church of **Santa Maria della Greca** as their sun-baked centrepiece.

You can enjoy inspiring views of the surrounding valley from the **Villa Comunale**, while for inspiration of another kind, make sure to try some of the town's celebrated white wine.

The Drive: Yet another short drive. Follow the southbound SS172 as it undulates to Martina Franca, passing more *trulli*, rock walls and giant *fichi d'India* (prickly pears).

05 Martina Franca

The main town in the Valle d'Itria, Martina Franca is known for its graceful baroque buildings and lovely old quarter, a picturesque ensemble of winding alleys, blinding white houses and curlicue wrought-iron balconies.

Passing under the **Arco di Sant'Antonio** at the western end of pedestrianised Piazza XX Settembre, you emerge into Piazza Roma, dominated by the 17th-century rococo **Palazzo Ducale**, whose upper rooms have semi-restored frescoed

Alberobello (p195)

THEGRIMFANDANGO/SHUTTERSTOCK

walls and host temporary art exhibitions. From the piazza, Corso Vittorio Emanuele leads to Piazza Plebiscito and the centre's baroque heart. The square is overlooked by the 18th-century **Basilica di San Martino** and at its centre a statue of city patron, St Martin, swings a sword and shares his cloak with a beggar.

The Drive: This quick 9km leg takes you off the main roads onto the quiet back-country SP61 and its continuation the SP13. All around extends bucolic farmland littered with rocks and the ubiquitous olive trees.

06 Cisternino

An appealing, whitewashed hilltop town, slow-paced Cisternino has been designated as one of Italy's *borghi più belli* (most beautiful towns). Beyond its bland modern outskirts, it harbours a charming kasbah-like *centro storico*. Highlights include the 13th-century **Chiesa Matrice** and the **Torre Civica**, a defensive tower dating to the Norman-Swabian period (11th to 12th centuries). There's also a pretty communal garden with rural views. If you take Via Basilioni next to the tower you can amble along an elegant route right to the central piazza, **Vittorio Emanuele**.

Cisternino is also famous for its *fornelli pronti* (literally 'ready ovens') and in many butchers' shops and trattorias you can select a cut of meat and have it grilled to eat straight away.

> PHOTO OPPORTUNITY
>
> Alberobello's *trulli* from the Belvedere Trulli.

The Drive: From Cisternino, the SP17 makes for an attractive drive as it passes through yet more typically Puglian countryside en route to Ostuni, 15km away.

07 Ostuni

Surrounded by an ocean of olive trees, chic Ostuni shines like a pearly white tiara, extending across three hills. The town, which marks the end of the *trulli* region and the beginning of the hot, dry Salento, heaves in summer as crowds flock to its excellent restaurants and stylish bars.

The historic centre is a great place to hang out, but if you're in the mood for exploring there are a couple of worthy sights. First up, there's the dramatic 15th-century **Concattedrale di Ostunil** with an unusual Gothic-Romanesque facade. Then there's the **Museo di Civiltà Preclassiche della Murgia** *(ostunimuseo.it)*, a small museum showcasing finds from a nearby Palaeolithic burial ground, including the skeleton of a 25,000-year-old woman nicknamed Delia.

The Drive: This last 76km leg takes you south of the Valle d'Itria to the sun-scorched Salento district and the handsome city of Lecce. From Ostuni head seawards on the SP21 to join up with the SS379, which parallels the coast down to Brindisi. Continue south, following signs to Lecce and hook up with the fast-flowing SS613 for the final push.

08 Lecce

Lecce, the so-called Florence of the South, is a lively, laid-back university city celebrated for its extraordinary 17th-century baroque architecture. Known as *barocco leccese* (Lecce baroque), this local style is an expressive and hugely decorative incarnation of the genre replete with gargoyles, asparagus columns and cavorting gremlins. Swooning 18th-century traveller Thomas Ashe thought Lecce was Italy's most beautiful city, but the less-impressed Marchese Grimaldi said the facade of the **Basilica di Santa Croce** made him think a lunatic was having a nightmare.

For a taste, head to **Piazza del Duomo**, the city's prized focal square overlooked by a 12th-century cathedral and the 15th-century **Palazzo Vescovile** (Episcopal Palace) with an arched arcade loggia.

33

SALENTO SURPRISES

DURATION: 5-7 DAYS

DISTANCE: 177KM/110 MILES

GREAT FOR: FOOD AND DRINK, HISTORY, NATURE

BEST TIME TO GO: SUMMERS ARE SCORCHING AND CROWDED, BUT GOOD FOR BEACH LOVERS.

★ BEST FOR

ARCHITECTURE

Gape at Lecce's hypnotic baroque treasures.

Basilica di Santa Croce, Lecce

Until quite recently the Salento was a poor, isolated region littered with the relics of a better past, from crumbling Greek ports to Bronze Age dolmens. Nowadays, it's a fashionable summer destination, attracting crowds of sun-seeking Italians and celebrity holidaymakers. This trip highlights the area's great cultural and natural treasures, taking you from Lecce's baroque splendours to some of Italy's finest beaches.

LINK YOUR TRIP

31 Puglia's Pilgrim Trail
From Lecce, head about 130km north along the SS613, SS379 and SS16 to Conversano, which kicks off this exploration of northern Puglia's great castles and churches.

35 The Calabrian Wilderness
From the wild snowcapped peaks of the Pollino to Tropea's violet-coloured seas, get lost in Italy's least-explored region – about 290km from Lecce along the SS106, SP653 and SP4.

01 Lecce

As you stare open-mouthed at Lecce's madcap baroque architecture, it's almost hard not to laugh. It's so joyously extravagant that it can be considered either grotesquely ugly or splendidly beautiful. The 18th-century Irish traveller Thomas Ashe called it the most beautiful city in Italy, while the Marchese Grimaldi called the facade of Santa Croce the nightmare of a lunatic. What is certain is that, with more than 40 churches and at least as many palazzi from the 17th and 18th centuries, the city has an extraordinary cohesion.

A baroque feast, **Piazza del Duomo** is the city's focal point and a sudden open space amid the surrounding enclosed lanes. However, the most hallucinatory spectacle has to be the **Basilica di Santa Croce**, a swirling allegorical feast of sheep, dodos, cherubs and unidentified beasties. A short walk away, the **Museo Faggiano** *(museofaggiano.it)* is an archaeological treasure trove revealing layers of local history dating back to the 5th century BCE.

MARTINA DE PASCALI/LONELY PLANET

The Drive: Head south for 26km, first on the SS101, then on the SS367 and SP362 through fertile plains to Galatina.

02 Galatina

With a charming historic centre, Galatina is the capital of the Salento's Greek-inflected culture. It is almost the only place where the ritual of tarantism – a folk cure for the bite of a tarantula – is still remembered. The **taranta folk dance** evolved from it, and each year the ritual is performed on the feast day of Sts Peter and Paul (29 June). However, most people come to Galatina to see the incredible 14th-century **Basilica di Santa Caterina d'Alessandria**, its interior a kaleidoscope of Gothic frescoes set off by the serenity of a pure-white altarpiece.

The Drive: Head to the SS16 and strike east for a total of 34km, mostly through flat agricultural fields and olive orchards.

03 Otranto

Overlooking a pretty harbour on the blue Adriatic, whitewashed Otranto is today a pocket-sized resort town, but for 1000 years it was Italy's main port to the East. The small historic centre is watched over by a beautiful 15th-century **Castello Aragonese**. Long a target of jealous neighbours, Otranto was besieged by Turks, in league with Venezia (Venice), in 1480. They brutally murdered 800 of Otranto's faithful who refused to convert to Islam. Their bones are preserved in a chapel of the 11th-century Norman **cathedral**. The cathedral also features a vast 12th-century mosaic of a stupendous tree of life balanced on the back of two elephants. The town itself has a pretty beach, though there are much longer strands just outside of town.

The Drive: It is a fairly straight shot for 7km through the farmland south of Otranto to Capo d'Otranto. As you get close, you'll see the white lighthouse against the blue Adriatic.

04 Capo d'Otranto

As you head down Salento's dreamy coast, take a pit stop on this small peninsula, which is the official division between the Ionian and Adriatic Seas. Its restored 19th-century lighthouse sits picturesquely at its tip. On clear days you can see Albania across the sparkling blue Adriatic Sea.

The Drive: Heading south for 13km, the coastal road (the SP87 and its continuation the SP358) starts twisting as the coastline turns more rugged, with broad rocky flatlands.

05 Santa Cesarea Terme

Santa Cesarea Terme has a number of Liberty-style (art nouveau) villas, reminiscent of the days when spa-going was all the rage. There are still hotels that cater to the summer crowds of Italians who come to bathe in the thermal spas. But don't have visions of stylish hammams and soothing massages; here spa-going is a serious medical business, and the **Terme di Santa Cesarea** feels like a fusty old hospital with a lingering smell of sulphur about it. Still, this makes a great stop to ease the aches of life on the road.

The Drive: From Santa Cesarea Terme to Castro, it is a 7km drive along the coastal SP358.

06 Castro

Almost midway between Santa Maria and Otranto lies the town of Castro, which is dominated by an austere, Romanesque cathedral and forbidding castle. Just downhill, its marina serves as a popular boating and diving hub for the rocky coastline, which is riddled with fascinating sea caves. Most famous is the **Grotta Zinzulusa**, which is filled with stalactites that hang like sharp daggers from the ceiling. It can only be visited on a guided tour. Note that in summer it gets maniacally busy. Get details at *visitcastro.com*.

The Drive: Keep hugging the coastline south along SP358 for 31km as you pass pine and eucalyptus groves, farmland and a series of small resort towns until you reach the southernmost point of the peninsula.

07 Santa Maria di Leuca

At the very tip of Italy's high heel, the resort town of Santa Maria di Leuca occupies what Romans called *finibus terrae,* the end of the earth. The spot is marked by the **Basilica Santuario di Santa Maria di Leuca**, an important place of pilgrimage built over an older Roman temple dedicated to Minerva. These days, with its Gothic- and Liberty-style villas, this is a holiday resort, pure and simple. Many people come here to take one of the boat trips to visit sea grottoes like the **Grotta del Diavolo**, the **Grotta della Stalla** and the **Grotta Grande di Ciolo**. Trips depart from the little *porto* between June and September.

The Drive: Head 29km inland on the SS274 through seemingly endless olive groves and sunburnt farms to around Ugento, then 10km along the SP72 to Casarano.

08 Casarano

Sitting amid the Salento's rich olive groves, laid-back Casarano is home to the **Chiesa di Santa Maria della Croce**. One of the oldest sites in Christendom, it holds mosaics that date to the 5th century as well as frescoes from the Byzantine period.

The Drive: From Casarano to Gallipoli, head west on the SP321 and SS274 roadways. You'll drive 20km through olive trees and ochre-coloured fields, passing Taviano and Macchiaforte en route.

09 Gallipoli

Kallipolis, the 'beautiful city' of the Greeks, may be a faded beauty now, but it still retains its island charm. The Salentines see it as a kind of southern Portofino, and its weathered white *centro storico* (historic centre) has a certain grungy chic: part fishing village, part fashion model. In the 16th and 17th centuries, Gallipoli was one of the richest towns in the Salento, exporting its famous olive oil to Napoli (Naples), Paris and London to illuminate their street lamps. That explains the rather elegant air of the old town, which is divided into two distinct halves: the patrician quarter, which housed the wealthy merchant class, to the north of Via Antonietta de Pace; and the popular quarter, with its rabbit-warren of streets to the south.

DETOUR

Parco Regionale Porto Selvaggio

Start: 09 Gallipoli

The Ionian coast can be holiday hell in July and August, but head about 25km north from Gallipoli and you'll soon find the real belle of the region, the Parco Regionale Porto Selvaggio, a protected area of rocky coastline covered with umbrella pines, eucalyptus trees and olives. Right in the middle of the park is elegant **Santa Caterina**, a summer seaside centre.

Lecce (p198)

MARTINA DE PASCALI/LONELY PLANET

PUGLIA ON YOUR PLATE

Puglia's bold, brawny cuisine adheres very closely to its roots in *cucina povera* – literally, 'cooking of the poor'. Yet that cuisine is built on an incredibly rich set of raw ingredients: seafood from the long coastline; durum wheat, olives and extraordinary produce from its rich plains; abundant grapes that are being turned into rapidly improving wines; and some of the world's best almonds. For pasta, Puglians tend to favour broccoli or *ragù* (meat sauce) topped with the pungent local *ricotta forte*. Like their Greek forbears, they're also partial to lamb and kid. Also, raw fish (such as anchovies or baby squid) are marinated to perfection in olive oil and lemon juice.

34

SOUTHERN ITALY

ACROSS THE LUCANIAN APENNINES

DURATION: 5–7 DAYS

DISTANCE: 288KM/179 MILES

GREAT FOR: MEDIEVAL VILLAGES, HISTORY, NATURE

BEST TIME TO GO: SPRING AND AUTUMN FOR SUN WITHOUT SUMMER HEAT AND CROWDS.

★ BEST FOR

FOODIES

Heavenly local cheeses in Castelmezzano's Al Becco della Civetta.

Castelmezzano (p204)

This trip begins on Basilicata's Tyrrhenian coast, which may be diminutive but rivals Amalfi for sheer drama. The trip ends in a completely different world – the chalky, sunburnt landscape around Matera, a strange and remarkable city with timeless troglodyte dwellings that are UNESCO-protected. In between, you'll cross the dramatic peaks of the Lucanian Apennines, a gorgeous land of alpine forests, green valleys and bristling hilltop towns.

LINK YOUR TRIP

30 Cilento Coastal Trail
From Maratea, take the coastal SS18 north to Sapri to explore this wild coastline.

35 The Calabrian Wilderness
From Rivello take the A3 south to Mormanno to get lost in Italy's least-explored region.

01 Maratea

Sitting in stately fashion above the cliffs and pocket-sized beaches of the Golfo di Policastro, Maratea is Basilicata's only bijou resort town. Uphill, the enchanting medieval centre has elegant hotels, pint-sized piazzas, wriggling alleys and startling coastal views. Still further up, a 22m-high statue of **Christ the Redeemer** lords it over the rugged landscape. Down at sea level, the town's harbour shelters sleek yachts and bright-blue fishing boats. The deep-greenhillsides that encircle this tumbling conurbation offer excellent walking trails, while the surrounding coastline hides dozens of tiny beaches.

The Drive: The 23km to Rivello takes you into the heights of the coastal range. From Maratea, follow signs north to Trecchina. Expect great sea views along the way. At Trecchina, head down to a short but blessedly straight stretch of highway SS585. Rivello will appear quickly on your right.

DALIU/SHUTTERSTOCK

02 Rivello

Perched on a high ridge and framed by the southern Apennines, Rivello is not just another picture-pretty medieval village. Due to its strategic position, it was contested for centuries by both Lombards and Byzantines. Eventually, they reached an unlikely compromise – the Lombards settled in the lower part of town, the Byzantines in the upper. This resulted in two separate centres with two diverse cultures developing in a single town. Today, Rivello's charm lies in its narrow alleys, where homes both grand and humble are graced with wrought-iron balconies.

The Drive: For the 40km to Padula, return to the SS585 and head to the northbound A3 *autostrada*. Rugged mountains will suddenly open out into the wide, fertile Vallo di Diano. Take the Padula exit and follow signs to the abbey.

03 Padula

In the plains just below hilltop Padula lies one of southern Italy's most extraordinary sites. The **Certosa di San Lorenzo** *(padula.eu)* is among the largest monasteries in southern Europe, with 320 rooms and halls, 13 courtyards, 100 fireplaces, 52 stairways, 41 fountains and the world's largest cloisters. Founded in 1306, its buildings represent more than four centuries of construction, though primarily it is a 17th- and 18th-century baroque creation.

The Drive: From Padula, take the SS19 back instead of the A3. Just past Montesano Scalo, follow signs to Sarconi along the SP ex SS103. Here begins a beautiful, winding ascent into the Lucanian Apennines, then a descent towards the verdant Val d'Agri. Reckon on just over an hour for the 44km journey to Grumentum.

04 Grumentum

Set amid the fertile Val d'Agri, Grumentum was once an important enough Roman city that the invading Hannibal made it his headquarters. Eventually it was abandoned for hilltop Grumento Nova in the 9th century. Today, its ruins sit humbly amid agricultural fields and leave much to the imagination. Still, they make for a fascinating and atmospheric ramble, especially the miniature version of the Colosseum.

The Drive: Head back to the SP ex SS103 for a 15km drive along the pastoral valley floor following signs to Viggiano. The last few kilometres are pure switchback.

05 Viggiano

Hilltop Viggiano stands guard above the beautiful Val d'Agri. Aside from its fine views, the town has an illustrious music history. Since the 18th century, it has been celebrated for its harp makers and players, and has a long tradition of producing lively street musicians.

Viggiano is also a historic pilgrimage destination thanks to its ancient statue of the Black Madonna, the *Madonna Nera del Sacro Monte.*

The Drive: The 63km ride to Castelmezzano is breathtaking. Head back down the switchback and look for the SP ex SS103 and signs to the town Corleto Perticara. At Corleto Perticara, pick up the SS92 and wind past Laurenzana with its beautiful Romanesque church and castle. Then catch the SP32 and head north. After passing a pretty reservoir signs will lead to Castelmezzano.

06 Castelmezzano

Clinging to a series of impossibly narrow ledges, the houses of tiny Castelmezzano look like something out of a fairy tale, bounded on one side by rocky spires and on the other by the vertigo-inducing gorges of the Caperrino river. When the mist swirls in (as it often does) the effect is otherworldly. For an adrenaline rush, fly across the gorge to neighbouring Pietrapertosa at 120km/h attached to a steel cable via **Il Volo dell'Angelo** *(volodellangelo.com).*

This region is also known for its incomparable goat's and sheep's milk cheese, the best of which is on the menu at **Al Becco della Civetta** *(beccodellacivetta.it).*

The Drive: Though you could practically throw a stone across the gorge separating Castelmezzano from Pietrapertosa, the 10km drive requires dozens of hairpin turns and a strong stomach. But views of the gorges are gorgeous indeed. The way is well marked.

07 Pietrapertosa

As the highest town in Basilicata, Pietrapertosa is possibly even more dramatically situated than neighbouring Castelmezzano. Pietrapertosa literally translates as 'perforated stone' and, indeed, the village sits in the midst of bizarrely shaped rocky towers.

Literally carved into the mountainside, its 10th-century **Saracen fortress** is difficult to spot, but once you've located it you won't regret the long climb up. The views are breathtaking.

The Drive: After the meandering descent from Pietrapertosa, take SS407 to the Tricàrico exit, 29km from Pietrapertosa. You'll notice the peaks of the Dolomiti Lucani disappear in favour of the chalky plains and gorges that define the landscape around Matera.

Matera

SEAN PAVONE/SHUTTERSTOCK

08 Tricàrico

Perched on a ridge above the Basento river valley, Tricàrico may not be as dazzlingly odd as Castelmezzano and Pietrapertosa, but it does have one of the best-preserved medieval cores in Basilicata, with Gothic and Romanesque religious buildings capped by a picturesque Norman tower.

Its ramparts also proffer lovely views over the surrounding countryside.

The Drive: Head back to the SS407 and continue east along the snaking Bassento river valley, until you see the castle of Migliònico far off on your left. Shortly after, exit the main road onto the SS7 and follow the signs to Matera.

09 Matera

Haunting and beautiful, Matera's unique *sassi* (districts of cave houses and churches) sprawl below the rim of the steep-sided Gravina gorge like a giant nativity scene.

The houses' rock-grey facades once hid grimy, filthy abodes, but in recent years many have been converted into restaurants and swish cave hotels.

> PHOTO OPPORTUNITY
>
> Capture Matera's ancient cave dwellings at sunset.

Overlooking the *sassi* – divided into the **Sasso Barisano** and **Sasso Caveoso** – the new town is a lively place, with its elegant baroque churches, exquisite Romanesque cathedral and elegant palazzi.

Matera is said to be one of the world's oldest towns, dating back to the Palaeolithic Age and continuously inhabited for around 7000 years. The simple natural grottoes that dotted the gorge were adapted to become homes, and an ingenious system of canals regulated the flow of water and sewage.

In his great book, *Christ Stopped at Eboli,* Carlo Levi describes the appalling poverty he saw in the city in the 1930s and how children would beg passers-by for quinine to stave off the deadly malaria.

Such publicity finally galvanised the authorities into action and in the late 1950s about 15,000 inhabitants were forcibly relocated to new government housing schemes. For a fascinating glimpse into Matera's past, search out the **Casa Noha** *(fondoambiente.it/casa-noha-eng)* in the Sasso Caveoso.

DETOUR

Carlo Levi Country

Start: 09 Matera

Aliano, a tiny and remote village about 80km south of Matera, would still languish unknown had not writer, painter and political activist Carlo Levi been exiled here in the 1930s during Mussolini's regime. In his extraordinary book *Christ Stopped at Eboli*, Levi graphically describes the aching hardship of peasant life in 'Gagliano' (in reality, Aliano) where 'there is no definite boundary between the world of human beings and that of animals and even monsters'.

Today, Aliano is a sleepy town that only seems to come alive late in the afternoon when old men congregate on the park benches in the pleasant tree-lined Via Roma, and black-shrouded women exchange news on the streets.

STAY AWHILE

MATERA

BY GREGOR CLARK

For an unforgettable detour, linger a few days in the ancient city of Matera, in Italy's less-visited Basilicata region. Human settlement here dates back several millennia, thanks to the natural shelter provided by the region's easily sculptable limestone cliffs. Long a desperately poor part of Italy, Matera has experienced a renaissance in recent decades. The relatively more modern upper town, with architectural flourishes ranging from Romanesque to baroque, presides over cliffs pockmarked with ancient rock-hewn dwellings, many now converted to hotels, restaurants, bars and museums. It's an enchanting spot, suffused with the peaceful, unhurried pace of southern Italy.

The labyrinthine staircases and narrow passageways of Matera's two cave dwelling districts, **Sasso Barisano** and **Sasso Caveoso**, make an atmospheric spot for aimless wandering. Stop off first at **Casa Noha** *(fondoambiente.it/casa-noha-eng)*, where videos projected onto the rock walls offer an excellent introduction to the history of Matera's stone dwellings, the ravages of its rural poverty and the region's cultural evolution.

I find myself inevitably drawn deeper, into the adjacent **Matera Gravina gorge**, a 200m-deep cleft riddled with the remains of abandoned villages and more than 150 rupestrian churches, now preserved as the **Parco della Murgia Materana** *(parcomurgia.it)*. Another 15km south, the region's crowning artistic glory is the **Benedictine Cripta del Peccato Originale** *(criptadelpeccatooriginale.it)*, known as Matera's Sistine Chapel for its exquisite Byzantine-era religious frescoes.

After a day exploring Matera's wonders, my favourite aperitivo spot is the panoramic terrace at **Crialoss** *(palazzodegliabati.it/crialoss)*, where you can relish the golden glow of Matera's cityscape at sunset before heading off to dinner at any number of cave restaurants, from low-key **Osteria La Lopa** *(lalopa.com)* to the Michelin-starred Vitoantonio Lombardo *(vlristorante.it)*.

LINK YOUR TRIP

Matera is the final destination of the **34 Across the Lucanian Apennines** road trip.

FROM LEFT: WR7/SHUTTERSTOCK, SYLVIEPM/GETTY IMAGES

Left & right: Matera

PLACES TO STAY

Casa Diva
This boutique hotel in the Sassi features traditional dwellings with contemporary renovations and breathtaking views from the rooms. *(casadivamatera.it)*

Ai Terrazzini Residence
Ai Terrazzini offers a series of large and comfy apartments and a plush hostel with beautiful views on the Sassi and a curated breakfast. *(aiterrazzini.it)*

Hotel Sant'Angelo
Carved out of tufa rocks and mirroring the layout of a traditional Matera neighbourhood, this complex comprises multiple historical dwellings whose rooms and courtyards are laid out on a steep slope and connected by stairways and landings. *(santangelomatera.it)*

35

SOUTHERN ITALY

THE CALABRIAN WILDERNESS

DURATION: 8-10 DAYS

DISTANCE: 606KM/376 MILES

GREAT FOR: HISTORY, NATURE

BEST TIME TO GO: SPRING AND AUTUMN FOR SUNNY WEATHER WITHOUT SUMMER HEAT AND CROWDS.

From the alpine Pollino to the thickly forested slopes of the Aspromonte, Calabria possesses some of Italy's wildest landscapes. Avoid the overbuilt coast and you'll often feel you have the place to yourself. Plagued by earthquakes, poverty and organised crime, its artistic heritage is limited, yet its rough beauties are gripping. Besides three sprawling national parks, ancient towns seem to grow out of craggy hilltops, while amethyst waters wash Tropea's beaches.

LINK YOUR TRIP

34 Across the Lucanian Apennines
From Mormanno, head north 66km to seaside Maratea to begin your adventure into the beautiful interior of Basilicata.

36 Wonders of Ancient Sicily
From Reggio Calabria, it's a 30-minute ferry ride to Messina on Sicily. Continue 50km south to Taormina taking in the island's Greek, Norman and Arab heritage.

01 Mormanno

In the heart of the **Parco Nazionale del Pollino** *(parconazionalepollino.it)*, this bristling hilltop town of 3000 stands guard over the narrow Lao river valley. Mormanno makes a convenient base from which to explore the peaks and forests of the surrounding national park. Don't miss its prized local lentils, best served in a deliciously simple soup loaded with oregano.

The Drive: Instead of the A3 *autostrada*, take the pleasant SP241, which winds its way for 21km through forested hills and green valleys as you sneak up on the back side of Morano Calabro.

02 Morano Calabro

One of the most dramatic hill towns in southern Italy, Morano Calabro is a dense, steeply rising medieval labyrinth capped by the dramatic ruins of a Norman castle. Just as extraordinary is its setting at the foothills of a dramatic stretch of the Pollino mountain range. Morano

★ BEST FOR

OUTDOORS

From Cupone, strike out into the wilds of Calabria's Sila mountain range.

MARCO FINE/SHUTTERSTOCK

Parco Nazionale della Sila (p211)

makes a good jumping-off point for the beautiful Gole del Raganello canyon.

The Drive: Head down the A3, dramatically framed by the Pollino mountain range, until you reach the exit for Altomonte, which is about 30km from Morano Calabro. The town itself sits at the end of a series of well-marked country roads, a further 10km away.

DETOUR

Gole del Raganello

Start: 02 Morano Calabro

Located just outside the town of Civita, about 20km east of Morano Calabro, the dramatic gorges carved by the Raganello river are well worth seeking out. In addition to the majesty of their sheer limestone walls, the gorges are also home to rich flora and fauna, from foxes and martens to soaring golden eagles. Note also that the towns in this region still preserve traces of Albanian culture more than five centuries after their ancestors fled to Calabria when Turks invaded Albania.

03 Altomonte

The views from this well-preserved hilltop town encompass the snowy heights of the Pollino range, the rich patchwork of farms that covers its foothills and even a glimpse of the blue Mediterranean off to the east. Don't miss the 14th-century **Chiesa di Santa Maria della Consolazione**, one of the finest examples of Gothic architecture in Calabria.

The Drive: For this 51km leg, head back to the A3, then south to the Montalto exit, where you'll then twist and turn along SS559 as you head for Santa Maria Assunta in Sambucina.

04 Santa Maria Assunta in Sambucina

Tucked in the foothills of the Sila mountains, this once-vast abbey has, over the centuries, been reduced to just a few atmospheric remnants, thanks to a devastating combination of earthquakes and landslides. Today, all that is left is a transept of the original church, which incorporates both Romanesque and Gothic elements.

The Drive: After getting back on the SS559, you will soon wind your way up to the SP247, then along a high plain, where pastureland alternates with pine and oak forests offering a distinct alpine flavour. Signs lead you the 38km to Camigliatello Silano.

05 Camigliatello Silano

A popular ski-resort town with 6km of trails, Camigliatello Silano looks much better under snow – think Swiss chalets in poured concrete. However, even in the summer it makes a comfortable base from which to explore the Sila mountains, with their upland meadows, pine and oak forests and well-marked hiking trails.

The Drive: As you gently make your way along the 10km jaunt on the SP250 to Cupone, you will soon see the blue waters of Lago Cecita appear through the trees.

06 Cupone

Home to the headquarters of the **Parco Nazionale della Sila** *(parcosila.it)*, Cupone sits on the edge of pretty, meandering Lago Cecita. Well-marked hikes into the surrounding heights radiate out from here, and there is a helpful visitors centre and small museum devoted to the local ecology and geology.

The Drive: Head back to Camigliatello Silano then catch the SS107, which twists its way down to Cosenza, for a total distance of 43km. The last part of the drive is particularly beautiful.

07 Cosenza

Though surrounded by uninspiring sprawl, Cosenza's medieval

> PHOTO OPPORTUNITY
>
> Sweeping views of mountains and sea from Capo Vaticano.

core is one of the best-preserved historic centres in Calabria, one of the few areas to have survived the constant earthquakes that have ravaged the region over the centuries. Its narrow, winding lanes have a gritty feel with their antiquated shopfronts and fading, once-elegant palazzi. Follow Corso Telesio and you eventually reach Piazza XV Marzo, an appealing square fronted by the Renaissance-style **Palazzo del Governo** and the neoclassical **Teatro Rendano**. Behind the piazza, the lovely **Villa Vecchia** park provides some welcome shade.

The Drive: Head south on the A3 until you reach sweeping views of the Golfo di Sant'Eufemia. Pizzo sits at its southern end, 90km away.

08 Pizzo

Stacked high on a sea cliff with sweeping views down to the Tropean peninsula, Pizzo has a distinct ramshackle charm. On its main square, cafes compete to offer the town's best *tartufo,* a death-by-chocolate ice-cream ball. A kilometre north of town, the **Chiesa di Piedigrotta** is a rock church that was first carved into the tufa rock by Neapolitan shipwreck survivors in the 17th century. It has since been filled with tufa saints as well as less godly figures like Fidel Castro and JFK.

The Drive: Head 30km south along coastal route SS522, which makes its way through uninspired beach resorts that alternate with farmland prized for its sweet red onions.

09 Tropea

Much of the Calabrian coast has been decimated by poorly planned mass development. Tropea is a jewel-like exception. Set on a rocky promontory, the town's small but well-preserved historic centre sits above a sugary, white-sand beach. At sunset, the clear turquoise waters are known to turn garish shades of purple. And don't miss the sweet fiery taste of the region's prized red onions, which come from the surrounding peninsula.

Note that the town's attractions are compromised in high summer by teeming crowds, when parking can become a blood sport.

The Drive: It is a lovely drive to Capo Vaticano for 13km along SP22, mostly following the coastline. When you reach the little town of San Nicoló, follow signs to Faro Capo Vaticano.

10 Capo Vaticano

Even if you don't have time to explore its beaches, ravines and limestone sea cliffs, stop at this cape on the southwestern corner of the Promontorio di Tropea for its jaw-dropping views. On a clear day, you can see past the Aeolian Islands all the way to Sicily.

The Drive: For this 83km drive, wind your way along the coastal SP23, skirting Rosarno until you reach the SS682. Take this and head across the pretty northern reaches of the Aspromonte to the Ionian coast. Push on south to Locri, from where hilltop Gerace is a short inland hop – follow signs from Via Garibaldi and follow the tortuously winding SP1.

Capo Vaticano

ALIAKSANDR ANTANOVICH/SHUTTERSTOCK ©

PARCO NAZIONALE DEL POLLINO

Connecting southern Basilicata and northern Calabria, the **Parco Nazionale del Pollino** *(parconazionalepollino.it)* is Italy's largest national park. The 'Mountains of Apollo' (Pollino) encompass a 1960-sq-km wedge of varied landscapes that are a repository of rare flora and fauna – including Italus, a gigantic 1300-year-old tree said to be the oldest in Europe. Now enshrined as a UNESCO Geopark, the Pollino offers endless hiking, biking and Nordic skiing opportunities, along with mountain villages where you can experience a way of life little affected by development. You'll find the park's main information office in Rotonda, 13km from Mormanno.

11 Gerace

A spectacular medieval hill town, Gerace is worth a detour for the views alone. On one side lies the Ionian Sea, and on the other the dark, dramatic heights of the Aspromonte mountains. It also has Calabria's largest Romanesque **cathedral**, a majestically simple structure that dates to 1045 and incorporates columns pilfered from nearby Roman ruins.

The Drive: After heading back down the SP1, turn south on the SS106, which parallels the blue Ionic coast. At the town of Bova Marina, follow signs inland along the sharply twisting road to hilltop Bova. The total distance is 77km.

12 Bova

Perched at 900m above sea level, this mountain eyrie possesses a photogenic ruined castle, plus stupendous surf-and-turf views that rival Gerace's. Don't miss the bilingual signage – the townspeople are among the few surviving speakers of Griko, a Greek dialect that dates at least to the Byzantine period and possibly to the times when ancient Greeks ruled here.

The Drive: The 19km road from Bova to Roghudi Vecchio features the most stunning stretch of driving on this trip – though it's also the most tortuous – and has some pretty rough patches. Note that it's important to ask about road conditions before setting out as roads can be washed out. It may be advisable to skip Roghudi and head straight to Gambarie.

13 Roghudi Vecchio

The wild, winding ride to Roghudi Vecchio takes you through a stunning stretch of the Aspromonte mountains. This ghostly town clings limpet-like to a steep, craggy slope above an eerily white bed of the Amendolea river, which is formed by limestone washed down from the surrounding peaks. The river is barely a trickle most of the year, but two terrible floods in the 1970s caused the town itself to be abandoned.

Note that the town is still uninhabited and unpoliced, so wandering off the main road is not recommended.

The Drive: On the 59km drive to Gambarie, it's more dramatic switchbacks down to the Amendolea river and back up, past the town of Roccaforte del Greco and back to the SS183, which climbs quickly from the olive trees and cacti of the lower altitudes to pines, oaks and chestnut trees along the flat peaks of the Aspromonte.

14 Gambarie

Headquarters of the **Parco Nazionale dell'Aspromonte** *(parco nazionaleaspromonte.it)* and the park's largest town, faux-Swiss Gambarie is more convenient than charming. It does make a great base to explore the pine-covered heights that surround it.

This is wonderful walking country, and the park has several colour-coded trails. There is also skiing in winter, with a lift right from the town centre.

The Drive: It's now time to return to sea level. This 32km leg begins on the SP7 as it passes through the towns of San Stefano and Sant'Alessio in Aspromonte, all the way to the A3. On the way down, gape across the Strait of Messina to Sicily, weather permitting.

15 Reggio Calabria

Reggio is the main launching point for ferries to Sicily, which sparkles across the Strait of Messina. Though the city's grid of dusty streets has the slightly dissolute feel shared by most port cities, Reggio's wide, seafront promenade, lined with art deco palaces, is delightful.

The city is also home to what are, probably, the world's finest examples of ancient Greek sculpture: the spectacular **Bronzi di Riace**.

Dating from around 450 BCE, these two full-sized Greek bronze nudes now reside at the **Museo Nazionale di Reggio Calabria** *(museo archeologicoreggiocalabria.it)*.

Gerace
POLONIO VIDEO/SHUTTERSTOCK

39
Palau
Stintino
Olbia
Castelsardo
Sassari
SARDINIA
Alghero
Nuoro
Dorgali
40
Oristano
Laconi
Sanluri
Muravera
Iglesias
Cagliari
38
Mediterranean Sea
0 100 km
0 50 miles
Tyrrhenian Sea
Golfo di Gaeta
Naples
CAMPANIA
BASILICATA
Sorrento
Amalfi
Salerno
Paestum
Padula
Palinuro
Sapri
Aeolian Islands
Lipari Town
Milazzo
Palermo
Trapani
A29
A29dir
Cefalù
A20
Marsala
SICILY
Petralia Soprana
Taormina
A18
A19
Catania
Selinunte
Sciacca
Enna
37
Agrigento
Gela
Syracuse
Ragusa
Noto
36
Pantelleria

DAMIANO MARIOTTI/SHUTTERSTOCK

The Emerald Coast (p234)

THE ISLANDS

EXPLORE

THE ISLANDS

Sicily and Sardinia, Italy's two main islands, are an enticing prospect. Sicily, the larger of the two, thrills with its Greek temples, exquisite baroque architecture, Arab-inflected cuisine and explosive volcanoes. Sardinia, some 200km west of the Italian mainland, is best known for its dreamy beaches and stunning coastlines, but rove inland and you'll discover it has a rugged, often beautiful, interior and troves of prehistoric treasures to unearth. Our trips take in the best the islands have to offer, leading from historic cities like Palermo, Syracuse and Cagliari through unforgiving hinterlands to dazzling shores and shimmering blue waters.

Palermo

Palermo, Sicily's regional capital and largest city, is in the island's northwest. It's served by international and domestic flights and regular car ferries sail in from Naples and Civitavecchia. Once in town, you can whet your appetite for the road ahead by exploring its heady streets and captivating sights – the Cappella Palatina and teeming Mercato di Ballarò are two not to miss. Palermo's food also delights, particularly its decadent *dolci* (sweets) and terrific street food – for a taste, try one of its legendary *arancine* (fried rice balls).

For somewhere to stay, there's a decent choice of hotels or, better still, excellent B&Bs.

Catania

Catania, Palermo's east coast rival, makes an excellent base for Sicily's eastern reaches. Mt Etna and Taormina are both within easy striking distance and Syracuse, gateway to the southeast, is only an hour's drive away.

It's a lively city with a striking baroque centre, a fabulous fish market and a distinct black-and-white look, courtesy of the volcanic rock used to build its monumental buildings. It's also an important transport hub: its Fontanarossa airport is Sicily's largest, trains run to/from Palermo and Messina (for ferry services to the mainland), and long-distance buses reach towns across the island.

WHEN TO GO

The islands' beach resorts heave in the torrid months of July and August, lending the coast a real holiday vibe. On the downside, accommodation rates peak and coastal roads are congested. Better for driving, as well as sightseeing, is spring (May and June) and autumn (September and early October), when prices are lower and the crowds thinner.

Cagliari

Rising from the sea in a jumble of roofs, facades and domes, Cagliari is Sardinia's historic capital. A port since ancient times, it can be reached by ferries from the Italian mainland and year-round flights to Elmas Airport. Accommodation is plentiful, but for charm and value for money, B&Bs are the way to go.

From Cagliari, the road leads west along Sardinia's southern coast or north toward Oristano and the island's rural centre.

Before heading off, take a day or two to explore the city's hilltop citadel and the colourful streets of the Villanova and seafront Marina districts.

Olbia & Alghero

On Sardinia's northeastern coast, Olbia is the main gateway to the Emerald Coast.

It's not a big place but it's well connected with ferries from the mainland and a small airport serving domestic and seasonal European flights.

Hotels and B&Bs provide lodgings while batteries of bars, restaurants and cafes cater to the summer crowds. Over in the northwest, Alghero is another possible base for northern Sardinia. A popular resort town, it's well set up for visitors with its own international airport, an arresting old town and a wide range of accommodation.

TRANSPORT

Flights from the Italian mainland and European cities serve airports at Palermo and Catania (on Sicily) and Cagliari, Olbia and Alghero (on Sardinia). Alternatively, year-round ferries sail from Civitavecchia, Naples and Genoa to ports on both islands. To get around the islands, buses are better than trains, and cars are better than buses.

WHERE TO STAY

Much of the accommodation in Sicily and Sardinia is concentrated in the main cities and summer resorts. In the cities, you'll find B&Bs are often your best bet with everything from modest family digs to boutique apartments in historic palazzi (mansions). Coastal options include beachside campgrounds, self-catering apartments and all-inclusive resort hotels. Many of these are well set up for families, offering half- and full-board packages. But note that much resort accommodation closes between November and March.

Outside the cities and holiday centres, accommodation tends to be simple, often in B&Bs and rural *agriturismi* (farm stays).

RESOURCES

- **Tourist offices**
  You'll find tourist offices in cities, towns and villages which can provide local info and basic maps.

- **Sardegna Turismo**
  Sardinia's official tourist website is comprehensive and up-to-date with ideas and practical information. *sardegnaturismo.it*

- **Visit Sicily**
  Official website that's chock-full of island information and suggestions. *visitsicily.info*

WHAT'S ON

- **Festa di Sant'Agata**
  Huge crowds cram into Catania to celebrate its patron saint every year from 3 to 5 February.

- **Sa Sartiglia**
  Oristano stages carnival parades and acrobatic horse riding in February.

- **Festival del Teatro Greco**
  (indafondazione.org) In May and June, classical plays are staged in Syracuse's ancient Greek theatre.

- **Festa di Sant'Efisio**
  Cagliari celebrates St Ephisius every 1 to 4 May, parading his effigy on a bullock-drawn cart.

36

★ BEST FOR

HISTORY

Exploring layers of Sicily's past in Syracuse.

THE ISLANDS

WONDERS OF ANCIENT SICILY

DURATION: 12–14 DAYS

DISTANCE: 664KM/412 MILES

GREAT FOR: FOOD AND DRINK, HISTORY, NATURE

BEST TIME TO GO: SPRING AND AUTUMN ARE BEST. AVOID THE HEAT AND CROWDS OF HIGH SUMMER.

Syracuse (p223)

A Mediterranean crossroads for 25 centuries, Sicily is heir to an unparalleled cultural legacy, from the temples of Magna Graecia to Norman churches made kaleidoscopic by Byzantine and Arab artisans. This trip takes you from exotic, palm-fanned Palermo to the baroque splendours of Syracuse and Catania. On the way, you'll experience Sicily's bucolic farmland, smouldering volcanoes and long stretches of aquamarine coastline.

LINK YOUR TRIP

35 The Calabrian Wilderness
To experience the wild peaks of the Pollino, head over to Reggio Calabria on the mainland via Messina.

38 Sardinia's South Coast
From Palermo, car ferries sail to Cagliari, the starting point for a journey through some of Sardinia's most beautiful, less-trodden landscapes.

01 Palermo

Palermo is a fascinating conglomeration of splendour and decay. Unlike Florence or Rome, many of its treasures are hidden rather than scrubbed up for endless streams of tourists. The city's cross-cultural history infuses its daily life, lending its dusty backstreet markets a distinct Middle Eastern feel and its architecture a unique East-meets-West look. A trading port since Phoenician times, the city, which is best explored on foot, first came to prominence as the capital of Arab Sicily in the 9th century CE. When the Normans rode into town in the 11th century, they used Arab know-how to turn it into Christendom's richest and most sophisticated city. The **Cappella Palatina** *(federicosecondo.org)* is the perfect expression of this marriage, with its gold-inflected Byzantine mosaics crowned by a honeycomb muqarnas ceiling – a masterpiece of Arab craftsmanship. For an insight into Sicily's long and

SAIK03P/SHUTTERSTOCK

turbulent past, the **Museo Archeologico Regionale Antonio Salinas** *(turismo.comune.palermo.it)* houses some of the island's most valuable Greek and Roman artefacts.

The Drive: The 82km trip to Segesta starts along the fast-moving A29 as it skirts the mountains west of Palermo, then runs along agricultural plains until you reach the hills of Segesta. The Greek ruins lie just off the A29dir.

02 Segesta

Set on the edge of a deep canyon in the midst of desolate mountains, the 5th-century-BCE ruins of Segesta are a magical sight. The city, founded by the ancient Elymians, was in constant conflict with Selinunte, whose destruction it sought with dogged determination and singular success. Time, however, has done to Segesta what violence inflicted on Selinunte; little remains now, save the theatre and the never-completed Doric temple. The latter dates from around 430 BCE and is remarkably well preserved. On windy days its 36 giant columns are said to act like an organ, producing mysterious notes.

The Drive: Keep heading along A29dir through a patchwork of green and ochre fields and follow signs for the 40km to Trapani. As you reach its outskirts, you'll head up the sinuous SP31 to Erice, with great views of countryside and sea.

03 Erice

A spectacular hill town, Erice combines medieval charm with astounding 360-degree views from atop the legendary **Mt Eryx** (750m) – on a clear day, you can see as far as Cape Bon in Tunisia. Wander the medieval streets interspersed with churches, forts and tiny cobbled piazzas. Little remains from its ancient past, though as a centre for the cult of Venus, it has a seductive history.

The best views can be had from the **Giardino del Balio**, which overlooks the rugged turrets and wooded hillsides down to the saltpans of Trapani and the sea. Adjacent to the gardens is the Norman **Castello di Venere** *(fondazioneericearte.org/il-castello-di-venere)*, built in the 12th and 13th centuries over the ancient Temple of Venus. And while Venus may be the goddess of love, Erice's goddess of all things sweet is Maria Grammatico, whose eponymous **pasticceria** *(mariagrammatico.it)* is revered around the globe. Don't leave town without savouring one of her cannoli or lemon-flavoured *cuscinetti* (small fried pastries).

The Drive: For the 12km to Trapani, it's back down the switchbacks of the SP31.

04 Trapani

Once a key link in a powerful trading network that stretched from Carthage to Venice, Trapani occupies a sickle-shaped spit of land that hugs its ancient harbour. Although Trapani's industrial outskirts are rather bleak, its historic centre is filled with atmospheric pedestrian streets and some lovely churches and baroque buildings. The narrow network of streets remains a Moorish labyrinth, although it takes much of its character from the fabulous 18th-century baroque of the Spanish period. Make time for the **Chiesa Anime Sante del Purgatorio**, home to the 18th-century *Misteri*, 20 life-sized effigies depicting the Passion of Christ.

The Drive: For the 33km trip from Trapani to Marsala, head south on the SS115. Small towns alternate with farmland until you reach Marsala on Sicily's west coast.

05 Marsala

Best known for its namesake sweet dessert wines, Marsala is an elegant town of stately baroque buildings within a perfect square of city walls. Founded by Phoenicians escaping Roman attacks, the city still has remnants of the 7m-thick ramparts they built, ensuring that it was the last Punic settlement to fall to the Romans.

Marsala's finest treasure is the partially reconstructed remains of a Carthaginian *liburna* (warship) – the only remaining physical evidence of the Phoenicians' seafaring superiority in the 3rd century BCE. You can visit it at the **Museo Archeologico Baglio Anselmi**.

The Drive: For this 52km leg, once again head down the SS115, passing through farmland and scattered towns until you reach the A29. Continue on the *autostrada* to Castelvetrano, then follow the SS115 and SS115dir for the last stretch through orchards and fields to seaside Selinunte.

THE 1693 EARTHQUAKE

On 11 January, 1693, a devastating 7.4-magnitude earthquake hit southeastern Sicily, destroying buildings from Catania to Ragusa. The destruction was terrible, but it also created a blank palette for architects to rebuild the region's cities and towns out of whole cloth, in the latest style and according to rational urban planning – a phenomenon practically unheard of since ancient times. In fact, the earthquake ushered in an entirely new architectural style known as Sicilian baroque, defined by its seductive curves and elaborate detail, which you can see on display in Ragusa, Modica, Catania and many other cities in the region.

06 Selinunte

Built on a promontory overlooking the sea, the Greek ruins of **Selinunte** *(parchiarcheologici.regione.sicilia.it)* are among the most impressive in Sicily, dating to around the 7th century BCE. There are few historical records of the city, which was once one of the world's most powerful, and even the names of the various temples have been forgotten and are now identified by letters. The most impressive, **Temple E**, has been partially rebuilt, its columns pieced together from their fragments with part of its tympanum. Many of the carvings, which are on a par with the Parthenon marbles, particularly those from **Temple C**, are now in Palermo's archaeological museum.

The Drive: Head back up to the SS115 and past a series of hills and plains for the 37km trip to Sciacca.

07 Sciacca

Seaside Sciacca was founded in the 5th century BCE as a thermal resort for nearby Selinunte. Until 2015, when financial woes forced the spa to shut down indefinitely, Sciacca's healing waters continued to be the big drawcard, attracting coachloads of Italian tourists who came to wallow in its sulphurous vapours and mineral-rich mud. Spas and thermal cures apart, it remains a laid-back town with an attractive medieval core and some excellent seafood restaurants.

The Drive: Continue eastwards on the SS115 as it follows the southern coast onto Porto Empedocle and then, 10km inland, Agrigento's hilltop centre. In all, it's about 62km.

GIOVENDAFM/SHUTTERSTOCK

Greek ruins, Selinunte

08 Agrigento

Seen from a distance, Agrigento's unsightly apartment blocks loom incongruously on the hillside, distracting attention from the splendid **Valley of Temples** *(parcovalle deitempli.it)* below. In the valley, the mesmerising ruins of ancient Akragras claim the best-preserved Doric temples outside of Greece.

The ruins are spread over a 13-sq-km site divided into eastern and western halves. Head first to the eastern zone, where you'll find the three best temples: the **Tempio di Hera**, the **Tempio di Ercole** and, most spectacularly, the **Tempio della Concordia**. This, the only temple to survive relatively intact, was built around 440 BCE and was converted into a Christian church in the 6th century.

Uphill from the ruins, Agrigento's **medieval centre** also has its charms, with a 14th-century cathedral and a number of medieval and baroque buildings.

The Drive: For this 133km leg head back to the SS115, which veers from inland farmland to brief encounters with the sea. Past the town of Gela, you will head into more hilly country, including a steep climb past Comiso, followed by a straight shot along the SP52 to Ragusa.

DETOUR

Villa Romana del Casale

Start: 08 Agrigento

Near the town of Piazza Armerina in central Sicily, the stunning 3rd-century **Roman Villa Romana del Casale** *(villaromana delcasale.it)* is thought to have been the country retreat of Diocletian's co-emperor Marcus Aurelius Maximianus. Buried under mud in a 12th-century flood, the villa remained hidden for 700 years before its floor mosaics – considered some of the finest in existence – were discovered in the 1950s. Covering almost the entire floor, they are thought unique for their range of hues and natural, narrative style.

09 Ragusa

Set amid the rocky peaks northwest of Modica, Ragusa has two faces. Atop the hill sits **Ragusa Superiore**, a busy town with all the trappings of a modern provincial capital, while etched into the hillside is **Ragusa Ibla**. This sloping area of tangled alleyways, grey stone houses and baroque palazzi is Ragusa's magnificent historic centre. Like other towns in the region, Ragusa Ibla collapsed after the 1693 earthquake. But the aristocracy, ever impractical, rebuilt their homes on exactly the same spot. Grand baroque churches and palazzi line the twisting, narrow lanes, which then open suddenly onto sun-drenched piazzas. Piazza del Duomo, the centre of town, is dominated by the 18th-century baroque **Duomo di San Giorgio**, with its magnificent neoclassical dome and stained-glass windows.

The Drive: Follow the SS115 for this winding, up-and-down 15km drive through rock-littered hilltops to Modica.

PHOTO OPPORTUNITY

Mt Etna from Taormina's Greek theatre.

10 Modica

Atmospheric Modica recalls a *presepe* (traditional Nativity scene), its medieval buildings climbing steeply up either side of a deep gorge. But unlike some of the other UNESCO-listed cities in the area, it doesn't package its treasures into a single easy-to-see street or central piazza; rather, they are spread around the town and take some discovering. Its star attraction is the baroque **Duomo di San Giorgio**, which stands in isolated splendour atop a majestic 250-step staircase.

The city's nerve centre is **Corso Umberto**. A wide avenue flanked by graceful palaces, churches, restaurants and bars, the thoroughfare is where the locals take their evening *passeggiata* (stroll). Originally a raging river flowed through town, but after major flood damage in 1902 it was dammed and Corso Umberto was built over it.

The Drive: Head back onto the SS115, which becomes quite curvy as you close in on Noto, 40km away.

11 Noto

Flattened by the 1693 earthquake, Noto was rebuilt quickly and grandly, and its sandstone buildings make it the finest baroque town in Sicily, especially impressive at night when illuminations accentuate

Mt Etna & Teatro Greco, Taormina

BERND REHORST/SHUTTERSTOCK

its carved facades. The pièce de résistance is **Corso Vittorio Emanuele**, an elegantly manicured walkway flanked by thrilling baroque palazzi and churches.

Transformed into a plush design hotel in 2026, **Palazzo Castelluccio** *(palazzocastelluccio.it)* reveals the luxury to which local nobles were accustomed. Its suite of lavish rooms is awash with murals, evocative paintings, gilded settees and worn glazed floors revealing the paths of long-gone servants.

The Drive: The 39km drive to Syracuse from Noto takes you down the SP59 and then northeast on the A18/E45, past the majestic Riserva Naturale Cavagrande del Cassibile as you parallel Sicily's eastern coast.

12 Syracuse

Syracuse is a dense tapestry of overlapping cultures and civilisations. Ancient Greek ruins rise out of lush citrus orchards, cafe tables spill out onto baroque piazzas and medieval lanes meander to the sea. Your visit, like the city itself, can be split into two easy parts: one dedicated to the archaeological site, the other to Ortygia, the ancient island neighbourhood connected to the modern town by bridge.

It's difficult to imagine now but in its heyday Syracuse was the largest city in the ancient world, bigger even than Athens and Corinth. The **Parco Archeologico della Neapolis** is home to well-preserved Greek (and Roman) remains, with the remarkably intact **Teatro Greco** – constructed in the 5th century BCE and rebuilt two centuries later – as the main attraction. In the grounds of **Villa Landolina**, about 500m east of the archaeological park, is the exceptional **Museo Archeologico Paolo Orsi** *(parchiarcheologici.regione.sicilia.it)*.

Compact, labyrinthine **Ortygia** encompasses 25 centuries of history. At its heart, the city's 7th-century CE **Duomo** looms over Piazza del Duomo, one of Italy's most magnificent squares. The cathedral was built over a pre-existing 5th-century-BCE Greek temple, incorporating most of the original Doric columns in its three-aisled structure. The sumptuous baroque facade was added in the 18th century.

The Drive: From Syracuse to Catania, it is a 66km drive north along the A18/E45. This is orange-growing country and you will see many orchards, which can be gorgeously fragrant when in bloom.

♥ WHY I LOVE THIS TRIP

DUNCAN GARWOOD, WRITER

Sicily claims some of the most spectacular artistic and archaeological treasures you've never heard of. The great Greek ruins of Agrigento and Syracuse might be on many travellers' radars but what about Palermo's Cappella Palatina or Noto's flamboyant baroque streets? These masterpieces are all the more rewarding for being so unexpected, and make this round-island trip an unforgettable experience.

13 Catania

Gritty, vibrant Catania is a true city of the volcano, much of it constructed from the lava that poured down on it during Mt Etna's 1669 eruption. The baroque centre is lava-black in colour, as if a fine dusting of soot permanently covers its elegant buildings, most of which are the work of Giovanni Battista Vaccarini. The 18th-century architect almost single-handedly rebuilt the civic centre into a stylish, modern city of spacious boulevards and set-piece piazzas.

Long buried under lava, the **Graeco-Roman Theatre** & **Odeon** reminds you that Catania's history goes back much further. Picturesquely sited in a crumbling residential area, the ruins are occasionally brightened by laundry flapping on the rooftops of vine-covered buildings that appear to have sprouted organically from the half-submerged stage.

The Drive: The 53km drive to Taormina along the A18/E45 is a coast-hugging northern run, taking in more orange groves as well as glimpses of the sparkling Ionian Sea.

14 Taormina

Over the centuries, Taormina has seduced an exhaustive line of writers and artists, from Goethe to DH Lawrence. The main reason for their infatuation? The horseshoe-shaped **Teatro Greco**, an ancient marvel looking out towards Mt Etna and the Ionian Sea. Built in the 3rd century BCE, the *teatro* is the most dramatically situated Greek theatre in the world and the second largest in Sicily (after Syracuse).

The 9th-century capital of Byzantine Sicily, Taormina also has a well-preserved, if touristy, medieval town, its streets dotted with fashionable cafes and bars.

STAY AWHILE

TAORMINA

BY GREGOR CLARK

Sicily's charismatic hilltop village of Taormina is a seductive place, with front-row views of Europe's most massive active volcano and a stunning sweep of Ionian coastline sparkling below. It's tailor-made for the Italian art of *dolce far niente* (sweet downtime), with cafes, restaurants and shops galore, and a plethora of hotels in hillside garden settings.

Taormina's resort-town renown dates back to the 18th century, when it was an obligatory stop on the European Grand Tour, yet its roots run much deeper. For a taste of Taormina's ancient history, my favourite spot is the spectacularly perched **Teatro Antico** *(parchi archeologici.regione.sicilia.it)*. Catching a summer performance here during the **Taormina Arte festival** *(taorminaarte.org)*, with Mt Etna smoking or erupting in the background, is a phenomenal experience – though this 3rd-century-BCE Greek theatre is a must-see attraction year-round. Come early (9am) to beat the crowds.

Taormina's pedestrianised main street **Corso Umberto** – framed by the medieval gates of Porta Messina and Porta Catania – snakes for 1km past shops specialising in everything from marzipan fruit to Sicilian ceramics to high-end fashion. It's worth a wander anytime, but it really hits its stride towards sunset. When the daylight starts fading, I love joining the throngs for Taormina's traditional *passeggiata* (evening stroll). Halfway down, **Piazza IX Aprile**, paved in gleaming black-and-white checkerboard marble, and framed on all sides by aesthetic beauties like the baroque San Giuseppe church and the crenellated 12th-century clocktower, is a prime people-watching spot.

For an impromptu beach day, take the funicular **Funivia Mazzarò-Taormina** *(asmtaormina.com/funivia-mazzaro-taormina)* down to Mazzarò (five minutes). Photogenic swim spots abound, but my favourite is enchanting **Isola Bella** *(visitsicily.info/attrazione/riserva-naturale-isola-bella)*, a rocky islet cradled between two green capes, adjoined by a nature reserve protecting peregrine falcons and red-bellied lizards.

LINK YOUR TRIP

Relax and unwind in Taormina after completing the **36 Wonders of Ancient** Sicily road trip.

Left & right: Taormina

FROM LEFT: LARASLK/SHUTTERSTOCK, GARY YEOWELL/GETTY IMAGES

PLACES TO STAY

Casa Turchetti
Every detail is perfect at this painstakingly restored former music school, on a back alley near Piazza IX Aprile. Vintage furniture and fixtures, handcrafted woodwork and homespun sheets exude an understated elegance. Topping it off is a breathtaking rooftop terrace. *(casaturchetti.com)*

Hotel Villa Belvedere
Built in 1902, this was one of Taormina's original grand hotels, with fabulous views, luxuriant gardens and a swimming pool shaded by a centenarian palm tree. *(villabelvedere.it)*

Villa Nettuno
Conveniently located just steps from the funicular to Mazzarò beach, this family-run spot with salmon pink walls and a flowery private garden is well priced, if a bit faded. *(hotelvillanettuno.it)*

37

THE ISLANDS

SICILIAN BAROQUE

DURATION: 5 DAYS

DISTANCE: 213KM/132 MILES

GREAT FOR: FOOD AND DRINK, HISTORY

BEST TIME TO GO: SPRING AND AUTUMN BRING FEWER CROWDS AND BETTER WEATHER FOR HIKING IN THE HILLSIDES OF THE MONTI IBLEI.

Shattered by a devastating earthquake in 1693 (p222), the towns of the Val di Noto rose collectively as reinvented beauties, becoming 18th-century poster kids for Sicily's own exuberant brand of baroque. The result is a rare example of aesthetic cohesion, a vision of honey-coloured towns sitting delightfully in a landscape of citrus and olive groves, and checkerboard fields shot through with limestone cliffs and rocky gorges.

LINK YOUR TRIP

30 Cilento Coastal Trail
From Catania, car ferries sail to Salerno, a short drive from Paestum, the launching pad for this spectacular coastal jaunt.

36 Wonders of Ancient Sicily
In Catania, you can join the grand tour of ancient Sicily, which begins in Arab-inflected Palermo and ends at Taormina's spectacular Greek theatre.

01 Catania

Though surrounded by ugly urban sprawl, Sicily's second-largest city is a thriving metropolis with a large university and a beautiful, UNESCO-listed centre. Brooding on the horizon, snowcapped Mt Etna is a powerful presence.

The volcano is deeply set in Catania's DNA. Much of the city's historic core was built from lava that poured down Etna's slopes during a massive eruption in 1669. From its exuberant baroque palazzi to grand set-piece squares, this is a city dressed in shades of charcoal and ashen grey. At its heart is elegant **Piazza del Duomo**, the city's collective living room. It's also where you'll find Catania's majestic **Cattedrale di Sant'Agata**, final resting place of homegrown composer Vincenzo Bellini. Just off the square is the famous fish market, **La Pescheria**, serving up more colour, noise and theatrics than any Bellini opera.

The Drive: From Catania to Syracuse, it is a 66km drive down

★ BEST FOR

HISTORY

Wander the labyrinthine lanes of Ragusa Ibla.

Ragusa Ibla (p229)

the A18/E45 *autostrada*. This is orange-growing country and you'll see many orchards, which are gorgeously fragrant when in bloom. Exit onto the SS124 for the last 4km into central Syracuse.

02 Syracuse

Settled by colonists from Corinth in 734 BCE, Syracuse (Siracusa) was considered the most beautiful city of the ancient world, rivalling Athens in power and prestige. You can explore the city's ancient heart at the extraordinary **Parco Archeologico della Neapolis**, the star attraction of which is the huge 5th-century-BCE **Greek theatre**.

In the wake of the 1693 earthquake, Syracuse, like most cities in the region, underwent a baroque facelift. While you'll find a number of baroque paintings at the **Galleria Regionale di Palazzo Bellomo**, the city's true period masterpiece is **Piazza del Duomo**, home of numerous architectural masterpieces. Top billing goes to the **Duomo**, its 18th-century facade considered a masterpiece of high Sicilian baroque. Look beneath the baroque veneer, though, and you can still see traces of the city's Greek origins, including 5th-century-BCE temple columns embedded in the Duomo's exterior.

The Drive: From Syracuse, head through rolling and unspoilt countryside along the SS124 for 42km to Palazzolo Acreide.

DETOUR

Valle dell'Anapo

Start: 02 Syracuse

For some beautifully wild and unspoilt countryside, turn off the SS124 between Syracuse and Palazzolo Acreide and head down into the beautiful **Valle dell'Anapo** – a deep limestone gorge. Follow signs to **Ferla**, with its small but lovely baroque centre. Another 11km past Ferla, you'll find the **Necropoli di Pantalica**, an important Iron and Bronze Age necropolis. Dating from the 13th to the 8th century BCE, it is an extensive area of limestone rocks honeycombed by more than 5000 tombs. There's no admission fee – just a car park at the end of the long, sinuous road down from Ferla.

03 Palazzolo Acreide

A charming town of baroque architecture and ancient ruins, Palazzolo Acreide's focal point is **Piazza del Popolo**, a striking square dominated by the ornate bulk of the **Chiesa di San Sebastiano** and **Palazzo Municipale**, an impressive town hall. A 20-minute uphill walk from Piazza del Popolo leads to the archaeological park of **Akrai**, once a thriving Greek colony and one of the area's best-kept secrets. You'll discover an ancient Greek theatre and Christian burial chambers with exquisitely carved reliefs.

The Drive: Head southeast along the SS287 for a 30km drive through more beautiful countryside. The road becomes curvier as you head into Noto.

04 Noto

Rebuilt after being flattened by the 1693 earthquake, Noto claims one of Sicily's most beautiful baroque centres. The golden-hued sandstone buildings and churches that flank **Corso Vittorio Emanuele**, many designed by local architect Rosario Gagliardi, are especially impressive in the early evening light and at night when they are illuminated.

Particularly eye-catching is the **Basilica Cattedrale di San Nicolò**, crowned by a distinctive dome. For an elevated view of the cathedral, hit the panoramic terrace at **Palazzo Ducezio** *(comune.noto.sr.it/la-cultura/la-sala-degli-specchi)*.

To see how the local aristocracy lived in baroque times, wander through nearby **Palazzo Nicolaci di Villadorata** or settle in for the night at **Palazzo Castelluccio** *(roccofortehotels.com)*, an ornate neoclassical mansion turned luxury hotel.

The Drive: Head southwest 22km along SS115 through more fields and orchards, passing through the town of Rosolini. Hilltop Ispica will rise up in front of you. Catch the sharply winding SP47 to the town centre.

05 Ispica

Between Noto and Modica, this hilltop town claims a number of fine baroque buildings. However, the real reason to stop is to peer into the **Cava d'Ispica** *(cavadispica.org)*, a verdant, 13km-long gorge studded with thousands of natural caves and grottoes. Evidence of human habitation here dates to about 2000 BCE, and over the millennia the caves have served as Neolithic tombs, early Christian catacombs and medieval dwellings.

The Drive: Start this 17km leg on the SS115 through relatively flat agricultural land. As you reach the suburbs of Modica, follow signs to Modica Centro and then to Corso Umberto I, the town's main thoroughfare.

06 Modica

With its steeply stacked medieval centre and lively central strip, **Corso Umberto I**, Modica is one of southern Sicily's most atmospheric towns. The highlight is the **Chiesa di San Giorgio**, a spectacular baroque church considered to be architect Rosario Gagliardi's great masterpiece. It stands in isolated splendour atop a majestic 250-step staircase in **Modica Alta**, the high part of town.

Modica is also famous for its distinctly grainy chocolate, worked at low temperature using an ancient method. To stock up on it, hit **Antica Dolceria Bonajuto** *(bonajuto.it)*, Sicily's oldest chocolate factory, or visit award-winning **Caffè Adamo** *(adamocaffe.it)*.

The Drive: From Modica to Scicli, wind your way southwest along the SP54 for 10km through rugged, rocky countryside.

06 Scicli

Compact Scicli is the most authentic of the Val di Noto towns, with an easy, salubrious vibe favoured by a growing number of VIP residents.

Its wealth of baroque churches includes the **Chiesa di Santa Teresa**, home to a 16th-century fresco featuring a rare inscription in Sicilianised Latin. Pedestrianised Via Francesco Mormino Penna claims a number of interesting sights, including **Palazzo Bonelli Patanè**, charming apothecary **Antica Farmacia**

HITTING THE HIGH NOTE

Catania's most famous native son, Vincenzo Bellini (1801–35), was the quintessential composer of *bel canto* opera. Hugely successful in his lifetime, he was known for his inimitable ability to combine sensuality with melodic clarity and his works still woo audiences today. The **Museo Belliniano**, in the composer's former Catania home, has an interesting collection of his memorabilia. Catania's lavish, 19th-century **Teatro Massimo Bellini** *(teatromassimobellini.it)* is the place to hear *I Puritani, Norma* and his other masterworks.

TRABANTOS/SHUTTERSTOCK

Corso Vittorio Emanuele, Noto

Cartia and **Palazzo Municipio**, home to sets from TV series *Inspector Montalbano.*

The Drive: The first half of this 26km stretch winds north on SP94, passing along the rim of a pretty canyon typical of the region. Then catch the winding SS115 as it heads up to Ragusa. Across a small canyon, you will see the old, hillside historic centre of Ragusa rising grandly.

PHOTO OPPORTUNITY

A nighttime shot of Noto's Corso Vittorio Emanuele.

08 Ragusa

Set amid rocky peaks, **Ragusa Ibla** – Ragusa's historic centre – is a joy to wander, with its labyrinthine lanes weaving through rock-grey palazzi, then opening suddenly onto beautiful, sun-drenched piazzas. It's easy to get lost but sooner or later you'll end up at **Piazza Duomo**, Ragusa's sublime central space.

At the top end of the sloping square is the 1744 **Duomo di San Giorgio**, one of Rosario Gagliardi's finest accomplishments.

Up the hill from Ragusa Ibla is **Ragusa Superiore**, the town's modern and less attractive half.

38

★ BEST FOR

FAMILIES

Splashing about on the beaches at Chia.

THE ISLANDS

SARDINIA'S SOUTH COAST

Beaches near Chia, Sardinia

DURATION: 4-5 DAYS

DISTANCE: 168KM/104 MILES

GREAT FOR: HISTORY, FAMILIES

BEST TIME TO GO: JUNE AND SEPTEMBER FOR PERFECT BEACH WEATHER WITHOUT THE AUGUST CROWDS.

From Cagliari's cultural gems to ancient ruins and stunning stretches of coastline, this trip is a real eye-opener. Outside the peak months of July and August, the roads are quiet and you'll be able to concentrate on the natural spectacle as it unfurls before you: spectacular coastal vistas on the Costa del Sud; searing Mediterranean colours on the Isola di San Pietro; melancholy woods and *macchia* (Mediterranean scrub)-clad hills around Iglesias.

LINK YOUR TRIP

39 The Emerald Coast
From Cagliari take the SS131 up to Alghero, 250km away, to join up with this tour of Sardinia's gorgeous, wind-whipped north coast.

40 Historic Sardinia
About 100km along the SS131 from Cagliari, Oristano is the start point for this compelling drive through Sardinia's wild and mysterious hinterland.

01 Cagliari

Rising from the sea in a helter-skelter of golden-hued palazzi, domes and facades, Cagliari is Sardinia's regional capital and most cosmopolitan city. As a working port it exudes an infectious energy, particularly down by the waterfront where Vespas buzz down wide boulevards, locals stop by busy cafes and diners crowd into popular trattorias. The big trophy sights are huddled in the **Castello** district, where the hilltop citadel rises above the city's sturdy battlements. Up here you'll find the graceful 13th-century **Cattedrale di Santa Maria** *(duomodicagliari.it)*, and Cagliari's premier museum, the **Museo Archeologico Nazionale**, whose collection casts light on Sardinia's ancient and mysterious nuraghic culture. For stunning views, head down to the **Bastione di Saint Remy**, a monumental viewing platform.

A short hop east of the city, **Poetto** beach is the hub of summer life with its limpid waters and upbeat party scene.

MARISA ESTIVILL/SHUTTERSTOCK

The Drive: Once you've cleared central Cagliari, it's a straightforward 32km drive along the SS195 to Pula. From Pula, the archaeological site of Nora is signposted, 4km away to the southwest. As you approach it, look out for pink flamingos in the nearby lagoon.

02 Pula

The village of Pula makes a good base for exploring the southern beaches and the nearby archaeological site of Nora. There's little to see in the village itself, but in summer visitors throng its vibrant cafes and various restaurants lending it a bubbly holiday atmosphere. A short drive out of Pula, the ruins of **Nora** *(nora.beniculturali.unipd.it)* are all that remain of what was once one of Sardinia's most powerful cities. Highlights include a beautifully preserved Roman theatre and an ancient baths complex, the **Terme al Mare**.

Just before you get to the site, keep an eye out for the beachside **Chiesa di Sant'Efisio**, a 12th-century Romanesque church that plays a starring role in Cagliari's big May festival, the **Festa di Sant'Efisio** *(festadisantefisio.com)*.

The Drive: From Pula, push on along the SS195 for the 18km drive to Chia, which is signposted off to the left shortly after the village of Santa Margherita di Pula. For much of the way the sea view is blocked by trees and foliage, but don't worry as there are plenty of vistas to be had on the next leg.

03 Chia

Extending from Chia to Porto di Teulada, the **Costa del Sud** is one of southern Sardinia's most beautiful coastal stretches.

At its eastern end, Chia is a hugely popular summer hang-out. More a collection of hotels, holiday homes and campsites than a traditional village, it has two ravishing beaches – to the west, the **Spiaggia Sa Colonia**, and to the east, the smaller **Spiaggia Su Portu**. Running the length of the Costa, the **Strada Panoramica della Costa del Sud** is a stunning drive, with dreamy views at every turn and a succession of bays capped by Spanish-era watchtowers.

The Drive: This 56km drive is the most spectacular leg of the trip. From Chia, the SP71, aka the Strada Panoramica della Costa del Sud, snakes along the coast, offering ever more beautiful views as it winds on to Porto di Teulada. Shortly before Porto, turn inland towards Teulada and pick up the northbound SS195 to Tratalias.

04 Tratalias

Now a sleepy backwater, Tratalias was once a major religious centre. When the town of Sant'Antioco was abandoned in the 13th century, the local Sulcis archdiocese was transferred to Tratalias and the impressive **Chiesa di Santa Maria** was built. A prime example of Sardinia's Romanesque-Pisan architecture, the church today presides over the town's lovingly renovated *borgo antico,* a medieval quarter that was abandoned in the 1950s after water from the nearby Lago di Monte Pranu started seeping into the subsoil.

The Drive: From Tratalias, it's a short 14km haul over to the Isola di Sant'Antioco via the SS126, which runs over a causeway to the island's main settlement, Sant'Antioco.

05 Sant'Antioco

The **Isola di Sant'Antioco** is the larger and more developed of the two islands off Sardinia's southwestern coast. Unlike many Mediterranean islands, it's not dramatically beautiful – although it's by no means ugly. Instead it feels very much part of Sardinia, both in character and look, with a happy, casual vibe.

The animated main town, **Sant'Antioco**, was established by the Phoenicians in the 8th century BCE. Evidence of its early history lies all around, and the town's small centre is riddled with Phoenician necropolises and fascinating archaeological litter. Just outside the centre, the **Museo Archeologico** *(mabsantantioco.it)* is one of the best museums in this part of southern Sardinia. It has a fascinating collection of local archaeological finds, as well as models of nuraghic houses and Sant'Antioco as it would have looked in the 4th century BCE.

The Drive: To get to the neighbouring island of San Pietro requires a ferry crossing from Calasetta, 10km northwest of

Capo Sandalo

IVAN CANAVERA/SHUTTERSTOCK

Sant'Antioco on the island's north coast. There are not many roads to choose from, so just head north and follow the signs through the green, rugged interior.

06 Isola di San Pietro

With an elegant main town and some magnificent coastal scenery, the Isola di San Pietro is a hugely popular summer destination.

The island's principal port of call is **Carloforte**, a refined town with an elegant waterfront, graceful palazzi and a reputation for excellent seafood – tuna is a local speciality. There are no must-see sights as such, but a slow wander through the quaint, cobbled streets makes for a pleasant prelude to an *aperitivo* (pre-dinner drink) and a fine restaurant meal.

Over on the island's west coast, **Capo Sandalo** is well worth searching out. A superb vantage point, it commands breathtaking coastal views and offers some relaxed walking. From the car park near the lighthouse, marked trails head through the rocky, red scrubland that carpets the cliffs.

The Drive: Once the ferry from Carloforte has docked at Portovesme, head northeast towards Gonnesa to pick up the SS126 for the final run in to Iglesias. The 35km route is not the most scenic, but there is something atmospheric about the dark, *macchia*-cloaked hills of Sardinia's traditional mining heartland south of Iglesias.

PHOTO OPPORTUNITY

Isola di San Pietro's coastline from Capo Sandalo.

07 Iglesias

Surrounded by the skeletons of Sardinia's once-thriving mining industry, Iglesias is a historic town that bubbles in the summer and slumbers in the colder months. Its historic centre, an appealing ensemble of lived-in piazzas, sun-bleached buildings and Aragonese-style wrought-iron balconies, creates an atmosphere that's as much Iberian as Sardinian – a vestige of its time as a Spanish colony. In the heart of the *centro storico* (historic centre), the 13th-century **Cattedrale di Santa Chiara** is the most impressive of the city's many churches with its Pisan-flavoured facade and checkerboard stone bell tower.

DETOUR

Tempio di Antas

Start: 07 Iglesias

From Iglesias the SS126 twists and turns for 17km through wooded hills up to the **Tempio di Antas** *(startuno.it)*, an impressive 3rd-century Roman temple set in lush bucolic greenery.

Built by the emperor Caracalla, the temple was constructed over a 6th-century-BCE Punic sanctuary, which was itself set over an earlier nuraghic settlement. It lay abandoned for centuries until it was discovered in 1836 and extensively restored in 1967. Most impressively, the original Ionic columns were excavated and re-erected.

From the site several paths branch off into the surrounding countryside. One of them, the Strada Romana, leads from near the ticket office to what little remains of the original nuraghic settlement and on to the **Grotta di Su Mannau** *(sumannau.it)*, 2.5km away.

39

★ BEST FOR

OUTDOORS

Dive into the crystalline waters of the Maddalena Archipelago.

THE ISLANDS

THE EMERALD COAST

DURATION: 5–7 DAYS

DISTANCE: 253KM/157 MILES

GREAT FOR: FOOD AND DRINK, NATURE

BEST TIME TO GO: MAY, JUNE, SEPTEMBER AND OCTOBER FOR BEACH WEATHER WITHOUT HUGE CROWDS.

Parco Nazionale dell'Arcipelago di La Maddalena (p236)

From unassuming Olbia, this trip rockets you into the dazzling coastline that the Aga Khan turned into a playground for oligarchs and their bikini-clad admirers. Head further north, however, and the coast grows wilder, with rocky coves washed by the startlingly blue waters of La Maddalena marine reserve. Rounding Sardinia's northwest corner, popular resorts alternate with timelessly silent stretches of coast, until finally you arrive at lovely, Spanish-inflected Alghero.

LINK YOUR TRIP

27 Shadow of Vesuvius
Regular ferries sail from Cagliari to Naples where you can join this journey around the Bay of Naples.

40 Historic Sardinia
This trip into the Sardinian heartland starts in Oristano, 110km south of Alghero on the SS292.

01 Olbia

Scratch Olbia's industrial outskirts and find a fetching city with a *centro storico* crammed with boutiques, wine bars and cafe-rimmed piazzas. Olbia is also a refreshingly authentic and affordable alternative to the purpose-built resorts stretching to the north and south.

To get a feeling for old Olbia, head south of Corso Umberto to the tightly packed warren of streets that represents the original fishing village. You'll find it has a special charm, particularly in the evening when the cafes and trattorias fill with locals.

The Drive: Heading north on the SS125 and then the SP13 for this 29km leg, you'll pass through a rocky, sun-bleached landscape that alternates with patchwork farmland.

02 Cannigione

Cannigione sits on the western side of the Golfo di Arzachena, the largest *ria* (inlet) along this coast. Originally a fishing village

TRAVELWILD/SHUTTERSTOCK

established in 1800 to supply the Maddalena islands with food, it is now a prosperous, and reasonably priced, tourist town. Down at the port, various operators offer excursions to the Arcipelago di La Maddalena, plus fantastic opportunities for diving, snorkelling and boat trips that nose around the gorgeous and complex shoreline.

The operators here include **Consorzio del Golfo** *(consorziodelgolfo.it)* and **Anthias** *(anthiasdiving.com)*.

The Drive: Hugging the coast as you head north along the SP13 and SP121, this beautiful 8km drive is defined by the famously beautiful blue-green waters of the Costa Smeralda (Emerald Coast). Near the village of Le Saline, you'll see the inlet on which the Capo d'Orso sits.

03 Capo d'Orso

Watching over the strait that separates Sardinia from the Isola della Maddalena, Capo d'Orso (Cape Bear) owes its name to a giant granite rock that resembles a rather ferocious-looking bear. The ursine lookout commands a dramatic view that, in a single sweep of the eye, takes in Sardinia's rugged northern coast, the Arcipelago di La Maddalena and, to the north, the mountains of Corsica.

The Drive: From Capo d'Orso, head northwest along the SP121 to Palau, just 5km away.

04 Palau

Palau is a lively summer resort and also the main gateway to the granite islands and jewel-coloured waters of the Arcipelago di La Maddalena. Three kilometres west of town, you can tour the **Fortezza di Monte Altura**, a 19th-century sentinel standing guard over the rocky crag. **Dea del Mare** *(deadelmare.com)* offers sailing excursions around the Maddalena islands. If diving is your thing, there's excellent diving in the marine park. **Nautilus Diving Centre** *(divesardegna.com)* runs dives to up to 40 sites.

The Drive: Actually, it's a boat trip. From Palau, there are at least hourly passenger and car ferry services to Isola della

Maddalena. The journey takes 15 minutes.

05 Isola della Maddalena

Just over the water from Palau, the pink-granite island of La Maddalena lies at the heart of the Arcipelago di La Maddalena. From the moment you dock at **Cala Gavetta** (La Maddalena's main port), you'll be in the thrall of its cobbled piazzas and infectious holiday atmosphere.

Beyond the harbour, the island offers startlingly lovely seascapes. A 20km panoramic road circles the island, allowing easy access to several attractive bays.

The ravishing **Parco Nazionale dell'Arcipelago di La Maddalena** *(lamaddalenapark.it)* consists of seven main islands, including La Maddalena, and 40 granite islets, plus several small islands to the south. They form the high points of a (now underwater) mountain range that once joined Sardinia and Corsica. Over the centuries, the *maestrale* (northwesterly wind) has moulded the granite into bizarre natural sculptures. But the great delight lies in its crystalline waters, which are rich in marine life and also assume priceless shades of emerald, aquamarine and sapphire.

To explore the archipelago and some of the smaller, lesser-known islands, **Elena Tour Navigazioni** *(elenatournavigazioni.com)* is one of various outfits offering boat cruises.

The Drive: Hop on the ferry back to Palau, then head northwest on the SS133, which will veer off as the SS133bis. Along the 24km, mostly inland, journey you'll pass Mediterranean scrub and granite boulders, with a brief seaside encounter at Porto Pozzo.

DETOUR

Isola Caprera

Start: 01 Isola della Maddalena

Just over a causeway from the Isola della Maddalena, Isola Caprera was once Giuseppe Garibaldi's 'Eden' – a wild, wonderfully serene island, covered in pines, which look stunning against the ever-present seascape and ragged granite cliffs. The green, shady Caprera is ideal for walking, and there are plenty of trails weaving through the pines. The island's rugged coast is indented with several tempting coves. You can also tour the **Compendio Garibaldino**, the serene compound the Italian revolutionary built for himself here.

MUST-TRY

SARDINIAN DISHES

Zuppa gallurese
Layers of bread and cheese drenched in broth and baked to a crispy crust.

Porceddu
Suckling pig, often spit roasted.

Aragosta alla catalana
Alghero's lobster speciality, with tomato and onion.

Fregola con cozze e vongole
Sardinian semolina pasta (similar to couscous) with mussels and clams.

Seadas
Light pastry turnovers filled with *pecorino* (sheep's milk cheese) and lemon zest and drizzled with honey.

06 Santa Teresa di Gallura

Bright, breezy and relaxed, Santa Teresa di Gallura bags a prime seafront position on Gallura's north coast. The resort gets extremely busy in high season, yet somehow retains a distinct local character. When not on the beach, most people hang out at cafe-lined **Piazza Vittorio Emanuele**. Otherwise, you can wander up to the 16th-century **Torre di Longonsardo**, a defensive tower near the entrance to **Spiaggia Rena Bianca**, the town's idyllic (but crowded) beach.

Well worth the 4km hike west of Santa Teresa, the small peninsula known as **Capo Testa** resembles a bizarre sculpture garden. Giant boulders lay strewn about the grassy slopes, their weird and wonderful forms the result of centuries of wind erosion. The walk itself is also stunning, passing through boulder-strewn scrub and affording magnificent views of rocky coves and the cobalt Mediterranean. Stop en route for a swim and to admire the views of not-so-distant Corsica.

The Drive: It's rugged, hilly terrain on this 70km southwestern route along the SP90, with a brief stint along the winding SS134 to Castelsardo and the sea.

07 Castelsardo

Medieval Castelsardo huddles atop a high, cone-shaped promontory that juts picturesquely into the Mediterranean. Originally designed as a defensive fort by a 12th-century Genoese family, the dramatic, hilltop *centro storico* is an ensemble of dark alleyways and medieval buildings seemingly melded into the rocky grey peak.

LARRAEND/SHUTTERSTOCK

📷 PHOTO OPPORTUNITY

The bizarre shapes of Capo Testa's natural sculpture garden.

Capo Testa

The Drive: Hug Sardinia's rugged northern coastline as you head west to Porto Torres along the SS200 and SP81. Then turn inland into desolately beautiful country to reach Stintino, 63km from Castelsardo, on the SP34.

08 Stintino

With its saltpans and hard-scrabble landscape, the northwest corner of Sardinia has a particularly desolate feel, especially when the *maestrale* wind blows in, whipping the *macchia* (Mediterranean scrub) and bleak rocks. But it also shelters the welcoming and laid-back resort town of Stintino, gateway to the **Isola dell'Asinara**, formerly home to one of Italy's toughest prisons. Nearby, the fabulous **Spiaggia della Pelosa** is one of Sardinia's most celebrated beaches.

The Drive: For this 54km drive, head back down south along the SP34 to the coastal SP57, followed by the SP69. Soon you will reach the flat agricultural plain just north of Alghero, then it's a straight shot on the SS291 into Alghero itself.

09 Alghero

For many people a trip to Sardinia means a trip to Alghero, the main resort in the northwest and an easy flight from a host of European cities. Although largely given over to tourism, the town has managed to avoid many of its worst excesses, and it retains a proud and independent spirit.

The main focus is the spectacular **centro storico**, one of the best preserved in Sardinia. Enclosed by robust, honey-coloured seawalls, this is a tightly knit enclave of shady cobbled lanes, Spanish Gothic palazzi and cafe-lined squares.

Below, yachts crowd the marina and long, sandy beaches curve away to the north. Hanging over everything is a palpably Spanish atmosphere, a leftover of the city's past as a Catalan colony. Even today, more than three centuries after the Iberians left, the Catalan tongue is still spoken and street signs and menus are often in both languages.

40

★ BEST FOR

OUTDOORS

Great hikes abound around Dorgali.

THE ISLANDS

HISTORIC SARDINIA

DURATION: 7 DAYS

DISTANCE: 239KM/148 MILES

GREAT FOR: FOOD AND DRINK, NATURE

BEST TIME TO GO: MARCH TO MAY FOR WILDFLOWERS AND GREEN HILLSIDES.

Dorgali (p241)

This trip takes you into the wild heart of Sardinia, a strange and hauntingly beautiful landscape. You'll discover remnants of the prehistoric nuraghi (Bronze Age fortified settlements) and the lonesome villages of the Barbagia, which are still steeped in bandit legend. Finally, you'll end up in the wilds of the eastern coast, where limestone mountains and deep canyons roll down to the aquamarine waves of the Golfo di Orosei.

LINK YOUR TRIP

38 Sardinia's South Coast
Some 97km southeast of Oristano on the SS131 Cagliari is the start point for this visually stunning tour of the island's south coast.

39 The Emerald Coast
Starting 90km up the coast from Orosei, this trip reveals Sardinia's wind-carved northern coast.

01 Oristano

One of Sardinia's most important medieval cities, Oristano has a historic centre that retains traces of its former greatness, most notably the 13th-century **Torre di Mariano II**. The centre is a pleasant place to wander, with its elegant shopping streets, ornate central square – **Piazza Eleonora d'Arborea** – and crowded cafes.

The region around Oristano was an important centre of the Bronze Age nuraghic people, and the **Museo Archeologico Antiquarium Arborense** *(antiquariumarborense.it)* is home to one of Sardinia's major archaeological collections.

Located 3km south of town, the 12th-century **Basilica di Santa Giusta** – one of Sardinia's finest Tuscan-style Romanesque churches – is worth seeking out.

The Drive: Your main routes on the 58km drive to Laconi will be the meandering SP35 and SS442. You'll traverse a widely

MARTIN FLORENT/SHUTTERSTOCK

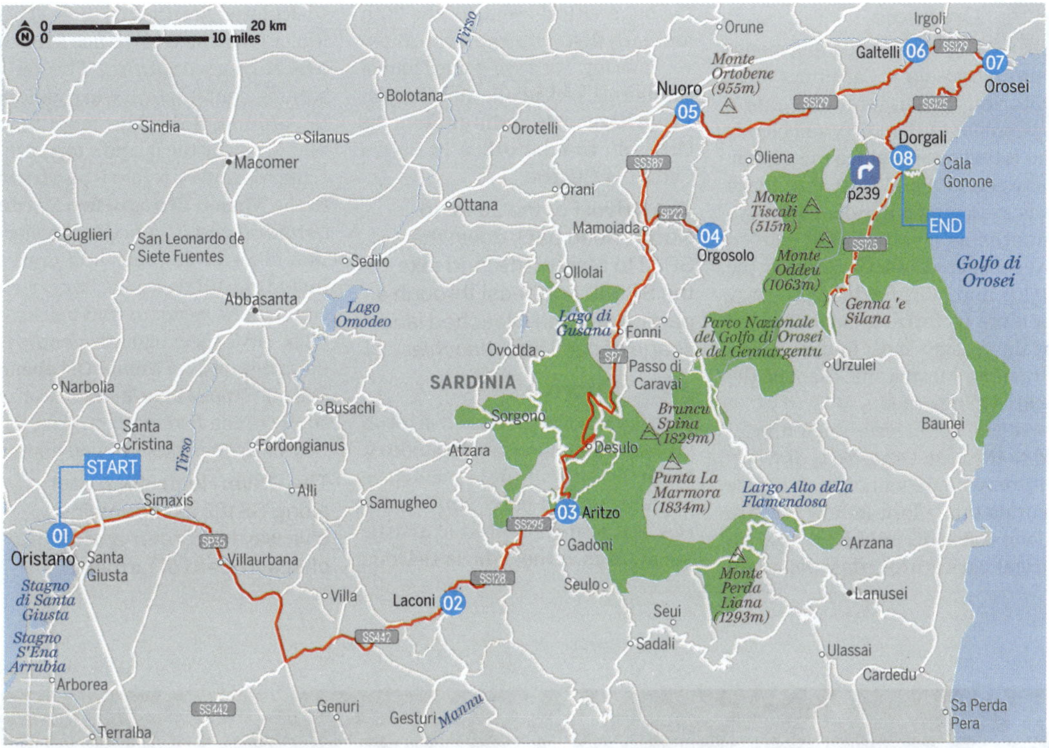

varied land of patchwork farms, small towns, rocky crags and wooded slopes.

02 Laconi

Laconi is a charismatic mountain town with a blissfully slow pace of life and bucolic views of rolling green countryside. Its cobbled lanes hide some genuine attractions, including an intriguing archaeological museum, the **Menhir Museum**. Occupying an elegant 19th-century palazzo, this museum beautifully exhibits a collection of 40 menhirs – stark anthropomorphic slabs probably connected with prehistoric funerary rites.

Just outside town, the **Parco Aymerich** is a gorgeous 22-hectare park with exotic trees, lakes, grottoes, great views and the remains of 11th-century **Castello Aymerich**.

The Drive: For this 27km leg, you'll head northeast along the SS128 and then the SS295 as you enter a wilder, more barren landscape, eventually reaching the pine-covered slopes around Aritzo.

03 Aritzo

With its cool climate and alpine character, this vivacious mountain resort (elevation 796m) has been attracting visitors since the 19th century, when it caught the imagination of boar-hunting Piedmontese nobility. But long before tourism took off, the village flourished thanks to its lucrative trade in snow gathering.

For five centuries, Aritzo supplied the whole of Sardinia with ice, and snow farmers, known as *niargios*, collected the white stuff from the slopes of **Punta di Funtana Cungiada** (1458m) and stored it in straw-lined wooden chests before sending it off to the high tables of Cagliari.

The Drive: Heading northeast along Via Marginigola, turn onto the sharply curving SP7 for the 65km to Orgosolo through the deserted mountains and valleys of central Sardinia. At the town of Mamoiada, take the winding SP22 for the last 10km up to Orgosolo.

04 Orgosolo

High in the brooding mountains, Orgosolo is Sardinia's most notorious town, its name long a byword for the banditry and bloody feuds that once blighted this region. Between 1901 and 1950, the village was averaging a murder every two months as rival families feuded over disputed inheritances. In the 1950s and '60s, feuding gave way to more lucrative kidnapping, led by the village's most infamous son, Graziano Mesina, nicknamed the Scarlet Pimpernel.

With its violent history now relegated to the past, Orgosolo is drawing visitors with the vibrant graffiti-style murals that adorn its town centre along **Corso Repubblica**. Like satirical caricatures, they depict all the big political events of the 20th and early 21st century and are often very moving. For a self-guided tour of the murals, pick up the multilingual **ScopriOrgosolo audio guide** at the Orgosolo **tourist office** in Piazza Caduti in Guerra.

The Drive: For the 26km to Nuoro, head back down the SP22 to Mamoiada, and take the SS389 northeast through a particularly sun-bleached landscape of cacti and *macchia*.

05 Nuoro

Once an isolated hilltop village synonymous with banditry, Nuoro had its cultural renaissance in the 19th and early 20th centuries, attracting a hotbed of artistic talent, from author Grazia Deledda to sculptor Francesco Ciusa. This legacy is reflected in the fine **Museo MAN** *(museoman.it)*. The only serious contemporary-art gallery in Sardinia, it displays more than 400 works by the island's top 20th-century painters. Nuoro is also home to the **Museo Etnografico Sardo** *(isresardegna.it)*, a peerless collection of Sardinian arts and crafts, including filigree jewellery, rich embroidery, weapons and masks.

The city's spectacular backdrop is the granite peak of **Monte Ortobene** (955m). Capped by a 7m-high bronze statue of the *Redentore* (Christ the Redeemer), it makes for good hiking.

The Drive: Head 33km east along SS129 as mountains give way to a green-and-ochre checkerboard of farmland.

Golfo di Orosei

PICS721/SHUTTERSTOCK

06 Galtelli

Crouched at the foot of Monte Tuttavista and hemmed in by olive groves, vineyards and sheep-nibbled pastures, Galtelli is quite the village idyll.

Its tiny medieval centre is a joy to wander, with narrow lanes twisting to old stone houses and sun-dappled piazzas. If you fancy tiptoeing off the map for a while, this is the place.

The Drive: It's a quick and relatively straight 9km jaunt along SS129 to Orosei, as rugged limestone peaks rear up again on your right.

07 Orosei

Scenically positioned at the northernmost point of the Golfo di Orosei and surrounded by marble quarries and fruit orchards, Orosei is an unsung treasure.

Over the centuries the silting of the Cedrino river – plus malaria, pirate raids and Spanish neglect – took its toll on the town, once an important Pisan port. However, its demise left behind an atmospheric historic centre laced with cobbled lanes, pretty stone houses, medieval churches and leafy piazzas.

The Drive: From the plains around Orosei, head southwest on the SS125 for 21km. Expect glimpses of both mountains and sea as you wind your way to Dorgali.

PHOTO OPPORTUNITY

The spectacular coastal scenery on the Golfo di Orosei.

08 Dorgali

Nestled at the foot of **Monte Bardia** and framed by vineyards and olive groves, Dorgali is a down-to-earth town with a grandiose backdrop. Limestone peaks loom above the centre's pastel-coloured houses and steep, narrow streets, luring hikers and climbers to their summits.

For more outdoor escapades, the dramatic **Golfo di Orosei** and spectacularly rugged **Supramonte** mountain range are within easy striking distance.

Just south of town lies one of Sardinia's most dramatically sited nuraghe. Follow signs along the Dorgali–Cala Gonone road to the **Nuraghe Mannu**.

First inhabited around 1600 BCE, the tower is a modest ruin, but it more than makes up for this by offering spectacular views of the gulf.

The site captured ancient Roman imaginations, too, and you can see the rectilinear remnants of their constructions alongside the elliptical shapes of earlier buildings.

DETOUR

Gola Su Gorropu & Tiscali

Start: 08 Dorgali

Dubbed the 'Grand Canyon of Europe', the **Gola Su Gorropu** *(gorropu.info)* is a spectacular gorge flanked by vertical 400m rock walls that, at their narrowest point, stand just 4m apart. The hike down to and through the canyon floor takes you into a strangely silent world of gnarled holm oaks, sheer limestone slopes and pockmarked cliffs. There are two main approach routes.

The shorter and more dramatic begins from the car park opposite Hotel Silana at the Genna 'e Silana pass on the SS125 at Km 183.

The easier, but longer, route is via the Sa Barva bridge over the Rio Flumineddu, about 15km from Dorgali.

Also at the Sa Barva bridge is the trailhead for the walk to one of Sardinia's archaeological highlights. Hidden in a mountaintop cave deep in the Valle Lanaittu is the nuraghic village of **Tiscali** *(museoarcheologicodorgali.it)*.

The hike up to the village is part of the pleasure, as you strike into the heart of the limestone Supramonte highlands.

You'll need sturdy footwear for some rock hopping, but most of the path is easy-going, and canopies of juniper and cork oaks afford shady respite.

Allow five hours for the return hike, including breaks and time for visiting Tiscali.

T3
T1

TOOLKIT

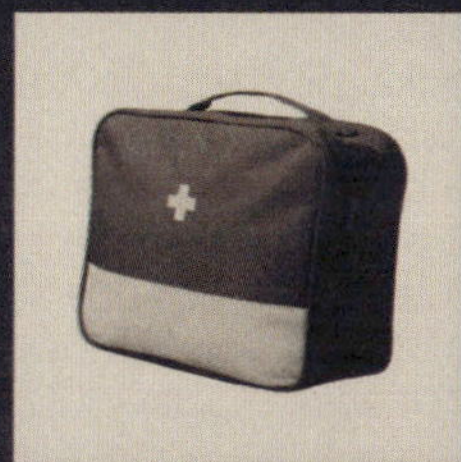

ARRIVING

Flights serve airports throughout the country. Italy's main intercontinental airports are Rome's Fiumicino (officially Leonardo da Vinci) and Milan's Malpensa. Both are well connected by public transport and offer a full array of services, including car hire. As an alternative to flying, there are excellent rail and bus links, especially to destinations in northern Italy, and ferries to Italian ports from across the Mediterranean.

CAR RENTAL AT AIRPORTS

Car hire is available at Italy's main airports. Agencies, signposted as Autonoleggio, are generally in or around the arrivals hall, although at Naples airport you have to take a shuttle bus to reach some offices. At Rome's Fiumicino airport, they're situated in Torre Uffici 2, which is linked to the terminals by passenger walkways.

Prebooking is advisable. You'll get a better rate and have a wider choice of vehicle. Make sure to specify in advance if you want an automatic car as the default will almost certainly be a manual.

As a rule, airport pick-ups cost slightly more than city-centre locations. But they have some advantages. For one thing, they'll save you the hassle of dealing with city-centre traffic and potentially troublesome ZTLs (Limited Traffic Zones) as you get to grips with your new car.

AIRPORT TO CITY CENTRE

	ROME FIUMICINO	MILAN MALPENSA	NAPLES CAPODICHINO
TRAIN	30min **€14**	1hr **€15**	No train
BUS OR SHUTTLE	1hr **from €7**	1hr **€10**	20min **€5**

MAIN AIRPORTS

Northern destinations: Milan (Malpensa, Linate), Venice, Bologna, Turin. Central areas: Pisa, Rome (Fiumicino, Ciampino) South and islands: Naples; Catania and Palermo (Sicily); Cagliari and Alghero (Sardinia).

VISAS

EU nationals don't need a visa. Travellers from the UK, Canada, New Zealand, the US and Australia can stay for up to 90 days without a visa. Other travellers should check requirements at vistoperitalia.esteri.it.

ETIAS

The European Travel Information and Authorisation System (etiasvisa.com) is due to come into effect in 2026. Non-EU travellers from visa-exempt countries will have to register online and pay a €20 fee before travelling to Italy.

WI-FI

Free wi-fi is usually available at airports, and is widely available in hotels, hostels, B&Bs and cafes. Signal quality can vary in older or rural properties.

GETTING AROUND

ROAD ETIQUETTE

Italian drivers are fast, aggressive and skilful. Lane hopping and late braking are the norm and it's not uncommon to see cars tailgating at 130km/h. Don't expect cars to slow down for you – as soon as you see a gap, go for it.

Headlight flashing is common and can mean 'Get out of the way' or 'There's a police check ahead'. Use of the car horn is also widespread, sometimes as a warning, sometimes as an expression of frustration.

DRIVING INFO

Drive on the right, overtake on the left

50

Speed limits: 50km/h in urban areas; 90–110km/h on secondary roads; 130km/h on motorways.

.05

Blood alcohol limit is 0.05%; it's zero for new licence holders and under-21s.

TRAVEL BETWEEN LOCATIONS

Trains are best between major cities and along the coast, while buses are better for rural inland areas. Major cities have good public transport systems, comprising buses, trams and, in some places, metros. You'll need a car to explore the countryside

ROAD CATEGORIES

Toll-charging motorways (autostradas) are indicated by an 'A' on a green sign. Fast-flowing state and regional highways (*strade statali* and *regionali*), as well as slower provincial roads (*strade provinciali*), are marked as SS, SR or SP on blue signs.

TOLLS & ZTLS

Most Italian autostradas require payment of a toll. Pick up a ticket at the entry barrier and pay (by cash or card) as you exit. In city centres, beware of Limited Traffic Zones (ZTLs) that can only be entered with a permit.

PARKING

Blue parking lines mean you'll need a ticket – get one from the nearest meter and display it on your dashboard. White lines often mean free parking, but can also mean for residents only. Yellow lines indicate that permits are needed.

TRAVEL COSTS

Car rental
From €30/day

Petrol
Approx €1.90/litre

EV charging
€0.50–€1/kWh

Train ticket from Rome to Milan
From €50

ACCOMMODATION

HOW MUCH FOR A NIGHT IN A...

Agriturismo
€50–100

Rifugio
€30–45

B&B
€60–140

FARM STAYS

From rustic country houses to luxurious rural retreats, Italian farm stays – known as *agriturismi* (or *masserie* in Puglia) – are hugely popular. Comfort levels, facilities and prices vary but the best offer top-notch accommodation as well as restaurants serving seasonal local fare. They are perfect for families, relaxation and cultural immersion experiences such as truffle hunting, olive harvesting and cookery classes.

CONVENTS & MONASTERIES

Continuing an age-old tradition, many Italian convents and monasteries provide modest accommodation. Some are open to all, while others only take in pilgrims or organised groups. As a rule, you can expect few frills and sometimes even curfews, but you're often rewarded with unforgettable settings and value-for-money rates.

RIFUGI

Italy's network of *rifugi* (mountain huts) provide high-altitude accommodation in the Alps and Apennines. Ideal for hikers and climbers, they range from rudimentary shelters (known as *bivacchi*) to hostel-like lodges with heating, electricity, hot meals and/or cooking facilities. They're usually only open from June to late September – for details check out the directory on the Club Alpino Italiano website (cai.it).

B&BS

Midrange and budget accommodation in Italy is largely made up of B&Bs. Ranging from rooms in historic *palazzi* (mansions) and city-centre apartments to restored farmhouses and seaside bungalows, they vary in size, quality and atmosphere but often provide value for money and a more personal touch.

UNIQUE OPTIONS

Italy has some charming offbeat accommodation. In Puglia you can stay in a *trullo*, a conical-roofed stone house unique to the Valle d'Itria, while in neighbouring Basilicata you can bed down in a boutique cave hotel in Matera. A good option for a taste of authentic village life is an *albergo diffuso*, a hotel with rooms spread across various sites.

AIRBNB DEBATE

The success of Airbnb-style rentals has been at the centre of political debate in recent years. Critics have spoken of rising rents pricing out locals and city centres being hollowed out. In response to these concerns, many Italian cities, including Florence, Venice, Milan, Bologna and Rome, have imposed regulations on short-term rentals, such as bans on self-serve key boxes and other measures for managing tourism.

CARS

ANTONELLO MARANGI/SHUTTERSTOCK

CAR RENTAL

Car-hire agencies are widespread and you'll find the big international firms and smaller local outfits at airports and major train stations.

When booking, bear in mind that a car is more hassle than it's worth in cities, so only hire for the time you'll be on the road. Note also that narrow streets, high fuel prices and tight parking mean that a small car is often your best bet.

To rent, you'll need a credit card, valid driving licence (with an International Driving Permit if necessary) and passport. You'll also need to be over 25. Some places will hire to 21- to 25-year-olds, but supplements will apply.

Rates generally include mandatory collision damage waiver insurance, although you can supplement this by purchasing additional coverage.

HOW MUCH TO HIRE A CAR?

Compact
€20–30 per day

Midsize
€35–50

EV
€35–70

EV

Electric cars are available at major Italian agencies, though book in advance to guarantee your choice.

EVs are best suited to city driving and short day trips rather than long-distance touring. As a rough guide, midsize cars have a range of about 200km, but you probably won't get that when driving on the autostrada.

To fully charge a car will generally take three to four hours on a slow charger (11–22kWh) or about 45 minutes on a fast charger (110kWh). You'll find chargers at select petrol stations, supermarkets and public car parks. Individual accommodation providers may also have them. Always check with the rental agency how to use chargers as you might have to download an app and set up an account.

OTHER GEAR

Hire cars come equipped with a warning triangle and safety vest, which you're legally obliged to carry in your vehicle. You might also need snow chains if you're going to be driving in mountainous areas between mid-November (possibly earlier) and mid-April. Google Maps means sat navs are not really necessary.

RESPONSIBLE TRAVEL

CLIMATE CHANGE & TRAVEL

Lonely Planet urges all travellers to engage with their travel carbon footprint, which will mainly come from air travel. While there often isn't an alternative, travellers can look to minimise the number of flights they take and use cleaner ground transport, such as trains.

One proposed solution – purchasing carbon offsets – unfortunately does not cancel out the impact of individual flights. While most destinations will depend on air travel for the foreseeable future, for now, pursuing ground-based travel where possible is the best course of action.

The **UN Carbon Offset Calculator** shows how flying impacts a household's emissions

The **ICAO's carbon emissions calculator** allows visitors to analyse the CO_2 generated by point-to-point journeys

Agriturismo.it
agriturismo.it
Book *agriturismi* (farm stays) across the country.

Legambiente
legambienteturismo.it
Travel ideas from Italy's top environmental organisation.

Addiopizzo
addiopizzotravel.it
Anti-mafia movement promoting tours, stays and shops.

STAY OFF THE TOURIST TRAIL

Italy's *alberghi diffusi* (scattered hotels; *alberghidiffusi.it*) offer an authentic slice of rural life. Designed to help resurrect 'dying villages', hotels such as Sextantio in Abruzzo have a central reception and rooms spread across a village.

EAT LOCAL

Kilometre-zero cuisine has long been central to Italian food culture. To keep it local, look for restaurants recognised by Slow Food *(slowfood.it)*, an organisation created to safeguard culinary traditions and promote local producers.

REUSE YOUR BOTTLE

Many popular Italian cities provide free drinking water. With a reusable bottle you can fill up at drinking fountains in Venice, Turin, Florence and Rome (where they're called *nasoni*, or 'big noses').

SAFE TRAVEL

HEALTH

Health care is readily accessible throughout Italy. EU nationals are entitled to reduced-cost, sometimes free, medical care; non-EU citizens should take out medical insurance. Pharmacists can advise on medical matters and sell medications for minor illnesses. Call 118 for an ambulance. Tap water is safe to drink unless marked *'acqua non potabile'* (water not suitable for drinking).

THEFT

Italy is a safe country but petty theft can be a problem. There's no need for paranoia, but always lock your car and never leave anything visible, particularly overnight. If possible, try to leave your car in a supervised car park. In case of theft, report the incident to the police within 24 hours and ask for a statement.

WEATHER

Episodes of extreme weather in Italy have increased in recent years. Hot, dry summers have led to drought, record-breaking temperatures and more frequent outbreaks of wildfires across the country. Similarly, storms and heavy rain have caused a rising number of floods and mudslides. If you're caught in a fire or flood, follow evacuation orders immediately.

EARTHQUAKES

Earthquakes are not uncommon in Italy, even if most cause little to no damage. Areas most at risk include the central and southern Apennines, southeast Sicily, Calabria and Friuli Venezia Giulia. Active volcanoes are another feature of Italy's seismic make-up. Mt Vesuvius might not have erupted since 1944, but Etna and Stromboli regularly blow their tops, often in spectacular style.

CAR BREAKDOWN

In the event of a breakdown, call your car-hire company. Roadside assistance might be included in your rental contract or it might be available as a paid extra. Italy's main motoring organisation, Automobile Club d'Italia (ACI), provides 24-hour roadside assistance (for a fee) – call 803 116 from an Italian phone, or 800 116800 from a foreign number.

IN CASE OF EMERGENCY

112
Any emergency General switchboard; will put you in touch with the most appropriate service

113
State police *(Polizia di Stato)* For thefts, road accidents etc

115
Fire brigade *(Vigili del Fuoco)* Fire and weather emergencies

118
Ambulance *(Ambulanza)*

NUTS & BOLTS

GOOD TO KNOW

Time zone
UTC plus one hour (plus two hours during summer)

Country code
39

Emergency number
112

CURRENCY: EURO (€)

MONEY

It always pays to have some cash on you. ATMs (known as *bancomat*) are widely available and most will accept cards tied to Visa/MasterCard/Cirrus/Maestro systems. Avoid Euronet ATMs, which charge inflated fees. Many banks impose a daily limit of €250 on withdrawals. Major credit cards are widely accepted (Amex less so). Businesses are now legally obliged to accept digital payments, although exceptions persist, particularly in bars, smaller shops and cheap restaurants. Don't rely on credit cards at small museums or galleries. At restaurants, *servizio* (service) is often included in the bill, meaning tipping is not necessary. If you want to leave something, a couple of euros is fine in pizzerias and trattorias; in smarter restaurants you can tip 5% to 10%. In bars, many people leave €0.10 or €0.20 when ordering coffee at the bar.

OPENING HOURS

Shops generally open 9am to 1pm and 3.30pm to 7.30pm (or 4pm to 8pm) Monday to Saturday. In cities, some shops are open all day. Restaurants open from noon to 3pm and 7.30pm to 11pm.

ALCOHOL & SMOKING

The legal age to be served alcohol in a bar or restaurant is 18. Smoking is banned in restaurants, bars, shops, public transport and all enclosed public spaces.

TOILETS

You'll find toilets at museums, major tourist sites, train stations and service stations. Many public facilities charge €1 to €1.50. Bars and cafes also have toilets, but you'll usually need to order something before using them.

ELECTRICITY

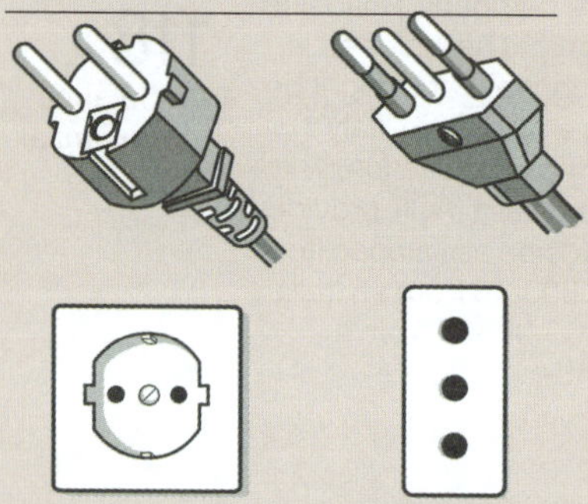

Type F
230V/50Hz

Type L
220V/50Hz

HOW MUCH FOR A...

Coffee (standing at a bar)
€1.10

Midrange meal
€25–35

Glass of wine
€5–8

Museum entry
€10–20

INDEX

Drives 000
Map pages **p000**

N

O

P

R

S

THE WRITERS

This is the 5th edition of Lonely Planet's Best Road Trips Italy guidebook, updated with new material by Gregor Clark.

Writers on previous editions whose work also appears in this book are included below.

Gregor Clark

Gregor is a lifelong polyglot with a special fondness for hiking, cycling and exploring Mediterranean and Alpine Europe; he has contributed to dozens of Lonely Planet guidebooks in his 25-year career as a travel writer. @thewideopenroad

Contributing writers

Brett Atkinson, Alexis Averbuck, Cristian Bonetto, Duncan Garwood, Peter Dragicevich, Paula Hardy, Virginia Maxwell, Stephanie Ong, Kevin Raub, Brendan Sainsbury, Regis St Louis, Nicola Williams

Send us your feedback

We love to hear from travellers – your comments keep us on our toes and help make our books better. Our well-travelled team reads every word on what you loved or loathed about this book. Although we cannot reply individually to your submissions, we always guarantee that your feedback goes straight to the appropriate writers, in time for the next edition.

BEHIND THE SCENES

This book was produced by the following:

Destination Editor
Darren O'Connell

Coordinating Editor
Gabrielle Innes

Production Editor
Graham O'Neill

Image Researcher
Leah Woodruff

Cartographer
Julie Dodkins

Assisting Editors
Soo Hamilton, Fionnuala Twomey

Cover Researcher
Sam Ubinas

Thanks to
Fergal Condon, Kellie Langdon, Ruth McLaughlin, Charlotte Orr, Glenn van der Knijff, Clifton Wilkinson

Product Development
Sofie Andersen, Melinda Anderson, Marc Backwell, Alison Killilea, Darren O'Connell, James Smart, Robin Yule

Acknowledgments

Digital Model Elevation Data
Contains public sector information licensed under the Open Government Licence v3.0 website nationalarchives.gov.uk/doc/open-government-licence/version/3/

Cover photographs
Front: Driving through the Dolomites; L_B_Photography/Shutterstock
Back: Pitigliano, Tuscany; Boris Stroujko/Shutterstock

Visit **lonelyplanet.com/contact** to submit your updates and suggestions or to ask for help. Our award-winning website also features inspirational travel stories and news.

Note: We may edit, reproduce and incorporate your comments in Lonely Planet products such as guidebooks, websites and digital products, so let us know if you are happy to have your name acknowledged. For a copy of our privacy policy visit **lonelyplanet.com/legal**

lonely planet

Published by Lonely Planet Global Limited
CRN 554153
Digital Depot, Roe Lane off Thomas Street, Dublin D08 TCV4, Ireland (EU authorised representative)
5th edition – Sep 2026
ISBN 9781837583881

10 9 8 7 6 5 4 3 2 1
Printed in Malaysia